LEADER'S GUIDE

Chris Stefanick & Ron Bolster

CHOSEN

YOUR JOURNEY TOWARD CONFIRMATION

ASCENSION PRESS

West Chester, Pennsylvania

Ascension Press
Post Office Box 1990
West Chester, PA 19380
1-800-376-0520
AscensionPress.com

Cover Design: Devin Schadt

Printed in the United States of America

ISBN: 978-1-935940-99-9

Contents

Welcome to *Chosen*

Thank you for responding to the call to prepare Catholic teens to take the next important step on their faith journey—Confirmation. I've spoken to people involved in youth ministry who are eager to reach this fast-paced, tech-savvy generation with the love of Christ—yet are wondering how, exactly, to communicate the teachings of the Church in a way that "speaks" to those caught up in an increasingly secular world.

If you feel like this, do not be afraid. While the "news of the day" gets old within twenty-four hours, and the latest tech gadget becomes obsolete in six months, the mercy of God is "new each morning" (Lamentations 3:23). That is truly "Good News."

Whether or not they know it, teens today have hearts and minds *made* to dive in to the Good News of the Gospel. In the words of St. John Paul II, "Jesus Christ is the answer to the question posed by every human life, and the love of Christ compels us to share that great Good News with everyone."[1]

Just as the God of the universe transformed human history two thousand years ago, he is fully "present" and seeks to transform the hearts of young people, here and now. This life-changing "divine encounter" is not a flashy event or a new philosophy; it is a person: Jesus Christ. Instead of encountering God on the crowded streets of Jerusalem, your candidates will encounter him in the sacraments, in the teachings of the Church, in their parish community, in experiences of service, and, in a special way, in *you*.

It is our prayer that the thousands of hours of work that went into *Chosen* will help you to facilitate an encounter with God himself. Like you, we do this work, not because of what we have to give young people, but because of what they have to give to the Church and the world when they open their hearts to God. In the words of the great pope who was such an important part of my own conversion: "I have seen enough evidence to be unshakably convinced that no difficulty, no fear is so great that it can completely suffocate *the hope that springs eternal in the hearts of the young, the young are our hope.*"[2]

Indeed, the young people we serve are not the Church of tomorrow any more than you are the Church of yesterday. The youth are the Church of today! And as you prepare them for the Sacrament of Confirmation, you are helping empower them to be the saints and kingdom builders they are called to be (as you become a saint and kingdom builder yourself).

We are honored to be on this journey with you. Know that we are praying for you as you do the most important work in human history: echoing the Good News that God has revealed to every generation.

Your friend in Christ,

Christopher J. Stefanick

About the Authors and Presenters

Chosen: Your Journey Toward Confirmation features some of the most passionate and inspiring Catholic youth-ministry experts and speakers from across the country.

Co-Authors

Chris Stefanick is a co-author and presenter for *Chosen*. He speaks to more than 50,000 teens, young adults, and parents every year. Chris has served at a parish in the East Los Angeles area and as director of youth and young-adult ministry for the Archdiocese of Denver. He is the founder and president of Real Life Catholic, a nonprofit organization dedicated to re-engaging a generation. Chris is a syndicated columnist, has authored or co-authored several books, and is a regular on Catholic TV and radio. Chris and his wife, Natalie, live with their children in Denver, Colorado.

Ron Bolster is director of the Office of Catechetics at Franciscan University. He was formerly the director of the Office of Catechetics for the Diocese of Peoria. He holds a master of arts degree in theology with catechetical certification from Franciscan University and an undergraduate degree from Cornell University. Ron has also served as a consultant for RCIA to the Archdiocese of Washington, DC. He and his wife, Andrea, reside with their children in Steubenville, Ohio.

Presenters

Jackie Francois Angel is a Catholic recording artist and speaker who travels both nationally and internationally, leading retreats and conferences for youth and young adults. Her debut album, *Your Kingdom Is Glorious*, was released through Spirit and Song, a division of OCP. Jackie and her husband, Bobby Angel, live in California.

Deacon Harold Burke-Sivers is the founder and director of Servant Enterprises Inc., dedicated to the promotion of Catholic values. He makes regular appearances in Catholic media and leads retreats, seminars, and conferences around the world. Deacon Harold and his wife, Colleen, live with their children in Portland, Oregon.

Brian Butler is co-author of *Theology of the Body for Teens* (both the high-school and middle-school editions). He is the co-founder and president of Dumb Ox Ministries, a nonprofit organization dedicated to chastity and vocation formation for teens and young adults. Brian and his wife, Lisa, live with their children in New Orleans, Louisiana.

The Dominican Sisters of St. Cecilia. The four Dominican sisters who participated in the *Chosen* program are from a congregation of nearly 280 religious sisters based in Nashville, Tennessee. The Dominican Sisters of St. Cecilia are committed to Catholic education and serve more than 12,000 students from preschool to college throughout the United States, as well as in Canada and Australia.

Jason Evert has spoken internationally to more than one million people about the virtue of chastity. He is the best-selling author or co-author of a dozen books, including *Theology of His/Her Body* and *Theology of the Body for Teens*. Jason and his wife, Crystalina, live with their children in Denver, Colorado.

Chris Padgett is a Catholic speaker and recording artist and travels around the world giving talks, missions, and concerts. He is also an author and has served as a professor of theology at Franciscan University of Steubenville in Steubenville, Ohio. Chris and his wife, Linda, live with their children in Syracuse, New York.

Fr. Michael Schmitz serves as both the director of youth and young-adult ministry for the Diocese of Duluth and as the chaplain for Newman Catholic Campus Ministry at the University of Minnesota-Duluth in Duluth, Minnesota. He also travels nationally and internationally giving talks and leading retreats and conferences.

Sarah Swafford is the director of special projects for Catholic Identity at Benedictine College in Atchison, Kansas. She is also a Catholic chastity speaker and author. She graduated from Benedictine College with degrees in theology and business marketing. Sarah and her husband, Dr. Andrew Swafford, live with their children in Atchison, Kansas.

Fr. Mark Toups is a priest for the Diocese of Houma-Thibodaux, where he serves as director of seminarians. In addition, he works with the Institute for Priestly Formation, specializing in communications, development, and spiritual direction. He received his master of divinity degree from Notre Dame Seminary in New Orleans, Louisiana.

Mary Ann Wiesinger is associate director of the department of evangelization and catechesis for the Diocese of Oakland. She is responsible for the basic and master catechist certification programs (English and Spanish) in Oakland, California.

Also Featuring

Leah Darrow is an international Catholic speaker. Before her debut on the reality TV show *America's Next Top Model,* and her subsequent years as a professional model in New York City, Leah earned a bachelor of arts degree in psychology from the University of Missouri-St. Louis. As a full-time apologist and speaker for Catholic Answers from 2010 to 2013, Leah brought both her experiences of reality TV and the fashion world to the masses. Leah lives with her husband, Richard, and their daughter in Denver, Colorado.

Br. Crispan Rinaldi **Fr. Richard Roemer**

Franciscan Friars of the Renewal. The Community of Franciscan Friars of the Renewal (CFR's) is a religious community whose twofold mission is to serve the poor and to evangelize through preaching, teaching, and witnessing the Catholic faith. The friars are located worldwide, with communities in New York City, Fort Worth (Texas), London (England), Nicaragua, and Honduras.

Chosen Program Overview

Chosen is a catechetical journey for teenaged Confirmation candidates (also called *confirmandi*). This program is designed to provide the essential intellectual and spiritual catechesis that is so vital to sacramental preparation.

Catechesis is different than an academic course, which seeks to impart knowledge about a given subject. While a catechist certainly teaches, and the student catechized certainly learns, the goal of catechesis is to bring about *a personal encounter with Jesus Christ*. It is teaching for conversion.[3] The end result of effective catechesis is not a classroom full of smart students, but a community full of disciples. Each lesson of *Chosen* has been carefully laid out with this aim in mind.

The name of this program, *Chosen,* is meant to convey that Confirmation, like the other Sacraments of Initiation (Baptism and the Eucharist), is not so much about us choosing God, as it is about him choosing *us* (see CCC 1).

Over the course of the next twenty-four lessons, your candidates will be invited first to hear, then to respond with faith to the voice of God who has called us to become his sons and daughters—simply because "he first loved us" (1 John 4:19).

The *Chosen* Catechetical Approach

Chosen follows the same three-phase catechumenal model used to prepare people to enter the Catholic Church through RCIA (Rite of Christian Initiation of Adults).* These stages are intended to facilitate conversion in the time leading up to the reception of the Sacraments of Initiation.

These three phases are expressed in the organization and structure of the catechetical presentation, following the classic Scripture passage in which Christ reveals his identity to Thomas and the other apostles: "Jesus said to him, 'I am the way, and the truth, and the life; no one comes to the Father, but by me'" (John 14:6). In *Chosen,* we discover that Jesus is ...

1. The Way

Pre-catechumenate, a time to remove obstacles to belief (pre-evangelization, Lessons 1 and 2) and present the basic Gospel message (evangelization, Lessons 3 to 6). The goal of this phase is conversion of the heart and to provide the "framework," or context, for every other lesson.

2. The Truth

Catechumenate, the time of formation (Lessons 7 to 17). When the heart discovers who Jesus is and is trained to follow him, the seeds of faith which were planted at Baptism and strengthened through Confirmation will flourish in new life.

3. The Life

Purification and enlightenment is a phase of more intense, interior formation in final preparation for the sacrament and for a life of discipleship (Lessons 18 to 24).

* General Directory for Catechesis (GDC), 59; see also CCC 1232–1233.

The *Chosen* program also provides candidates opportunities to encounter Jesus in his Church, such as a retreat, a Penance service, and suggested prayers for candidates, families, and sponsors that can be included in the general intercessions at Mass. These resources are available as free downloads at ConfirmationStudy.com.

Following the celebration of the Sacrament of Confirmation is a phase called *mystagogy*. This is the phase in which the newly initiated Christian is immersed in the mysteries he or she has received and in the life of the Christian community. For the newly confirmed teenager, we think the best way to provide an opportunity for *mystagogy* is through youth ministry. If you do not have a youth ministry program, check out great resources from Life Teen, the Dead Theologians Society, and YDisciple to implement youth ministry in your parish.

"Who's Who?" in Confirmation: Explaining the Roles

It takes a whole Church to raise a disciple. Each time a youth is confirmed, he or she takes his or her place in the wider community of faith—among those who have played a vital role in helping him or her to reach this sacramental milestone. This sacramental "support team" includes ...

The Candidate (Confirmand): Teens can live up to our expectations ... if we take the time to communicate what we expect clearly and consistently. Be sure to convey to your candidates, both individually and as a group that (next to God's) theirs is the most important role in their own preparation process.

Starting with the first class, communicate both verbally and in writing what you expect. Have your candidates and their parents sign the "Candidate Commitment" form (available as a free download at ConfirmationStudy.com) and bring it back to the next class. This pledge form includes essential commitments, such as:

- *Mass attendance* ... every Sunday (and on holy days of obligation).

- *Class participation.* Candidates must be on time and be attentive at every class, at prayer services and retreats, and at other required formation events.*

- *Service hours.* While specific requirements may vary from parish to parish and diocese to diocese, opportunities to serve in the community and parish should be provided and encouraged. These opportunities are most fruitful when supervised by team members and adult mentors.

- *Complete homework assignments.* Each lesson contains a "Taking It Home" section that reinforces what was learned in class and what will be covered in the "Review Game" the following week. Consider how you can best motivate your group.

- *Doing the "Challenge of the Week."* Each week, candidates will complete a personal challenge that will help them apply that week's material to their own lives.

---

* Discern, with your pastor, how to handle students who consistently miss class or who fail to follow through on other aspects of Confirmation preparation. In some cases, those who are unwilling to make Confirmation preparation a priority may not be ready to receive the sacrament. (That said, exceptions should be made if preparation is, in fact, a priority to the student, the sacrament is desired, and the requirements were not met for good reasons.)

Expect great things from this process, and let your prayers reflect that you are trusting God to work through this program, so that candidates who are Catholic "because I was raised that way" will become Catholic "because Jesus is the way, and I can't trust another; because Jesus is the truth, and I'm convinced; and because Jesus is the life, and I can't imagine life without him."

The Candidate's Family: Parents are not only the "primary educators" of their children; they are also the "first heralds of the Gospel."[4] In a recent study conducted by the National Study on Youth and Religion (a survey of thousands of teens), **the majority of teenagers named their parents as their number-one spiritual influence.** Parents provide a child's first glimpse at the unconditional love that is at the heart of the Gospel. They are also the first to show their children, by example, what it means to be a disciple of the Lord. For better or for worse, a teen's faith tends to mimic that of mom and dad.

In your correspondence and interaction with parents, be sure to communicate what you expect of them in their child's Confirmation preparation. Encourage parents and other family members to think about the example they are giving to their teens. It may be just the motivation some parents need to start coming back to weekly Mass or going to monthly Confession as a family. It may inspire others to increase at-home devotionals, like reading the Gospels together as a family or praying a weekly Rosary.

The *Chosen* program offers a detailed Parent Information Session, which includes a powerful twenty-minute video presentation with Chris Stefanick and Fr. Mike Schmitz. This session gives teachers the opportunity to engage parents at the very beginning of the program and gives them the opportunity to show their children the importance they place on preparing for the sacrament. A free PDF download is available featuring an outline for the sixty-minute session, instructions for preparing for and following up the session, and sample letters to parents. A short "Invitation to Parents" video from Chris Stefanick is also available, which encourages parents to be actively engaged and to attend the Information Session. (The free PDF outline and videos are available at ConfirmationStudy.com.)

The *Chosen* Parent's Guide includes an overview of what the child will be taught in class each week and provides some handy "table talk" discussion starters. Parents should take a few minutes each week to talk about their child's spiritual journey and what he or she is learning.

The Sponsor: Like a parent, a Confirmation sponsor's job is to be an up-close-and-personal witness of the Christian life for the candidate. The sponsor's task does not end when the teen is confirmed; rather, the sponsor is obligated to help the teen "grow in faith," to help in his or her Christian walk throughout life, and to seek out the candidate if he or she ever goes astray.

The *Chosen* Sponsor's Guide includes dozens of ideas and talking points to help each sponsor communicate the faith effectively to his or her candidate, who, through the sacrament, becomes in a very real sense, that sponsor's "spiritual child." Encourage sponsors to commit to praying daily for their candidates and to reminding their teens that they are praying for them. This support will mean a great deal to the youth, especially as they grow into young adulthood.

The Catechist: Since "catechesis" is teaching to bring about a personal encounter with Jesus Christ, the personal witness and pastoral guidance of the catechist is inseparable from the message. Remember, you are not just teaching but "making disciples" of young people as our Lord did with the apostles. He did not just share facts. He shared his life with them. He ate meals with them. He let them see how he lived. And what they saw was authentic.

A catechist should be more like a big brother or sister sharing life in Christ than a distant instructor sharing facts about God. While a catechist will spend most of his or her time leading the group, it is equally important to listen and remain patient, to demand respect, to give an example of what holiness means, and to take questions seriously. Even if you do not have the answers immediately available, you should tell them you will find them.

The *Chosen* program offers a number of resources for catechists and volunteers, including a seven-part Leader Training and Orientation Video series. This series of short and engaging videos featuring author and presenter Chris Stefanick provides a helpful introduction and overview of *Chosen*. Leaders can ask volunteers to watch the videos online before meeting or could choose to play the videos as part of a team-training meeting prior to running the program. Leaders should also encourage volunteers to view the detailed Frequently Asked Questions and to consider hosting or attending a *Chosen* Formation/ Training Day. (Visit ConfirmationStudy.com for the free training videos, FAQs, and information on Formation/ Training days.)

The Parish Community: The involvement of the entire parish community should be encouraged throughout the process of preparing for Confirmation. *Chosen* offers a retreat and a Penance service, and the parish community can offer support through the inclusion of intercessory prayers for the candidates at Sunday Mass. It is important for candidates to be introduced into the life of the parish, and they should be given opportunities to volunteer and experience the community through getting involved with service projects and other parish activities.

In addition to including intercessory prayers for the candidates and their sponsors at Sunday Mass (visit ConfirmationStudy.com for free downloadable samples), announcements can be made to keep the parish community informed as to the candidates' progress. Consider having your candidates read their Candidate Commitment Form before Mass at the beginning of the program. This gives the parish an opportunity to show their loving support. It is amazing what a little encouragement and kindness from the pulpit can do.

Chosen Program Components

The *Chosen* program is designed to guide you through every step of the sacramental preparation the teens in your parish will need for Confirmation. The catechesis is done through a plug-and-play video and student workbook combination that is both engaging and rich and is designed to lead candidates into a deeper relationship with Christ.

Chosen also features a Parent's Guide and a Sponsor's Guide, which we highly recommend you utilize. These guides are designed to draw parents and sponsors closer to the candidates and to the process of formation, which will both encourage and strengthen the teens on their journey. Confirmation also provides a great opportunity to evangelize sponsors and parents, and these guides include features like "The Top Ten Catholic Questions" and dozens of tips, suggestions, and ideas for ways to grow in the faith.

In addition to the printed and video materials, we offer two additional resources to help you adapt the *Chosen* program to meet the particular requirements of your diocese or parish:

1. The *Chosen* website (ConfirmationStudy.com) contains free downloadable resources, promotional materials, and program forms.

2. Ascension Press Study Consultants can answer any questions you have about how to adapt the *Chosen* program to your particular needs. Call us at 1-800-376-0520, or email your question to info@ascensionpress.com.

The following items are included in the *Chosen: Your Journey Toward Confirmation* Starter Pack. An asterisk (*) indicates that you will need to order additional copies for your candidates and others involved in the program. (Also note that a **Student Pack** is available, which includes the Student Workbook, Parent's Guide and Sponsor's Guide. Because the Parent's and Sponsor's Guides are considered integral parts of the program, these resources are offered in a bundled package at a discounted price.)

*   **Twenty-Four Part Video Series** – Twenty-four 15- to 25- minute lessons and a "Review Game" video for Lessons 3 through 24. Videos available for streaming at Evangelization.com. Also available on DVD (one set of DVDs is included in the Starter Pack).

*   **Student Workbook*** – Designed to be used in conjunction with the video lessons, the workbook includes fill-in-the-blank questions, saint stories, prayers, vocabulary words, and more. (Order one per candidate.)

*   **Leader's Guide*** – Includes a program overview, planning and scheduling resources, leader's notes, and more. (Order one per catechist.)

*   **Sponsor's Guide*** – Includes an overview of the sponsor's role, "Conversation Starters," answers to the "Top Ten Catholic Questions," and more. (Order one per sponsor.)

*   **Parent's Guide*** – Includes an overview of the parent's role, guidelines for support, tips for talking with the child, and more. (Order one per household.)

Getting Started

Step 1: Plan Your Schedule

Chosen is a twenty-four-lesson program that may be completed in one year or over the course of two years. (For more information, refer to "Scheduling Models" on page xii.)

As you schedule your weekly meetings, we suggest allowing 90 minutes per lesson (see "*Chosen* Session Format" on page xvi). The lessons can also be done in 60 minutes by adapting the time spent on particular components or by assigning suggested in-class activities as homework instead. In addition, you will want to schedule special meetings and group events (including the "Retreat," and the "Penance Service") and note how and when you will communicate with sponsors and parents regarding the times they will be required to be present.

Many find it helpful to create a detailed "master plan" that includes class times, administrative details (such as diocesan meetings), candidate requirement deadlines, and service opportunities. This plan will help you track details and communicate them in a timely manner to parents, sponsors, and candidates. (Be sure to add to your master plan—and put on the parish calendar—a "dress rehearsal" of the Rite of Confirmation, which sponsors and parents are invited to attend.)

To prevent double-booking your space with another parish group, be sure to confirm your proposed schedule with your parish office before communicating the details of the program to families.

Step 2: Recruit Your Team*

The *Chosen* model emphasizes small-group "discipleship." This is the way Jesus formed the faith of the first disciples. In an era where ninety-three percent of teens do not believe in absolute truth, a ministry that is entirely based on a large-group model is not sufficient to ensure that teens are "getting it."[5] We have found that most groups for teens work best when they are kept small (five to twelve teens per leader). Therefore, we recommend that, especially during small-group discussion times, each catechist be responsible for no more than twelve teens.

At parishes where videos are viewed as a large group, we still recommend seating candidates in smaller groups, each with its own catechist, who will ensure respectful and attentive behavior from the members of the group during the videos, lead small-group discussion times, and ensure that the teens in the group are grasping the topics being studied.

Here are a few tips for recruiting and forming the best team possible:

- *Decide how many team members you need*. Depending on where the group meets, plan on having one to two small-group leaders for every group of five to twelve teens. Two adults per small group is ideal and is necessary if the small group meets in a more private setting.

- *Do not start your program without your team.* It can be difficult to hand off work. It is easy to motivate people, however, if they feel they are part of the ministry from the start.

- *Approach with enthusiasm*. Instead of saying, "This won't take much time," start with the invitation, "Do you want to help me change the lives of young people?"

- *Pray hard*. Jesus prayed all night before recruiting his apostles. He knew how important that decision was.

- *Invite selectively*. Do not extend a general invitation to the whole parish. Handpick people you think will be effective with young people. They do not have to be young and cool. (Sometimes retirees are the most effective people with teens.) They do have to be authentic, holy, and normal. They should also have a love for young people.

- *Take your time*. It is easy to hire a volunteer. It is very difficult to fire one.

- *Recruit more people than you think you will need*. Do not set a goal of recruiting enough people to get the program done. Recruit enough people to invest in the formation of the teens. A one-to-seven leader-to-candidate ratio is ideal.

* Check with your diocese on what training and screening is required of adult leaders and what meeting space is permissible.

- *Once you have your team, take time to train them*. Schedule one or two evenings to go through the materials and talk about how to lead a small group and how to deal with questions or concerns that might arise. Give them a copy of your "master plan" so they will know what will be required of them well in advance. Have your volunteers watch the "Leader Training and Orientation" videos. (See page xv for more information.)

Step 3: Engage the Parish Community

A catechist wears many hats: teacher, mentor, role model ... and parish "development director." To do your job well, you need contributions from the whole parish community, not just in terms of financial support, but in terms of time and talent, too. Speak with your pastor about the best ways to get others involved and about who he would recommend for particular tasks.

When you involve your parish in Confirmation preparation, it is not just the candidates who benefit. Enlisting the help of others in your community in the service of young people offers them the blessing of putting their gifts to use in the parish. There are endless possibilities for the support roles the members of your community can take on. Here are just a few:

- *Hospitality*: Instead of buying snacks every week, consider finding a group of people willing to feed your teens at every meeting. A large group would mean that someone might only "cater" one meeting every few months. The hospitality team provides "God's love made edible." Make it good.

- *Prayer Support*: Encourage each team member to recruit and request the prayers of a personal intercessor who can spiritually support his or her work with the young people in the program. Include the Confirmation class in the weekly prayers of the faithful at Mass, and consider how you can encourage families in your parish to pray for each candidate individually. For example, you might hand out cards with the first names of the teens to parishioners after Mass to post on their refrigerators as a reminder to pray for specific teens. You could also create a bulletin board with the first name and picture of each candidate and post it in a common area. Another idea is to arrange for a prayer team to keep vigil for the teens while they are on retreat. Teens are very moved when they learn that adults from the parish have been praying for them throughout their retreat.

- *Money*: You would be amazed at the potential financial support hiding in every parish. With the pastor's permission, give parishioners the opportunity to sponsor a candidate, including covering program fees and funding ongoing spiritual growth opportunities, such as retreats and youth-ministry events. (Some people might simply make a donation toward your "prize bank" or incentive program.)

- *Environment*: If the program meets in one large space, consider having a small team decorate one corner of the room with pictures (images of candidates' patron saints, the Divine Mercy image, or other sacred images), cushions or other seating, electric candles, rosaries, prayer books, a CD player and instrumental music, and other appropriate items to create a "sacred space" for prayer.

Step 4: Create Your "Program Checklist"

In the weeks leading up to launching your program, keep your checklist handy to ensure that nothing gets overlooked. Your checklist might include ...

- *Schedule the date of Confirmation with your pastor and bishop's office.* Before beginning your planning, check with your pastor to see if the bishop has already scheduled a visit to your parish to celebrate Confirmation or if a request for possible dates needs to be made to the bishop's office.

- *Select and reserve your meeting space.* Consider how to create a welcoming atmosphere to help candidates feel comfortable. If yours is a large group, make sure the space is large enough to accommodate everyone for both the video presentation and the small-group discussions.

- *Order materials.* Be sure to order a few extra—you can always return unused materials if you do not need them.

- *Recruit and train your team.* At least a week ahead of time, schedule a training session for your entire team. Show the first video presentation and review the first lesson in the Student Workbook together. Talk about how to handle difficult questions or situations that may arise—such as what to do if a candidate professes not to believe in God or does not want to be confirmed. Seek your pastor's advice if needed.*

- *Promote the program.* Be sure to put an announcement in your parish bulletin well in advance. Depending on your parish's religious education model, consider promoting the program at least one full month (or possibly two or three months) before classes begin. Significant advance notice is the best way to minimize scheduling conflicts. Plan on hosting a Parent Information Session prior to the first lesson, to hand out the Parent's Guide and communicate your expectations in person. (For more information, see "Parent Information Session" on page xv.)

- *Outline program requirements and decide how to communicate those expectations.* If you are not already familiar with them, confirm sacramental preparation requirements with your pastor or diocesan office, and add them to your "master plan." Be sure to reinforce verbal communications with visual reminders, such as email blasts, paper newsletters (mailed or sent home), Facebook posts, parish bulletin announcements, a bulletin board ... Decide what works best for your group.

- *Prepare your first lesson.* Do you have the necessary audiovisual equipment ready and in good working order? Do you have the other materials and teaching aids (such as prizes**) that you will need for the first lesson? Print out the "Candidate Commitment" forms, which should be signed by candidates and their parents and returned at the second lesson. (Visit ConfirmationStudy.com to download the form.)

---

* If you need guidance on how to present something in a lesson, remember that Ascension Press Study Consultants are available to help. Just call 1-800-376-0520.

** Depending on your budget and personal preferences, you can offer individual or group incentives to keep kids engaged and motivated—anything from a "candy jar" to iTunes gift cards ... to an end-of-the-year pizza party or an iPad giveaway.

Scheduling Models

One-Year Plan

September

The Way: Pre-Evangelization (Remove obstacles and present the "big picture.")

Lesson 1 – "Why am I here?" (An Introduction to *Chosen*)

Lesson 2 – "What makes me happy?" (Discovering God as the Source)

October

The Way: Evangelization (Deliver life-changing kerygma/*Gospel message.)*

Lesson 3 – "What's your story, God?" (A Look at Salvation History)

Lesson 4 – "How do I know God is real?" (Understanding Divine Revelation)

Lesson 5 – "Who is Jesus?" (The Person and Mission of Christ)

Lesson 6 – "Why be Catholic?" (Discovering the Church Jesus Founded)

November

Retreat (downloadable resource)

The Truth: Catechumenate (Explain sacramental living and the power to answer the call.)

Lesson 7 – "Where am I going?" (A Look at the Four Last Things)

Lesson 8 – "How do I get there?" (The Power and Purpose of the Sacraments)

Lesson 9 – "When did my journey begin?" (Baptism, Your Initiation into God's Family)

December

Lesson 10 – "Why tell my sins to a priest?" (The Healing Power of Confession)

Lesson 11– "How does God help when it hurts?" (Anointing of the Sick and Redemptive Suffering)

January

Lesson 12 – "Who is the Holy Spirit?" (Meeting the Third Person of the Trinity)

Lesson 13 – "What does the Holy Spirit do for me?" (Gifts for the Journey)

Lesson 14 – "Why have I been *Chosen*?" (Sealed and Sent in Confirmation)

Lesson 15 – "Why do I have to go to Mass?" (Encountering Jesus in the Eucharist)

February

Lesson 16 – "What does it mean to say, 'I do'?" (Marriage, a Sign of God's Love)

Lesson 17 – "Who's calling?" (Holy Orders and Vocational Discernment)

The Life: Discipleship (Final preparation for a life of discipleship)

Lesson 18 – "Are you talking to me?" (Getting to Know God Through Prayer)

Lesson 19 – "Who is Mary?" (Meeting the Mother of God — and Your Heavenly Family)

March

Lesson 20 – "What would Jesus do?" (The Beatitudes as a Path to True Happiness)

Lesson 21 – "Do I have what it takes?" (Building Virtue — Your Spiritual Workout)

Lesson 22 – "Why wait?" (God's Plan for Love and Sex)

Lesson 23 – "How do I build the kingdom?" (Saying "Yes" to the Mission of Christ and His Church)

Penance Service (downloadable resource)

April

Pre-Confirmation Interviews (downloadable resource)

Lesson 24 – "Where do I go from here?" (The Journey Continues)

Have sponsors attend and do Confirmation rehearsal with Lesson 24.

Easter Season

Confirmation Rehearsal

Rite of Confirmation

Two-Year Plan

Year One

September

The Way: Pre-Evangelization (Remove obstacles and present the "big picture.")

Lesson 1– "Why am I here?" (An Introduction to *Chosen*)

October

Lesson 2 – "What makes me happy?" (Discovering God as the Source)

November

The Way: Evangelization (Deliver life-changing kerygma/*Gospel message.)*

Lesson 3 – "What's your story, God?" (A Look at Salvation History)

Lesson 4 – "How do I know God is real?" (Understanding Divine Revelation)

December

Lesson 5 – "Who is Jesus?" (The Person and Mission of Christ)

Lesson 6 – "Why be Catholic?" (Discovering the Church Jesus Founded)

January

Retreat (downloadable resource)

The Truth: Catechumenate (Explain sacramental living and the power to answer the call.)

Lesson 7 – "Where am I going?" (A Look at the Four Last Things)

February

Lesson 8 – "How do I get there?" (The Power and Purpose of the Sacraments)

Lesson 9 – "When did my journey begin?" (Baptism, Your Initiation into God's Family)

March

Lesson 10 – "Why tell my sins to a priest?" (The Healing Power of Confession)

Lesson 11– "How does God help when it hurts?" (Anointing of the Sick and Redemptive Suffering)

Year Two

September

Lesson 12 – "Who is the Holy Spirit?" (Meeting the Third Person of the Trinity)

Lesson 13 – "What does the Holy Spirit do for me?" (Gifts for the Journey)

Online Resources

The following is a list of online resources available at ConfirmationStudy.com. Visit the site regularly for updates, to check for additional resources, or to contact an Ascension Press Study Consultant.

- **Candidate Commitment Form** – Candidates and their parents sign this form, committing to undertaking the basic requirements of the program, such as Mass attendance, class participation, and homework assignments.

- **To the Heart — The *Chosen* Confirmation Retreat** – A retreat is recommended after the initial pre-evangelization and evangelization phases of the program (Lessons 1 to 6). The retreat is designed to reinforce the material and topics covered up to this point and to encourage the movement of the material from the head to the heart. This detailed retreat is offered in both a three-day and one-day format.

- **Penance Service** – A penitential service with the opportunity for individual Confession is recommended as the candidates make final spiritual preparation for receiving the Sacrament of Confirmation. This Penance service includes ideas for Scripture selections, reflections, and prayers. It is recommended that this service be done following the catechesis phase of the program (Lessons 7 to 17).

- **Parent Information Session** – Recognizing the primary role that parents are called to play in their children's faith formation, this session offers you an opportunity to engage with parents before their teen begins the program. A free downloadable PDF guide includes a sample framework for a one-hour Parent Information Session, sample letters for parents, and a checklist of things to consider prior, during and after the Parent Session. The session features a powerful twenty-minute video presentation with Chris Stefanick and Fr. Mike Schmitz. These resources, along with a five-minute video from Chris Stefanick inviting parents to the session, are all available for free at ConfirmationStudy.com.

- **Leader Training and Orientation Videos** – This series of seven short videos, featuring author and presenter Chris Stefanick, provides a helpful introduction and overview of *Chosen* and is perfect for leaders, volunteers, and anyone interested in learning more about the program. Leaders can ask volunteers to watch the videos online before meeting or could choose to play the videos as part of a team-training meeting prior to running the program.

- **Sample Intercessory Prayers** – The entire parish community can offer their support and encouragement by praying for candidates, families and sponsors during the intercessory prayers at Sunday Mass.

- **Examination of Conscience** – This examination of conscience outlines steps to prepare for making a good confession. Thoughtful questions and reflections, designed to resonate with teens, are provided.

- **Pre-Confirmation Interview** – This interview offers an important opportunity to assess candidates' spiritual understanding and readiness to receive the sacrament, as well as to answer their questions and encourage them as they make their final preparations for the Rite of Confirmation.

Session Outline

Below is a suggested format for a 90-minute lesson. You can adapt these recommended plans to meet the particular needs of your group (e.g., by adapting the time spent on particular components or by assigning suggested in-class activities as homework), but this provides a basic model to get you started.

Each lesson follows the same basic format: (1) Review of the previous lesson and an opening prayer, (2) video presentation, (3) small-group discussion, (4) group discussion and closing remarks, followed by a closing prayer, and (5) homework, which reinforces the material learned that week.

Chosen Session Format

90 minutes

 Step 1 **Welcome/"Review Game" (5 minutes, beginning with Lesson 3)***

A video-based review of the previous lesson's material. These questions are drawn from the "Watch It!" questions and the "Hero of the Week," "Wrap-Up," and "What's That Word?" features (located in the "Taking It Home" section at the end of each lesson).

In order to build interest and excitement about the game, leaders may ask for two candidates to "face off" at the front of the class to answer the questions. Whoever gets the most correct answers wins a prize, which could range from candy to a five-dollar bill or iTunes gift card. Think creatively—nothing makes a game a success like a great prize.

If your candidates seem to need a "change," consider adapting the game a bit using one of these variations—or one of your own.

- "Shout Out": See who can call out the answer first.
- "Family Feud/College Bowl": Divide into teams and have one member of each team "face off" for points.

Step 2 **"Challenge of the Week Review" (5 minutes)**

Students are encouraged to share their experiences of the "challenge" they chose to do the previous week. (See Step 8, "Challenge of the Week.")

Leaders can ask if anyone would like to share a "challenge experience." To break the ice, you might ask questions like, "Who chose the first challenge?" "Did you find it easy or difficult?" "Would any of you want to share what you wrote or any insights you gained?"

---

*   The first lesson starts with an icebreaker called "Autograph Chasers."

"Opening Prayer" (3 minutes)

This prayer is based on the lesson topic for the week. The Student Workbook contains the "group" part of the prayer, with directions and notes for the teacher printed in the Leader's Guide version.

 "Dive In" (5 minutes)

This feature is a thought-provoking story to draw candidates into the topic for the week. This can be read aloud by the leader or a candidate or silently by the class. This is done before the video presentation.

"Watch It!"/Small-Group Discussion – Video Presentation (50 minutes)

The video presentations are divided into three segments of 4 to 8 minutes each.* At the end of each segment, the video is paused and candidates fill in two or three questions in their workbooks.

After checking to be sure that everyone has the correct answers, the facilitator then leads candidates through the small-group discussion questions before viewing the next video segment. (Allow for about 10 minutes after each segment.)

Recommended questions are printed in the Leader's Guide; these can be adapted or modified to meet the needs of your group. Questions that are "open ended" or that could have several possible responses do not have an answer key. Other questions have *Catechism* references or other printed responses to assist you in facilitating the discussion.

"To the Heart" (10 minutes)

After the small-group discussion, the class is then brought back together to read the "To the Heart" story, either silently or aloud by the leader or a candidate. A thought-provoking question is included in the Leader's Guide in a red box to foster a brief class discussion.

In the first lesson, the "To the Heart" feature is omitted to give you time to communicate your expectations for the program to your group. A "Candidate Commitment" form is available in the "Online Resources" section of the Chosen *website (ConfirmationStudy.com).*

 "Hero of the Week" (5 minutes)

Each lesson highlights a saint whose life and work embodies that week's topic. This piece can be read either silently or aloud by the leader or by a candidate.

---

* Lesson 1 and Lesson 24 contain two segments.

Step 8 **"Challenge of the Week" (2 minutes)**

Each week, candidates will be asked to choose from one of three personal challenges to help them apply that week's lesson. They should read through the three options and then check the box next to the challenge they intend to complete. During the week, they will complete the challenge and write about it in the space provided in the Student Workbook.

Step 9 **"Homework Instructions and Updates" (2 minutes)**

Just before the closing prayer, remind candidates to read the "Wrap-Up" and the "What's That Word?" vocabulary section in the "Taking It Home" part of the workbook. They should also review the "Watch It!" questions and "Memory Verse" to prepare for the next lesson's "Review Game." Finally, remember the "Challenge of the Week."

Step 10 **"Closing Prayer" (3 minutes)**

This short prayer, included in the Student Workbook, reflects on the lesson's topic. Before beginning the prayer, leaders may want to ask if anyone has any special prayer intentions.

Note: The steps for Lessons 1, 2, and 24 are unique to those particular lessons.

Send Us Your Ideas and "Success Stories"

Do you have any Confirmation program "success stories"—service projects, special group activities, or program highlights—you would like to share? We would love to hear from you. Contact us at ConfirmationStudy.com. We know leaders and educators are creative and inventive people, so please send us *your* story or idea. (Remember to include pictures!)

For More Information

Please visit ConfirmationStudy.com for helpful information regarding *Chosen* and for free downloadable resources. If you have any questions regarding ordering materials or preparing for a study, call an Ascension Press Study Consultant at 1-800-376-0520, or visit AscensionPress.com.

We welcome your feedback. Please contact us at AscensionPress.com or by mail at Ascension Press, P.O. Box 1990, West Chester, PA 19380.

How to Use this Leader's Guide

This Leader's Guide is designed to walk you through each lesson using easy-to-follow Steps and Leader's Notes.

The first page of each lesson provides a "Leader's Overview" and the "Objectives" for that lesson. It is recommended that leaders and facilitators read through the entire lesson (and watch the corresponding video) before each lesson. However, if that is not possible, this "Overview" and the "Objectives" list will provide a basic outline of the themes and topics to be addressed in the lesson.

The text for the opening prayer is found here in the Student Workbook section each week.

Throughout the Leader's Guide, suggested words to say to the class are printed in WHITE text within the colored boxes in the margins.

The "Steps" at the bottom of the pages will explain and guide you through each general component of the lesson. Simply follow each step for a fruitful and engaging classroom experience.

Leader's instructions are printed in RED text in the margins.

Also provided in the margins are *Catechism* and Scripture references. You may use these in preparation for the class (e.g., to orient yourself further with the material and to assist you in leading discussions). You may also choose to refer to them during class, if time permits.

The answers to the "Watch It!" questions are provided in RED text.

The "Small-Group Discussion" questions for the video segments are found here each week in the blue box. "Leader's Notes" are found below.

The first time each Glossary word appears in the Student Workbook, it is called out with caps and gold text. Students are told they can check the Glossary in the back of the Student Workbook for a detailed definition.

Discussion questions for the "To the Heart" section are found here each week in the red box.

Each week, there is a "Find It!" question. We suggest you ask if anyone found the answer to the previous week's "Find It!" after playing the "Review Game." A prize could be awarded for the correct answer.

Overview

"Why am I here?" Depending on the student, this question may be answered several different ways. Naturally, most teens attend this class to prepare for the Sacrament of Confirmation, as their final Sacrament of Initiation into the Catholic faith. Some teens approach this sacrament eagerly; others are compelled by their parents, with varying degrees of willingness, and may be looking forward to "graduating" from religious education. *Chosen* has been developed to meet the needs of both types of students.

The question posed in the title of this introductory lesson also hints at its primary purpose: to convey that the journey of faith in general (and thus, of Confirmation preparation in particular) is not just something we do "on the side" of *real life*, but that it has everything to do with discovering the very meaning of life itself and learning how to live it to the full.

To the degree that you, as the teacher, are both welcoming and respectful of this process of discovery (asking the Holy Spirit to speak to and soften the hearts of those you are trying to reach with the truth of the Gospel), you have an opportunity to be part of a profound transformation in the lives of your students.

A crucial part of that process of transformation is for your students to discover the communal aspect of Christian life and to experience your patience, willingness to listen, and true concern for them, as well as an atmosphere of positive peer pressure. This is all part of "pre-evangelization," engaging the audience "where they are" in order to prepare them for true "evangelization"—that is, bringing them to where God wants them to be.

Objectives of this Lesson

1. *Get to know each other.* Make basic introductions; then ask, "Why are you here?" Use this exercise to help students find points of commonality and to be open to learning together. Encourage them to be accepting of one another by modeling this attitude yourself. Help them to see that you are all on a journey together.

2. *Disarm them.* Tell them your goal is their happiness, plain and simple. Let them know they do not need to sound "religious"—tell them to just be themselves—to be honest and real.

3. *Get them thinking about what they really want out of life.* Help them to identify how their hearts' longings ultimately reveal an underlying need for "something more." While we all desire many different things, in the end, we all want the same things out of life: love, a sense of purpose, and peace. In a word, we all want to be happy.

4. *Get them committed.* Communicate expectations and program requirements clearly, and send the "Candidate Commitment" form home for students and parents to read and sign.

"Why am I here?"

(An Introduction to *Chosen*)

✝

Opening Prayer

"Hail Mary, full of grace, the Lord is with thee.
Blessed art thou among women,
and blessed is the fruit of thy womb, Jesus.
Holy Mary, Mother of God, pray for us sinners,
now and at the hour of our death. Amen."

As you lead the "Opening Prayer," pay attention to how your students respond. Some may need to read this basic prayer from the book—and this may be a sign that they have not received much faith formation at home. As you teach, look for ways to encourage those who are not as advanced, so you can all enjoy the journey together.

Opening Prayer

Lord Jesus, you do not waste our time. You brought us here for a reason. Keep our hearts and minds open throughout this Confirmation class to whatever you want to give us.

Mother Mary, you were perfectly open to the grace of God. We entrust our time together to you. Pray for us. Help us to be as open to God as you were, so we too can be filled with the life he came to give us.

Together, let's pray the Hail Mary. In the name of the Father and of the Son and of the Holy Spirit …

This week you will need …

- Name tags (if desired)
- Game prize
- "Candidate Commitment" form (download at ConfirmationStudy.com)

 Step 1 **Opening Prayer** (3 minutes)

Lead the class in the "Opening Prayer," which is included in the Student Workbook. Leader's Guide notes are provided above: Red text provides direction and guidance, and white text is for you to read aloud to the class.

Explain that this game really has nothing to do with the lesson. Its purpose is to help them get to know each other.

If you would rather do another game, feel free to use any icebreaker you think would be effective. The key is to get them talking to each other.

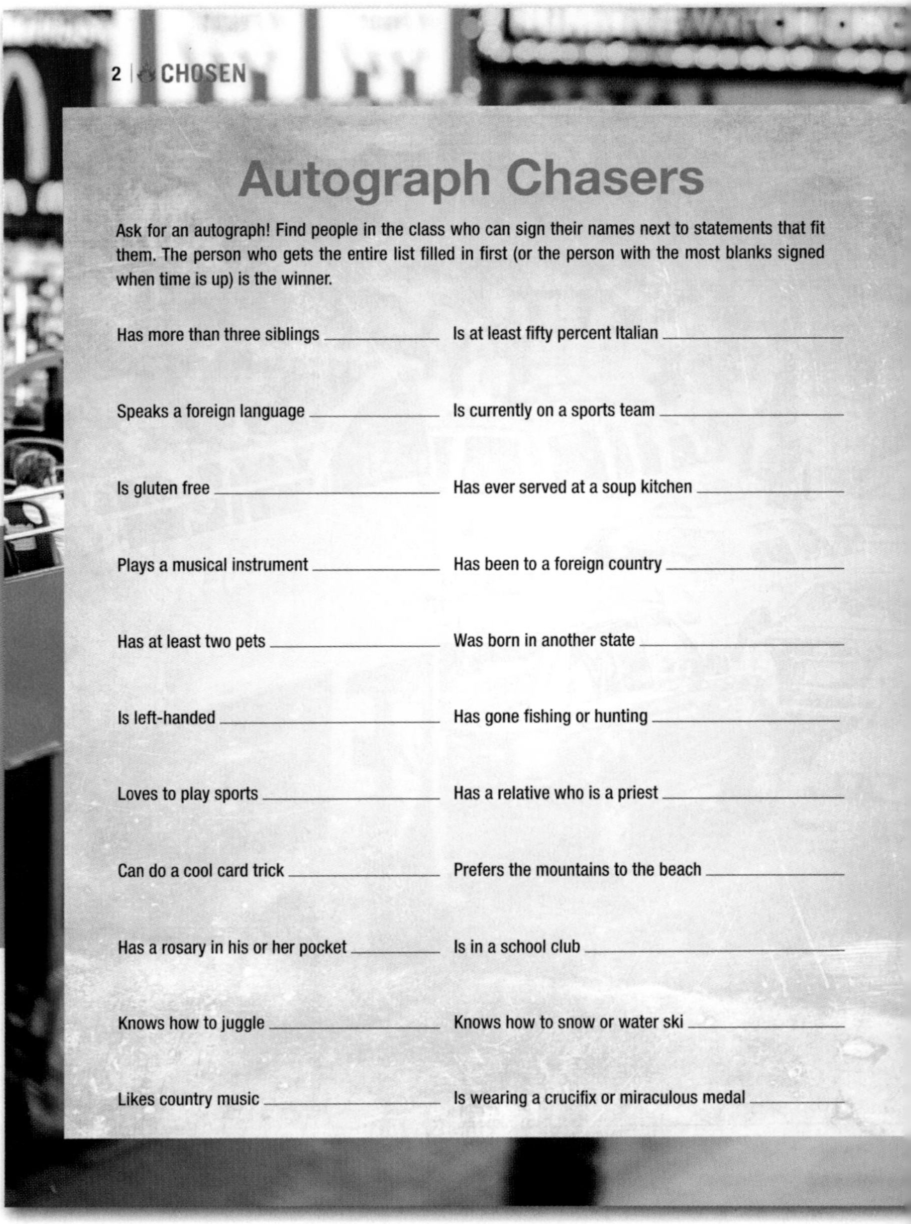
2 | CHOSEN

Autograph Chasers

Ask for an autograph! Find people in the class who can sign their names next to statements that fit them. The person who gets the entire list filled in first (or the person with the most blanks signed when time is up) is the winner.

Has more than three siblings ________	Is at least fifty percent Italian ________
Speaks a foreign language ________	Is currently on a sports team ________
Is gluten free ________	Has ever served at a soup kitchen ________
Plays a musical instrument ________	Has been to a foreign country ________
Has at least two pets ________	Was born in another state ________
Is left-handed ________	Has gone fishing or hunting ________
Loves to play sports ________	Has a relative who is a priest ________
Can do a cool card trick ________	Prefers the mountains to the beach ________
Has a rosary in his or her pocket ________	Is in a school club ________
Knows how to juggle ________	Knows how to snow or water ski ________
Likes country music ________	Is wearing a crucifix or miraculous medal ________

My Five Personal Goals

Think for three minutes about this simple question: "What do I want out of life?" Write the top five things that come to your mind. Do you want to be rich? Famous? Have a family? Meet the man/woman of your dreams? Become a leader in some scientific field? The sky's the limit.

Step 2 Icebreaker: Autograph Chasers (5 minutes)

The object is to get the students up and moving and meeting new people. Direct them to find people in the class who can sign their names next to statements that fit them. For example, if John is gluten free, he can sign in that blank, but he can only sign each student's workbook once. The person who gets the entire list filled in first (or the person with the most blanks signed when time is up) is the winner. **Note:** For smaller groups, you may choose to allow students to sign their names more than once, but still limit it to a set number of times.

Step 3 Watch It! (3 minutes)

Play Lesson 1, Segment 1. There is no "Small-Group Discussion" after this segment. The group will move right into Step 4.

Step 4 My Five Personal Goals (5 minutes)

Have the students complete the "My Five Personal Goals" exercise in their workbooks. Give them the instructions found in the orange box above.

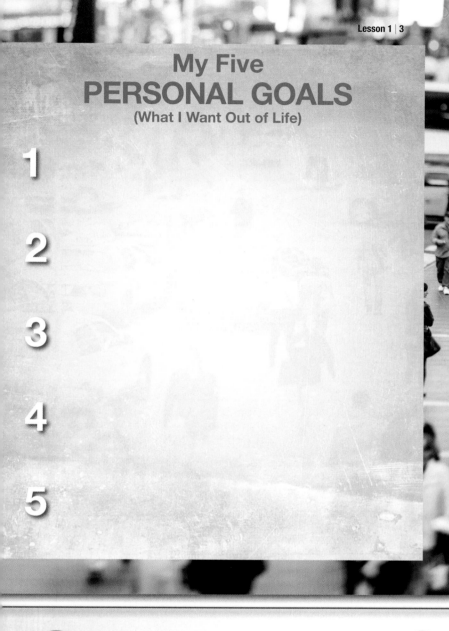

My Five
PERSONAL GOALS
(What I Want Out of Life)

1

2

3

4

5

Small-Group Discussion

Segment 2: Beginning the Journey

1. What struck you from the video?[1]

2. After the first segment, you had a chance to write down five personal goals, things most important to you. What did you write as a personal goal?[2]

3. How would you answer the question, "Why are you here?"

4. What is one big question you hope to get an answer to this year?

5. What do you think the title *Chosen* has to do with Confirmation?

Small-Group Discussion Leader's Notes

1. This question provides an opportunity for you to elaborate on any points the teens did not "get" while watching the video. Note that every human desire ultimately points to something intangible, but important: happiness, love, purpose, peace.

2. If no one volunteers, consider starting with yours—but give them a few seconds to think about their responses. Affirm and encourage— never criticize or show frustration. Be sure to point out that each person's answer reflects what he or she believes will lead to happiness and fulfillment.

Step 5 ## Watch It!/Small-Group Discussion (50 minutes)

Play Lesson 1, Segment 2. After the video, have them break into small groups. They should have their workbooks with them. Lead students in a small-group discussion using the questions provided in the blue box above.

Step 6 ## Lay Out Expectations (5 minutes)

Use this time to communicate your expectations of the program. Acknowledge that the students may have come to class for many different reasons, but that their presence there is no accident. God has chosen them to embark on this journey toward truth. He wants to help them find the "truth and happiness [they] never stop searching for" (CCC 27).

Tell them you expect great things of this process—namely, that those who are Catholic "because my parents made me" or "because there's a cute girl or boy in my church," will come to see that being Catholic is about, as Jesus

4 | CHOSEN

Challenge of the Week

☐ **Take the "What I Want Out of Life" list you wrote in class to the next level.** Take one action to bring you a tiny step closer to one of your dreams. Check out a related book, contact someone in your chosen field with a question, or do an extra workout or study session. Write about it here.

☐ **Pray a Hail Mary** each night before bed this week, for yourself and your fellow students, asking God to help you be open to what he has in store for you in the time of preparation that lies ahead. Put a note on your bedside table to help you remember.

☐ **Did you know that God speaks to us through the kindness of other people?** Think about all those people who help you figure out your life (parents, teachers, coaches, friends, and others), and thank one of them for something specific before our next class. Do it in person or by mail or email. Write about it in the space below.

_____

_____

_____

_____

_____

_____

_____

Closing Prayer

> Every time you see a word that looks like this, you can turn to the Glossary on page 234 for a detailed definition.

"For I know the plans I have for you, says the Lord, plans for welfare and not for EVIL, to give you a future and a hope."

—Jeremiah 29:11

Heavenly Father, you created every person in this room for a holy purpose. Your LOVE for us is real, and your plan for each of us is powerful. You reveal your plans in many ways, including through our talents, our dreams, and the encouragement of those who love us. Help us to find you in silence. Inspire us, Lord, to seek you with all our hearts.

promised, living "life to the full" (John 10:10, NIV). Similarly, those who cannot imagine not being in the Church will grow in their ability to love and serve God with all their hearts, minds, and strength.

Let them know there are certain things you expect from them. While they can expect an open heart and a listening ear from you, you expect them to show respect for you, for the other adult leaders, for their peers, and for the Confirmation preparation process in general.

Read through the "Candidate Commitment" form* with them and ask them to bring it back, signed by them and their parents, to the next class.

* Print a copy for each student from the download available at ConfirmationStudy.com.

Step 7 **Challenge of the Week** (2 minutes)

Ask your candidates to read the "challenges" at the top of page 4 and choose one of the three to complete this week. Have them check the box next to the challenge they intend to complete. Encourage them to write about their experiences in the space provided.

Step 8 **Closing Prayer** (3 minutes)

As a way of building up community, ask if there are any prayer intentions. Write them down (or have candidates share them aloud) and after praying for those intentions, have the class read the "Closing Prayer" together (provided in the Student Workbook).

**Lesson 2
Leader's Notes**

Overview

The purpose of this lesson is to consider the possibility that everything we need in life is ultimately found in God. Happiness, love, peace, purpose, and security are all qualities that are found in the lives of those who live according to the "master plan."

As young Catholic men and women, Confirmation candidates are on a quest for identity and personal significance. As the influence of their peers increases, they continue to look to the example of their parents to guide them. However, this group is extremely sensitive to any perceived hypocrisy or inconsistency. Therefore, finding and holding up authentic models of faith (and acknowledging the consequences of following the wrong role models) is of paramount importance.

Objectives of this Lesson

1. *Explain that what the world offers in terms of bringing us happiness will always fall short of our desires.* Our culture identifies success with fame, power, and wealth, yet it is clear that many who achieve these things are unhappy.

2. *We are all looking for God, and we are empty until we find him.* Though not everyone knows it, the search for God is our most pressing need (after satisfying our physical needs). The rational human soul is always reaching for the transcendent (see Psalm 42:1-2; CCC 27–28).

3. *"Come and See."* The *"kerygma,"* or core message of Christianity, answers our hearts' deepest longing as well as our most fundamental questions about life: "What is the meaning of life, and what comes after death?" In response to this simple invitation, the Savior always offers a singular invitation: "Come, and you will see" (John 1:39). He *is* the answer (see CCC 158).

"What makes me happy?"

(Discovering God as the Source)

✝

Opening Prayer

"Jesus turned and saw [Andrew and John] following him and said to them, 'What are you looking for?' They said to him, '[Teacher] ... where are you staying?'

"He said to them, 'Come, and you will see.'"

—*John 1:38-39, NAB*

Lord Jesus, you ask us, just as you asked Andrew and John, "What are you looking for?" So you stand before each heart in this room and ask the same question today.

And just as you invited *them* to "come and see," you're offering to lead *us* to the HAPPINESS we seek.

We accept your invitation. Help us to find what we're *really* looking for in life. Give us the wisdom to look for happiness in the right place. Amen.

Opening Prayer

Let's start with a reading from the Gospel of John.

> *Read John 1:38-39, NAB*

Jesus' first question to his followers was, "What are you looking for?"

Last week we discussed what we are all really looking for in life.

What are some of the things we came up with?

> *Pause briefly to allow a few to comment.*

This week we are going to take the next step. Let's pray. In the name of the Father ...

Step 1 — Welcome (2 minutes)

Welcome the class.

Step 2 — Challenge of the Week Review (5 minutes)

Ask if anyone would like to share a "challenge experience" from the previous week. Try to draw students out by prompting them with basic questions regarding the challenges from last week (e.g., "Did anyone choose the first challenge?").

Step 3 — Opening Prayer (3 minutes)

Lead the class in the "Opening Prayer," which is included in the Student Workbook. Leader's Guide notes are provided above: Red text provides direction and guidance, and white text is for you to read aloud to the class.

In presenting these examples of celebrities who struggled and ultimately met their untimely deaths as the result of substance abuse, no judgment on their persons or characters—or the eternal destiny of their souls—is being implied. The message you should convey to students is that the lives of many celebrities are unworthy of their emulation and imitation, and that a young Catholic should model his or her life after the true "heroes"—Jesus, Mary, and the saints.

Dive In:
The Price of Fame

Born in a two-bedroom house in a small town in Mississippi, Elvis Presley died one of the most famous people to walk the earth. He starred in thirty-three films, was on TV countless times, appeared in concert more than a thousand times all over the country, and sold more than one billion records worldwide. Yet, the "King of Rock and Roll" died on his bathroom floor from a drug overdose, with more than ten different prescription drugs in his system.

As a child, Jimi Hendrix was often seen carrying a broom, pretending it was a guitar. Jimi's school social worker told the boy's father that failure to get his son a guitar might eventually cause a mental breakdown! Jimi got his first guitar at age fifteen and became one of the greatest electric guitarists who ever lived. His genius left an indelible mark on the music industry—yet he also died of an overdose.

Kurt Cobain's band, Nirvana, was called "the flagship band of Generation X" by *Rolling Stone* magazine.

Almost overnight, it changed the music scene from "big-hair," glam bands to grunge. The band sold more than fifty million albums. Kurt had a tough time dealing with fame and depression, however. At the height of his success, he shot himself.

Every generation is packed with fallen idols, sad reminders of the high price of "success": Heath Ledger, Michael Jackson, Amy Winehouse, Whitney Houston. After rising to stardom and fame, each suffered a drug- or alcohol-related death. They seem to stand before us almost as warning signs that say, "STOP! This road does NOT lead to fulfillment!" And yet, according to one poll, twenty-nine percent of young people (up ten percent in recent years) said they'd rather be famous than happy![1]

As we'll discover in today's lesson, it takes something more than what this world can offer us to be really happy and truly fulfilled. Today we're going to take a look at that "something more."

Note: In presenting these examples of celebrities who struggled and ultimately met their untimely deaths as the result of substance abuse, no judgment on their persons or characters—or the eternal destiny of their souls—is being implied. Even famous people can struggle with difficult problems (e.g., drugs, alcohol, depression, etc.) and ultimately lose their battle. Not every action of a celebrity is worthy of emulation and imitation. You should model your life after the true "heroes"—Jesus, Mary, and the saints.

"There is a terrible hunger for love. We all experience that in our lives—the pain, the loneliness. We must have the courage to recognize it. The poor you may have right in your own family. Find them. Love them."
—*Blessed Teresa of Calcutta*

Step 4 — Dive In (5 minutes)

Read this story aloud, have a candidate read it aloud, or have the class read it silently before watching the video segments. This thought-provoking story ties in to the lesson's topic and serves to set up the video presentation.

Watch It!

Segment 1: The Goal of Life

1. Everyone wants to be _____happy_____.

Segment 2: Is There Something More?

1. In which television show did Leah appear?

   A) "Wheel of Fortune"   C) "Dancing with the Stars"

   B) "America's Next Top Model"   D) "Survivor"

2. **T** or F? Leah was raised as a Catholic.

Segment 3: Are We on Our Own?

1. Brian walks by a famous river that is hard to navigate. Which river is it? __The Mississippi__

2. Brian says that the source of all happiness may ultimately be found in _____God_____.

Small-Group Discussion

Segment 1: The Goal of Life

1. What struck you from the video?

2. What did you want to be as you were growing up? Has it changed?

Segment 2: Is There Something More?

1. Is there a difference between being rich and famous and being happy? Why do you think wealth and fame do not necessarily lead to happiness (and sometimes even seem to destroy it)?

2. What are some characteristics that make people famous today that you do not admire?

Segment 3: Are We on Our Own?

1. Do you know anyone who seems to be a happy person? What do you think makes them that way?

2. Who is someone (in your life, in the world, or from history) that you admire? What do you find most admirable about that person?

Step 5

Watch It!/Small-Group Discussion (50 minutes)

On the video, click on Lesson 2, Segment 1. When Segment 1 ends, have students fill in the "Watch It!" questions (2 to 3 minutes). Run through them to be sure they wrote the correct answers so they will have them to prepare for the next "Review Game."

Next, lead students in a small-group discussion for Segment 1. You may begin by asking general questions like: "What part of the video spoke to you the most?" Discussion questions for each segment are provided in the blue box above.

Follow the same steps for Segments 2 and 3. (Allow for about 10 minutes of discussion time after each segment.)

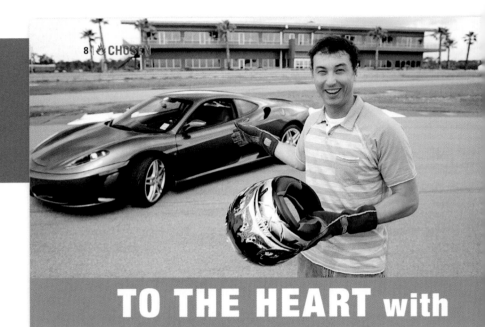

8 | CHOSEN

Question:
Why do you think that having faith and finding God made life more satisfying for Brian than having anything else could?

TO THE HEART with

When I was growing up, my dream was to be an NFL football player (just like 147 million other kids). Then, when I was fifteen, I discovered Psalm 37:4: *"Take delight in the Lord, and he will give you the desires of your heart."* That verse captured my imagination. I thought God was saying, "If you scratch my back, I will scratch yours."

The summer before my senior year, I met a girl at a youth event in Colorado. I liked her a lot, and when she told me of her plans to attend the University of Colorado in Boulder (CU), I got excited about the possibilities. CU had a good communications program and a nationally ranked football team. So I struck a deal with God: "If you let me walk on and make the team at Colorado, I will do whatever you ask of me and use my platform to share the Good News of the Gospel." *How could God refuse that deal?* I thought.

Shortly before making the long bus trip to attend CU, I called the girl I was pursuing ... and her *boyfriend* got on the phone. I was stunned—and a little hurt. She had *lied* to me! But at least I still had school and football to pursue. So that August, I drove from New Jersey to Colorado—and discovered I *loved* it out there! The mountains were beautiful, the people were friendly, the weather was great, and I couldn't wait to try out for the football team. I trained rigorously and had the time of my life. Finally, the day arrived ... and I did not make the team.

At the end of the semester, I transferred out of CU with failing grades, shattered dreams, and a broken heart. *God's sure not keeping his end of the deal,* I thought. I had faithfully gone to Sunday **MASS**, said my daily prayers, and avoided the wild party scene. *I'm the good guy,* I thought to myself. *So, what's up with this, God?*

 Step 6 **To the Heart** (10 minutes)

After the small-group discussions, read this story aloud, have a candidate read it aloud, or have the class read it silently. After the story (written by this week's video presenter), read the thought-provoking question(s) provided in the red "To the Heart" box above. Time permitting, ask follow-up questions and encourage discussion.

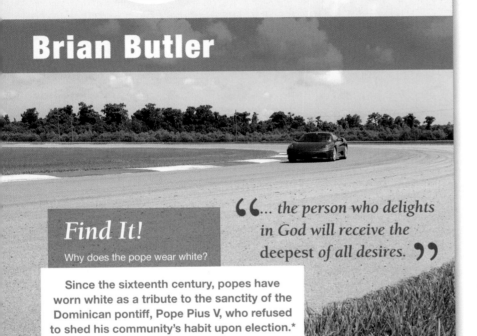

Re-reading Psalm 37:4, it finally occurred to me that I had badly misinterpreted this verse, treating God like a genie in a lamp. By relegating him to an "if this, then that" relationship, I was robbing myself of the freedom and love that God had created me to share with him.

Over the next few years, my FAITH grew; I pulled up my grades, played football at a smaller university, and later married the girl of my dreams. Life was pretty sweet, but *none* of these things gave me the lasting happiness that I discovered when I got things right with God. He loves us with a wild, faithful, bold love. His desire for us is deep, and this is why the psalmist says, "Deep calls to deep" (Psalm 42:7). We may never get that perfect date, straight A's, that new high-tech gadget, or a pile of money ... but the person who delights in God will receive the *deepest* of all desires. God will give *himself* to that person.

If you take some time to prayerfully consider God's desire for you, and stack all those other things against the world's greatest love, deep within you'll hear the "echo" that God placed in your heart, "O God, you are my God, I seek you, my SOUL thirsts for you ..." (Psalm 63:1).

Brian Butler

Find It!

Why does the pope wear white?

Since the sixteenth century, popes have worn white as a tribute to the sanctity of the Dominican pontiff, Pope Pius V, who refused to shed his community's habit upon election.*

❝ ... the person who delights in God will receive the deepest of all desires. **❞**

*Don't forget to make a note in your lesson plan each week of how many students found the answer to this question; give a little treat to those who followed through.

10 | CHOSEN

Hero of the Week

Born:
circa 251

Died:
356

Memorial:
January 17

Patron Saint of:
- skin diseases
- basket makers
- gravediggers

St. Anthony the Great
(Anthony of Egypt)

"Put your money where your mouth is!"

It's fairly easy to *say* you are a Christian, but what would you give up to get closer to Christ? Could you walk away from your Xbox? Put away Facebook? Lose your iPhone?

Listening to a homily on Matthew's Gospel, Anthony of Egypt (also known as "St. Anthony the Great") was moved by Jesus' call to sell everything and to "Come, follow me" (Matthew 19:21). So Anthony sold his family's estate, which he had recently inherited. He placed his younger sister with a group of Christian women and then moved to the outskirts of the town to live as a hermit. Just like that.

It was a radical move, even then.

Anthony was born in 251 in Coma, near Heracleopolis. He came from a wealthy family of landowners, and when he turned eighteen, his parents died, and he inherited the family estate. He could have lived a life of luxury ... but he left it all behind, gave everything he owned to the poor, and lived a life of simplicity and **PRAYER** in the desert. He dressed in animal skins and ate bread and insects. Anthony and others who followed his example (moving from the outskirts of town to the desert, to live in total isolation) became known as the "Desert Fathers."

In today's culture, such a demonstration of zeal for Christ is countercultural. But even then, many must have questioned the mental health of anyone wanting to live this way. For Anthony, it was the ultimate testament to his faith. He listened to God's call and followed. Immediately. Wholeheartedly. And with enthusiasm.

The devil tempted him often, and he suffered both spiritually and physically as a result of his radical commitment and lifestyle. In all of this, God stayed by his side, a source of strength and inspiration. And after each trial, Anthony pushed himself further in his spiritual journey. More than anything, he wanted to experience God's presence in his life and follow him perfectly.

St. Anthony's lessons are enduring. While few are called to be Christian hermits like he was, Anthony stands as a living message to us, that we are all called to give to the poor (rather than live for personal gain), and that we should seek happiness in God over and above anything this world has to offer.

St. Anthony, pray for us. Model for us the perseverance to live the life to which we aspire, moving closer and closer to God every day.

Step 7 — Hero of the Week (5 minutes)

This saint story will help to highlight and reinforce this lesson's topic. You may choose to read it aloud, have a candidate read it aloud, or have the class read it silently.

Challenge of the Week

 Inspired music: Come to class next week with a song or image that highlights a musician or other artist's quest for God. Write about it in the space below.

 Start a powerful new habit! Turn off all media for five minutes a day and relax in a quiet place. Ask God to help you to be open to his voice in your life. Write a little about what happened in the space below.

 Speak or write a sincere message of encouragement to someone you know who is sick or who is sad, worried, or upset about something. Say a prayer for his or her intentions. Is there something practical you can do to help this person this week?

_____
_____
_____
_____
_____
_____
_____
_____

Closing Prayer

"But seek first his kingdom and his righteousness, and all these things shall be yours as well."

—*Matthew 6:33*

Heavenly Father, many people spend their lives chasing wealth, power, status, or fame, hoping to find happiness. Yet, so often they end their lives in despair, having missed out on the greatest treasure of all: knowing and loving you. Show us our true selves, Lord, made in your image and likeness. And inspire us with a holy courage to live, not as the world dictates, but according to your perfect plan for our happiness. Amen.

Step 8 **Challenge of the Week** (2 minutes)

Ask your candidates to read the "challenges" above and choose one of the three to complete this week. Have them check the box next to the challenge they intend to complete. Encourage them to write about their experiences in the space provided.

Step 9 **Homework Instructions and Updates** (2 minutes)

Remind candidates to read the "Wrap-Up" and the "What's That Word?" sections in the "Taking It Home" section of the Student Workbook. They should also review the "Watch It!" questions to prepare for the next "Review Game."

Step 10 **Closing Prayer** (3 minutes)

As a way of building up community, ask if there are any prayer intentions. Write them down (or have candidates share them aloud) and after praying for those intentions, have the class read the "Closing Prayer" together (provided in the Student Workbook).

Explain that, starting this week, the group should review all these features at home in preparation for the "Review Game" that is at the start of each lesson. The "Review Game" feature will begin in the next lesson. The vocabulary words and Catechism references are in the Glossary. As time permits, or as homework, consider having students look up the indicated Catechism passages associated with each word.

² CCC 358

³ Jn 3:16

Taking It Home

For next week's "Review Game," be sure to read over the following …

1. **Watch It!** questions (page 7)
2. **Wrap-Up**
3. **"What's That Word?"**
4. **Memory Verse**

Don't forget to do your
Challenge of the Week (page 11)

Wrap-Up

Scripture tells us that "God is love" (1 John 4:8), and that he created us for himself. In this life and the next, we will find true fulfillment by knowing, loving, and serving God. That is how he created us to find ultimate happiness—not the passing kind of "happiness" the world gives, but an abiding joy that doesn't depend on circumstances.

God created the whole world out of love for us, and created us to reveal his image and likeness to the world.² God the Father exhibited the ultimate act of love when he gave his only Son, JESUS CHRIST, to die on the cross to atone for the sins of the world.³ Jesus loved us enough to give his own life for us. We are called to this type of unselfish love—to live in a way that reminds those we encounter of the amazing, unlimited love of God.

That's how we become fully human—fully alive! To the contrary, living for ourselves only leads to emptiness.

"What's That Word?"

HAPPINESS

Everyone wants to be happy. In fact, we could say that all of our actions are motivated by a desire to achieve happiness. We can be mistaken, though, about what will actually make us happy. Many people are confused about what it takes to be happy, and some despair, believing that lasting happiness is impossible.

We can only be happy if we fulfill the purpose for which we have been created: to love and be loved. But no human love can completely fill our hearts. In the fifth chapter of Matthew, Jesus provides us the "blueprint" for happiness in THE BEATITUDES, which give us the conditions we must fulfill for a truly blessed, happy life, living in God's own divine love.[4]

LOVE

We all want it. But what is it? To love someone is simply to will and to do what is good for that person. The ultimate love, expressed in a willingness to SACRIFICE for the sake of another *simply because it is best for that person,* is a theme throughout Scripture, found in more than 600 verses. God's greatest expression of love is found in Jesus Christ, especially in his sacrificial death on the cross.

The meaning of life is love: receiving love from God, showing our love for God through obedience to him, and loving others with God's own love that is within us.[5]

[4] Mt 5:3-12

[5] 1 Jn 4:19; Jn 13:34-35, 14:15, 15:12-17; CCC 1823

Memory Verse:

"But you are a chosen race, a royal priesthood, a holy nation, God's own people, that you may declare the wonderful deeds of him who called you out of darkness into his marvelous light."

—1 Peter 2:9

6   CCC 1716

7   Gal 5:22-23; CCC 736

8   CCC 2304

PEACE

In everyday use, PEACE is often used to describe the absence of war or conflict. The biblical understanding of peace, however, goes a bit deeper. The fifth Commandment ("you shall not kill") implies that we are to strive for peace in all of our relationships. As Jesus teaches in the Beatitudes, peace is a key goal of our life in him: "Blessed are the peacemakers, for they shall be called children of God."[6]

In his letter to the Galatians, St. Paul lists peace as a fruit of the HOLY SPIRIT.[7] St. Augustine describes peace as "the tranquility of order," which can only be achieved through peace with God and living a life of justice and CHARITY.[8] Peace can properly be understood, then, as a harmony existing between individuals and peoples, and within our souls. Given our fallen nature, true peace can only be achieved through the help of God's GRACE.

Did You Know?

The pope does not earn a salary and has no bank account.

Any questions?

What does God have to do with my finding happiness or fulfillment?

Your stomach growls because it needs healthy food to fill it—God designed your body to signal that need. If there were no need for food, that growling would make no sense. Similarly, there's a "growling" in the depths of every soul. But none of what the world offers really works to fill our growling souls. St. Augustine, who had tried out every SIN under the sun, said, "You have made us for yourself, O Lord, and our hearts are restless until they rest in you."[9]

Can't I just be a "good person" without God?

In some ways, yes. In other ways, not at all.

Think about it. If you woke up and found yourself surrounded by the most amazing gifts you can imagine—precious gems, the coolest video games, thousands of dollars in gift cards, (insert your favorite stuff here)—and it never even occurred to you to find out who gave you these gifts, and you had no urge to thank anyone for them, that would be a serious moral flaw!

God has given us life, breath, and our very existence. Whether from shallowness or sin, it's a serious moral flaw to fail to even look toward him, want to know him, or thank him.

Notes

**Lesson 3
Leader's Notes**

Overview

The purpose of this lesson is to introduce your class to an overview of salvation history. We begin the story by addressing the question, "How could a good God allow so much suffering and evil?" We explore the goodness of God's creation, how sin and evil entered the world, and God's redemptive plan (the "plot" of salvation history), which centered in the person and work of Christ and the establishment of the Church.

With this lesson, we move from "pre-evangelization" to authentic "evangelization," introducing students to the *kerygma*—the proclamation of the Gospel message that invites a response.

Objectives of this Lesson

1. *Review the salvation story, God's plan of redeeming love, as revealed to us through Scripture.* It is *our* story, from the creation of the world and the sin of our first parents; to the Incarnation, earthly ministry, and redemptive Death and Resurrection of Christ; to the coming of the Holy Spirit and the ongoing life of the Church (see CCC 107).

2. *Jesus is the fullest revelation of God, who introduces us to the idea that "God is love" (1 John 4:8).* God is not just the Creator of the universe, but a communion of Persons: an eternal exchange of love. Each of us is made in God's image; that is, we are made for love (see CCC 221, 358).

3. *God has given signs in every age to reveal his love for us.* In addition to Scripture and the sacramental life of the Church, God has raised up "witnesses," such as the martyrs and saints, to show his love in the world (see CCC 957, 2473).

4. *Hearing and responding to the* kerygma, *or proclamation of the core Gospel message, is essential to becoming the people God intends us to be.* The *whole* story has led to this moment, and the Church needs you. Christ needs you. We are all called to greatness, called to be saints (see CCC 1695).

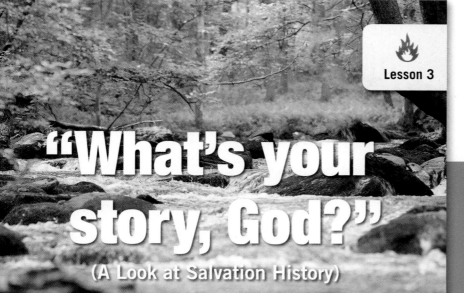

"What's your story, God?"
(A Look at Salvation History)

✝

Opening Prayer

God, I still have so much to learn about you, myself, my world. I know I don't say it enough, but "thank you" for all that you've done in my life so far and for all that I get to have and experience because of you. Even though at times it feels like you are very distant, and I question why you would allow bad things to happen, I'm sure you are working in ways that I do not always see or understand. So, please help me to be more aware of the good things you are doing and how I fit into your eternal "story" here and now. Amen.

Opening Prayer

Most of our prayers tend to center around asking God to do things for us. It is easy to overlook the good things God has done in the world and in our lives. We have much to be grateful for. We are part of something big—God's story. Despite what we might feel, he is not distant, but very active, and he wants us to participate intimately with him in his eternal work. Let's pray. In the name of the Father …

 Step 1 Welcome/Review Game (5 minutes)

Begin by welcoming the class and telling them that you will be starting with a review of the previous lesson's material. On the DVD menu, click on Lesson 3; then on the sub-menu, click on "Review Game."

Have students answer the questions based on the previous lesson. For more information about how to adapt this game to meet the needs of your group, see the "Review Game" section in the Introduction to this Leader's Guide (page xvi).

 Step 2 Challenge of the Week Review (5 minutes)

Ask if anyone would like to share a "challenge experience" from the previous week. Try to draw students out by prompting them with basic questions regarding the challenges from last week (e.g.,"Did anyone choose the first challenge?").

Step 3 Opening Prayer (3 minutes)

Lead the class in the "Opening Prayer," which is included in the Student Workbook. Leader's Guide notes are provided above: Red text provides direction and guidance, and white text is for you to read aloud to the class.

16 | CHOSEN

Dive In:
A Confusing Story

Once upon a time, there was a toad. After being coaxed out of the comfort of his hobbit hole by Gandalf the wizard, Toad went on a long journey with a talking donkey to find his pride (pack of lions) and become their king.

You see, Toad thought he killed his dad, but it was actually Mufasa who did it! When he became king, a princess kissed him, and he became a wooden puppet, but in the end, the fairy godmother made him a real boy ... and he lived happily ever after.

Notice anything strange about that story? There was no real beginning. No end. No meaning. It was just random images and events pieced together. You would wonder if the author was even awake while writing, or if the story just kind of wrote itself ...

That's life without God.

If there is no intelligent mind behind life, then the story of human history and each life in particular is no more than disjointed events thrown together by chance.

Thankfully, there is more. There is a larger, overarching story that the creation of the universe, the events of human history, and the story of your life fit within. It's written by the hand of God. It has a happy ending. And every character is a key player. That story offers us a deep sense of meaning and purpose.

Today we're going to take a look at that story, *"His-story,"* otherwise known as "salvation history."

"I arise today
Through a mighty strength, the invocation of the Trinity,
Through a belief in the Threeness,
Through Confession of the Oneness
Of the Creator of creation."
—St. Patrick

Step 4 **Dive In** (5 minutes)

Read this story aloud, have a candidate read it aloud, or have the class read it silently before watching the video segments. This thought-provoking story ties in to the lesson's topic and serves to set up the video presentation.

Watch It!

Lesson 3 | 17

Segment 1: Creation and the Fall

1. The Blessed Trinity is one God in three divine Persons: God the Father, God the ____Son____, and God the ____Holy Spirit____.

2. God created Adam and Eve in his ____image____ and likeness.

Segment 2: Jesus' Divine Rescue Mission

1. Unlike Eve, who disobeyed God, _____ said "yes" to God's plan. By her obedience, she became the "New Eve."

   A) Sarah (B) Mary) C) Elizabeth D) Esther

2. Jesus revealed to us the awesome truth that God is ____love____.

Segment 3: A Kingdom on Earth

1. The Church is both human and _____.

   (A) divine) B) angelic C) eternal D) earthly

2. ____Saints____ are men and women the Church recognizes for their heroic virtue. They are witnesses, intercessors, and examples of faith.

Small-Group Discussion

Segment 1: Creation and the Fall

1. What is your favorite movie? What makes the story good?

2. Pretend I have never heard of Christianity. Can you sum up the "story line" or at least share what you know of the history of Christianity?

Segment 2: Jesus' Divine Rescue Mission

1. Although Eve and Mary are both pivotal women in salvation history, they are very different in the way they trusted in God. Can you talk about those differences and how each woman strikes you?

2. What does it mean to you to hear the phrase, "God is love"? Did it mean something different to you when you were younger?

Segment 3: A Kingdom on Earth

1. What are some things that make salvation history a good story? What elements of the plot are engaging, redeeming, heroic, inspiring, or hopeful?

2. How does the story of salvation history impact the story of your own life?

3. Share something about your favorite saint.[1]

Step 5

Watch It!/Small-Group Discussion (50 minutes)

On the video, click on Lesson 3, Segment 1. When Segment 1 ends, have students fill in the "Watch It!" questions (2 to 3 minutes). Run through them to be sure they wrote the correct answers so they will have them to prepare for the next "Review Game."

Next, lead students in a small-group discussion for Segment 1. You may begin by asking general questions like: "What part of the video spoke to you the most?" Discussion questions for each segment are provided in the blue box above.

Follow the same steps for Segments 2 and 3. (Allow for about 10 minutes of discussion time after each segment.)

Small-Group Discussion Leader's Notes

1. If they have not chosen a saint name for Confirmation already, encourage students to start thinking about it.

Question:
In this story, Father Schmitz talks about how interesting and exciting his uncle was and how that made him want to get to know his uncle even better. Has that ever happened to you—have you ever met someone who seemed particularly interesting, making you want to get to know that person better? How do you think a person can get to know God better?

18 CHOSEN

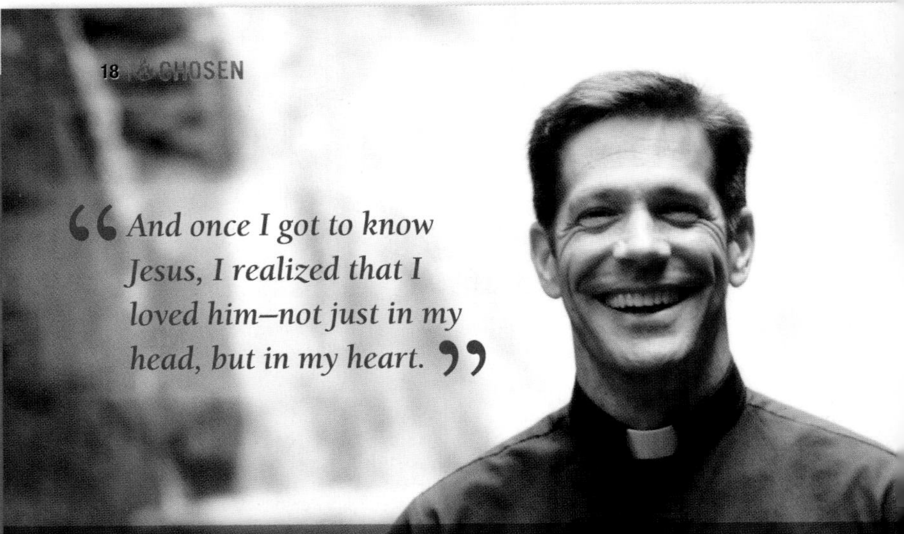

"And once I got to know Jesus, I realized that I loved him—not just in my head, but in my heart."

TO THE HEART with

My Uncle Tom lived in Los Angeles my entire life and worked on a number of TV shows and movies. He was a voice-over actor on *Titanic* and *Air Force One* and even wrote a couple of Hallmark movies that are still shown during the Christmas holidays!

I loved Uncle Tom. (After all, he was my uncle!) When he called, we would talk, and then I would tell him I loved him and hang up. Unfortunately, I never really *knew* my Uncle Tom, because I never got to fly hundreds of miles to California to spend time with him. (How cool would *that* have been—to go with him to "Take a Kid to Work Day"?)

If I had been able to get to know him in person, I think our phone conversations would have been different. I would have been able to say, "Uncle Tom, I love you," and know that what I was saying wasn't just in my head; it would have been in my heart as well.

For a long time, it was the same way with God. I was raised CATHOLIC, so I knew the story—God created the world and promised to set things right after sin wrecked everything. And I knew God loved me, and I guess I loved God back. But even when I came to *believe* in Jesus, I didn't feel close to God. I loved Jesus in my *head*, but it just didn't seem like I loved him in my *heart*.

So, I went on a thirty-day retreat with some Jesuit priests in the foothills of Colorado. They challenged me to spend thirty days in *silent prayer* with Jesus in the Gospels. They told me to just take my time and read a little from the Gospels each day. They taught me how to hear Jesus and get to know him in the Scriptures, like St. Ignatius of Loyola.

Step 6 To the Heart (10 minutes)

After the small-group discussions, read this story aloud, have a candidate read it aloud, or have the class read it silently. After the story (written by this week's video presenter), read the thought-provoking question(s) provided in the red "To the Heart" box above. Time permitting, ask follow-up questions and encourage discussion.

Lesson 3 19

Although I did not receive an incredible REVELATION in a blinding burst of light from God as St. Paul did, I did get to know Jesus by observing his actions in the Gospels, by talking with him in prayer, and by going to Mass. In simply spending time with Jesus, I got to know him. And once I got to know him, I realized that I loved him—not just in my head, but in my heart.

That experience taught me something important: If you want to get to know someone (instead of just "about" someone), you have to spend time with that person. And the best way to get to know the author of our SALVATION story is to spend time with him, talking to him and listening to him as you read that story together.

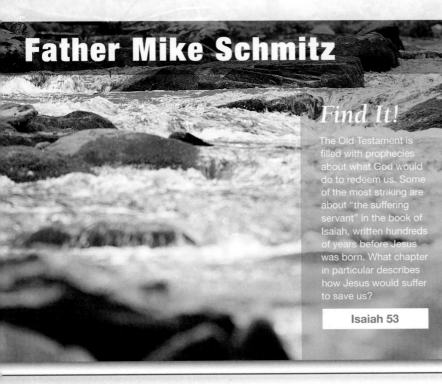

Father Mike Schmitz

Find It!

The Old Testament is filled with prophecies about what God would do to redeem us. Some of the most striking are about "the suffering servant" in the book of Isaiah, written hundreds of years before Jesus was born. What chapter in particular describes how Jesus would suffer to save us?

Isaiah 53

20 | CHOSEN

Hero of the Week

Born:
August 21, 1567

Died:
December 28, 1622

Memorial:
January 24

Patron Saint of:
- journalists
- educators
- confessors

St. Francis de Sales

It took a long time for Francis to believe that God really loved him. He didn't feel very lovable ...

In fact, at one time, he was pretty sure he was going to HELL. He didn't *want* this to happen, of course, but he didn't see any way around it. He lived during the time of the Protestant Reformation and was surrounded by people (called Calvinists) who believed that God creates some people for the sole purpose of sending them to hell.

Over time, with a lot of prayer, Francis came to see that God is love–and, even more amazing, he felt God calling him to become a *priest!*

A priest? Are you sure, God? It took God thirteen years to convince Francis that, yes, this was what he was supposed to do with his life–tell others about the God who loves them.

There was only one more problem: Nobody wanted to hear Francis preach. It wasn't that he was bad at public speaking–he had been educated for a brilliant public career. But after several years, he felt abandoned and hadn't converted one soul.

Still, he didn't give up. He once wrote, "Have patience with all things, but chiefly, have patience with yourself." Francis realized that those who most needed to hear about God's love were not flocking to the CHURCH. So he began writing notes and slipping them under doors. If people wouldn't hear what he had to say, perhaps they would read it. It was just a matter of getting their attention.

It worked. ... Thousands who had left the Church returned to practice the Catholic faith!

As BISHOP, Francis took to heart the need to minister to the people–not just the religious, but the regular, ordinary men and women who also needed spiritual direction. His greatest work, *Introduction to the Devout Life*, recounts what Francis learned about God's love through his own life experiences. This spiritual classic continues to inspire Christians today. Check it out!

St. Francis de Sales, pray for us. Help us understand that we are loved because we are God's.

 Step 7 **Hero of the Week** (5 minutes)

This saint story will help to highlight and reinforce this lesson's topic. You may choose to read it aloud, have a candidate read it aloud, or have the class read it silently.

Lesson 3 | 21

Challenge of the Week

 Make a cheerful sacrifice. Volunteer to do a sibling's chores for a day, help a neighbor with yard work, make a meal for your family, or babysit for free. Write about what you did.

 Create or find symbols of the Holy TRINITY. Explain the symbolism to someone in your family and write about it in the space below.

 Choose a saint to research, and jot down three interesting facts in the space below about his or her life to share with your small group at the next class.

_____
_____
_____
_____
_____
_____
_____
_____
_____
_____

Closing Prayer

"For God so loved the world that he gave his only-begotten Son, that whoever believes in him should not perish but have eternal life."

—*John 3:16*

Heavenly Father, you are powerful, but you don't force us to love you. Through the gifts of your grace and our FREE WILL, we can be heroes like the saints or experience the emptiness of sinful choices.

Help us, Lord, to always choose you. Thank you for giving us your son, Jesus, whom we receive in Holy Communion and who strengthens us to find the very best in ourselves. Amen.

Step 8 — Challenge of the Week (2 minutes)

Ask your candidates to read the "challenges" above and choose one of the three to complete this week. Have them check the box next to the challenge they intend to complete. Encourage them to write about their experiences in the space provided.

Step 9 — Homework Instructions and Updates (2 minutes)

Remind candidates to read the "Wrap-Up" and the "What's That Word?" sections in the "Taking It Home" section of the Student Workbook. They should also review the "Watch It!" questions to prepare for the next "Review Game."

Step 10 — Closing Prayer (3 minutes)

As a way of building up community, ask if there are any prayer intentions. Write them down (or have candidates share them aloud) and after praying for those intentions, have the class read the "Closing Prayer" together (provided in the Student Workbook).

22 | CHOSEN

Taking It Home

For next week's "Review Game," be sure to read over the following …

1. **Watch It!** questions (page 17)
2. **Wrap-Up**
3. **"What's That Word?"**
4. **Memory Verse**

Don't forget to do your
Challenge of the Week (page 21)

Wrap-Up

"In the beginning God created the heavens and the earth" (Genesis 1:1). From the very first verse of the Bible, all of Scripture recounts an epic story, full of real men and women who encountered the living God.

As we read the Scriptures, we discover that God has revealed himself again and again to the human race, making us his own children through a series of COVENANT promises. The final and most perfect covenant was made in the New Testament, through God's only-begotten Son, Jesus Christ, who created the Church.

We call this epic story "salvation history." Salvation history is the *true* story of God's relationship with the human race. This is a story with three parts.

In the Old Testament, God the Father particularly reveals himself in the creation of the world, in the sin of our first parents and the fall of the human race, in the promise of a redeemer, and in the covenants with Adam, Noah, Abraham, and David.

In the New Testament, God the Son is especially revealed. Through the life of Christ, God's promise of a redeemer is fulfilled in the INCARNATION, when God took on a human nature in the person of Jesus Christ. By his suffering (or "Passion"), Death, Resurrection, and Ascension into heaven, Christ showed us his love, paid the price for our sins, and restored our created purpose.

Finally, the Holy Spirit is more explicitly active in the life of the Church. By instituting the SACRAMENTS and passing his authority on to his apostles, Christ ensured that his presence would continue in the world until the end of time.[1] Today, he makes us co-workers in his mission to bring his kingdom to the world, until at last he will return in glory to bring our eternal reward.

Salvation history reveals the purpose of all natural and human history and of your life in particular. In this lesson, we took a closer look at this story of salvation history to show how God's story is our story, too.

[1] Mt 28:20

"What's That Word?"

MYSTERY

When people talk about a MYSTERY, they usually mean something that we do not—or cannot—understand. In this sense, it is synonymous with a riddle or an enigma. In Catholic terms, though, a mystery is something we would not have known unless God had revealed it. He revealed the mysteries to us because he wanted us to know him and his plan for us. Therefore, a mystery makes sense, and we *can* understand it, but not fully, because God is infinite, and we are not. One of the reasons that HEAVEN will never be boring is that we will have the opportunity to explore the mysteries without ever running out of new things to learn; that exploration can begin now. (Eastern Churches use the word "mystery" for sacrament (see CCC 774).

SIN

Sin is a deliberate thought, word, deed, or omission contrary to God's plan.[2] It is an offense against God and a failure in genuine love because it makes us less than we have been created to be. *Sin* is addictive and self-destructive; it weakens the sinner and makes it more difficult to find true happiness, which comes from pleasing God. Ultimately, if we are unrepentant, sin can destroy us.

The word for *sin* comes from a Greek archery term that means "missing the mark." We sometimes sin by deliberately planning evil against another and carrying it out, but more often than not, we sin out of weakness. Overcome by selfishness, emotion, or laziness, we hurt ourselves and others because we "fall short of the target," which is to act in a virtuous and loving way with the help of God's grace. The antidote to sin is RECONCILIATION.

[2] CCC 1849–1851

Memory Verse:

"For God so loved the world that he gave his only-begotten Son, that whoever believes in him should not perish but have eternal life."

—John 3:16

24 | 🔥CHOSEN

[3] CCC 234

TRINITY

The Blessed Trinity is the central mystery of the Christian faith,[3] the belief that the Father, the Son, and the Holy Spirit, three distinct Persons, are one God and share a single divine nature. The Trinity is an eternal communion of love: The Father loves the Son, and the Son loves the Father in return. The love between them is the very Person of the Holy Spirit. God invites each of us to share in this communion, both in this life (especially through the sacraments) and in heaven. This is why he created us. The Christian family (a husband and wife together with their children) uniquely images the life-giving love of the Trinity.

Did You Know?

In Greek, a common language of the New Testament writers, the word for "father" translates as "nourisher, protector, or upholder."

Any questions?

Could you give a quick explanation of the Holy Trinity?

"The mystery of the Most Holy Trinity is the central mystery of Christian faith and life. It is the mystery of God in himself" (CCC 234). The Trinity could never have been known by human reason; it had to be revealed to us by God through the person of Jesus.

In the Old Testament, the Israelites understood God to be one: "Hear, O Israel: The Lord our God is one Lord" (Deuteronomy 6:4). When we say God is one, we are saying he is complete and unchangeable, one in his essence, being, and substance. However, God is also a communion of Persons: *Father, Son, and Holy Spirit.* Although there are three Persons, there is one common, divine nature, which each divine Person fully possesses.

God invites each of us to share in the communion between the Father and the Son in their Spirit of love. That's why he created us.

Notes

**Lesson 4
Leader's Notes**

Overview

In the last lesson, we talked about salvation history. The purpose of this lesson is to focus on the ways in which God makes himself known to us and how we should respond to what he has revealed. We examine the relationship between faith and reason and how both of these things—properly understood—bring us to a right understanding of the truth. We also highlight the profoundly intimate nature of faith, which is an act of surrender to the God who first gave himself to us.

In school, in their communities, and through the media, students are bombarded with the idea that there is no such thing as objective moral or spiritual truth, but that these things are "relative" to what each person thinks. As a result of this "relativism" (which Pope Francis identified as "the spiritual poverty of our time"[6]), faith and morals have been reduced to personal opinion or sentiment rather than reality. "Jesus is God for me." "Abortion is immoral to the Catholic Church."

As they grow in their understanding of Catholicism, your students need to move toward a truly *adult* approach to faith, based on full intellectual assent to the teachings of the Church—which are not valid merely because they are our traditions, but because what God has revealed is true.

Objectives of this Lesson

1. *Explain how God can be known by what he has revealed in the order and diversity of nature, as perceived through human reason* (see CCC 50, 54). (Also clarify that claiming to know the truth is not incompatible with loving and respecting those with whom we disagree.)

2. *Explain divine revelation.* God reveals himself through Scripture and Tradition, culminating in the person and work of Christ (see CCC 53, 80–82).

3. *Discuss the gift of faith as our proper response to this revelation.* Though faith is a gift, it is also a virtue we strengthen through exercise (see CCC 142–143, 153).

"How do I know God is real?"

(Understanding Divine Revelation)

✝

Opening Prayer

As I begin to understand your story and how I fit into it, there are times when I'm struggling with what to do now. How do you want me to respond and live out my faith in my family, my school, and with my friends? I'm still learning to believe, but I'm now starting to see that you have a plan for me. So, even though I sometimes may feel a bit scared or unsure about what it all means, please help me to be open to you and how you want me to live. Amen.

Opening Prayer

This week we are going to look at how God reveals himself to us and how we respond to that revelation. Let's pray. In the name of the Father …

 Welcome/Review Game (5 minutes)

Begin by welcoming the class and telling them that you will be starting with a review of the previous lesson's material. On the DVD menu, click on Lesson 4; then on the sub-menu, click on "Review Game."

Have students answer the questions based on the previous lesson. For more information about how to adapt this game to meet the needs of your group, see the "Review Game" section in the Introduction to this Leader's Guide (page xvi).

 Challenge of the Week Review (5 minutes)

Ask if anyone would like to share a "challenge experience" from the previous week. Try to draw students out by prompting them with basic questions regarding the challenges from last week (e.g., "Did anyone choose the first challenge?").

Opening Prayer (3 minutes)

Lead the class in the "Opening Prayer," which is included in the Student Workbook. Leader's Guide notes are provided above: Red text provides direction and guidance, and white text is for you to read aloud to the class.

¹ Is 62:5; Jn 3:29; Mt 25:1; Mk 2:19

Dive In:
A God Who
Wants to Be Known

Imagine that someone has offered you a month-long, all-expenses-paid trip to ... your dream destination! Your passport is ready, your bag has been packed, your parents have said "yes." All you have to do is get on that plane and go. Would you? Right now?

It would be risky, being out on your own. Maybe you're afraid of planes. Maybe you'll eat something bad and get sick. Maybe you'll get lost. Maybe something will happen to someone in your family while you're gone. Do you risk it? It's up to you.

Love is the same way. Allowing ourselves to love and be loved, as we were created to be, is risky. And yet, each of us longs for the kind of love that allows us to be completely open and honest. There is such freedom in that kind of closeness.

Every human relationship involves different levels of intimacy—from the less intimate chats with acquaintances, to the more heartfelt talks and confidences of friendship, to the "got your back" trust we have with our closest friends and family members. Over time, we learn which people we can trust and which ones we can't—all from opening ourselves, bit by bit, to find the intimacy we crave.

Sometimes, that trust may be misplaced. A friend may break a confidence; the guy (or girl) you've had a crush on may break your heart. Even family members let us down sometimes (though they usually come through for us if we give them a chance).

Trust in God is never misplaced. God wants intimacy with us. Maybe you never thought of God as a lover or a friend, but he thinks of himself that way. He is referred to as "the Bridegroom" in Scripture¹ and told his apostles, "You are my friends" (John 15:14).

The Native American warrior and Catholic convert, Joseph Chiwatenhwa, once said about God, "Now I begin to see that the reason you made us is because you want to share your love. Nothing attracts you as much as your people."

Yes, God wants you to know him! And though he already knows everything about you, he wants you to open your heart and life up to him! We're going to talk about what God has done to make himself known and how he wants us to respond to what he has revealed. Just as it is with the risk of taking any journey or engaging in any relationship, the journey of faith requires trust.

Step 4 — Dive In (5 minutes)

Read this story aloud, have a candidate read it aloud, or have the class read it silently before watching the video segments. This thought-provoking story ties in to the lesson's topic and serves to set up the video presentation.

Segment 1: Evidence for God

1. Chris compares the probability of the universe forming out of nothing to the probability of a print shop explosion resulting in a _____.

   A) novel   C) movie script

   (B) dictionary)   D) newspaper

2. The fullness of divine revelation is found in
   _____ **Jesus Christ** _____

Segment 2: Scripture and Tradition

1. Both Sacred __**Tradition**__ and Sacred Scripture form the deposit of faith, God's revelation to us.

2. The Gospels, the four books in the Bible that tell us about the life of Jesus, are Matthew, Mark, __**Luke**__, and __**John**__.

3. The Bible is a collection of _____ books.

   A) 12   B) 76   C) 52   (D) 73)

Segment 3: Our Response to God

1. We respond to divine revelation with the gift of _____**faith**_____.

2. **T or F?** Faith is a one-time decision.

Small-Group Discussion

Segment 1: Evidence for God

1. Can you think of a time when God revealed himself to you? Maybe it was in prayer or through another person or an event.

2. Pretend you are talking to a nonbeliever. What "proofs" of God's existence can you share?[1]

Segment 2: Scripture and Tradition

1. How often do you read the Bible? What stops you from reading it more often?

2. Share your favorite story or verse from the Bible and the reason you like it.[2]

Segment 3: Our Response to God

1. Do you know anyone who does not believe in God? Why do you think he or she does not believe in God?

2. Do you ever find it hard to trust God or to remember that he loves you no matter what? If so, what have you done—or what could you do in the future—to work through this problem?

Step 5 **Watch It!/Small-Group Discussion** (50 minutes)

On the video, click on Lesson 4, Segment 1. When Segment 1 ends, have students fill in the "Watch It!" questions (2 to 3 minutes). Run through them to be sure they wrote the correct answers so they will have them to prepare for the next "Review Game."

Next, lead students in a small-group discussion for Segment 1. You may begin by asking general questions like: "What part of the video spoke to you the most?" Discussion questions for each segment are provided in the blue box above.

Follow the same steps for Segments 2 and 3. (Allow for about 10 minutes of discussion time after each segment.)

Small-Group Discussion Leader's Notes

1. See "Existence of God" in Glossary.

2. Consider presenting each candidate with a Catholic Bible and encouraging him or her to read a little bit every day as part of Confirmation preparation. A free online version is available at USCCB.org

28 CHOSEN

Question:

What part of nature "speaks" to you about God?

TO THE HEART with

Natalie was raised Catholic. Her mom had spent tens of thousands of dollars sending her to Catholic school. But she thought of the faith as nothing but an oppressive list of rules. There must be "something more" to life. Something deeper. Something SACRED. She went to college and looked outside of the faith for that "something."

"I entered the college party scene, but it left me empty," she remembers. "I took classes about world cultures, astronomy, and philosophy. I sought advice from renowned educators who had studied other religions. I tried meditation and eastern religions, hoping to 'break through' to a 'higher reality.' I found only disillusionment."

Eventually, she gave up faith altogether. She called her mom from college and said, "Mom, I'm an atheist." But her mom never stopped praying for her. (Beware the power of praying moms and grandmas!)

Natalie's faith returned at a most unexpected moment. She wasn't at church. She wasn't on a retreat. She wasn't in a CONFIRMATION class. She was on a beach in Hawaii at 2 AM. Here is how she described the moment.

There I was, sitting beneath a palm tree on a rocky point. I looked out and saw perfectly shaped waves, sea green in the moon's glowing light. The sky was full of stars, with scattered meteors shooting across. It was natural perfection. And, as if from some unknown place inside, my mind uttered the words, "Thank you."

I caught myself. Who was I talking to? I had rejected the notion of a God, so who was I talking to? But as I gazed

Step 6

To the Heart (10 minutes)

After the small-group discussions, read this story aloud, have a candidate read it aloud, or have the class read it silently. After the story (written by this week's video presenter), read the thought-provoking question(s) provided in the red "To the Heart" box above. Time permitting, ask follow-up questions and encourage discussion.

*again at the scene before me, something inside me melted. It was all too beautiful to account for itself. **Someone** had painted it! And despite my prior convictions, I began to believe again.*

A few months later, at the prodding of her family, Natalie decided to go on a retreat weekend. She felt out of place. She wanted to be away from everyone and went outside, but she couldn't stop crying. Wherever she went, she sensed Jesus standing in front of her with open arms.

She went to World Youth Day and, hearing the voice of John Paul II, she realized, "That's my shepherd, and I'm falling in love with Jesus and his Church again." But even as she said it, she knew it wasn't really "again," but for the first time.

Natalie's journey back to Jesus began with the natural world "evangelizing" her. I had the awesome blessing of marrying her five years later.

Chris Stefanick

❝It was natural perfection.❞

Find It!

What Augustinian priest and scientist is known as the "Father of Modern Genetics"?

Gregor Mendel

30 | CHOSEN

Hero of the Week

St. Thomas Aquinas

Thomas Aquinas was the kid who always got picked last in gym class.

He was big and slow, and he never said much—always lost in his thoughts. His classmates used to call him "that dumb ox." His teachers, though, had a different view. His mentor, St. Albert the Great, once said, "One day the bellow of that dumb ox will be heard around the world."

What Aquinas lacked in speed, he made up for in intelligence. At the age of five, he asked, "What is God?" His teacher was stumped ... so Thomas decided to become a theologian to find out. He was confident that the EXISTENCE OF GOD could be proven. In fact, he came up with *five* such proofs.

Thomas decided he wanted to become a Dominican priest. His family hated the idea. They had different career goals for Thomas. His brothers kidnapped and imprisoned him in a room with a prostitute to test his resolve. Aquinas picked up a burning stick from the fireplace and chased the woman away, then burned a cross on the door of his cell. He knew what he wanted—and he knew it wasn't to be found in the pleasures and riches of this world. He wanted truth ... plain and simple.

Aquinas spent his entire life trying to understand the mysteries of God, not in order to prove how smart he was, but out of a desire to *know God* and to make him known to others. He wrote some of the most important theological works ever written, more than 50,000 pages of text over a period of more than twenty-five years, keeping four scribes scribbling busily the entire time! His greatest work, the *Summa Theologica,* remained unfinished at his death. Seeing God's glory in a mystical vision, Aquinas said, "All I have written is like so much straw compared to what I have seen."

Toward the end of Aquinas' life, his confessor, Brother Reginald, witnessed the philosopher in a chapel, face down before a great crucifix. He heard Jesus speak to Aquinas from the cross, saying, "Thomas, you have written well of me. What will you have for your reward?"

Aquinas replied, "Only yourself, Lord."

It was the most perfect summary of his life's work. Declared a DOCTOR OF THE CHURCH in 1567 by Pope Pius V, the life story of St. Thomas Aquinas reminds us that God does not want even the most intellectually gifted of us merely to *understand* him. He wants us to *love* him ... and to let him love us.

St. Thomas Aquinas, pray for us, that we will have the humility to ask God for the faith to believe even when we cannot understand.

Born:
1225
Died:
March 7, 1274
Memorial:
January 28
Patron Saint of:
- universities
- students

Step 7 Hero of the Week (5 minutes)

This saint story will help to highlight and reinforce this lesson's topic. You may choose to read it aloud, have a candidate read it aloud, or have the class read it silently.

Lesson 4 | 31

Challenge of the Week

☐ **Read from one of the Gospels** for three minutes every day. Take two minutes afterward to think about what you read. Write about it in the space below.

☐ **Choose a prayer space at home for a daily conversation with God.** Make sure a Bible is handy for your use along with any images or items (natural or man-made) that help you focus your mind on God. Write about it in the space below.

☐ **Practice your listening skills.** Meet with a close friend or family member. For a full five minutes, listen attentively, asking questions as needed. In the space below, write about something you learned about that person and how it affected your relationship.

_____

_____

_____

_____

_____

_____

_____

Closing Prayer

"But as for you, continue in what you have learned … from childhood you have been acquainted with the sacred writings which are able to instruct you for salvation through faith in Christ Jesus."
—2 Timothy 3:14-15

Lord Jesus, you reveal yourself to us in so many ways: through the inspired words of the Bible, the teachings of the Church, the beauty of nature, and in the quiet of our own hearts. Give us the grace to respond enthusiastically to the many ways you invite us to come closer to you, and inspire us to shine as lights in a dark world. Amen.

Step 8 **Challenge of the Week** (2 minutes)

Ask your candidates to read the "challenges" above and choose one of the three to complete this week. Have them check the box next to the challenge they intend to complete. Encourage them to write about their experiences in the space provided.

Step 9 **Homework Instructions and Updates** (2 minutes)

Remind candidates to read the "Wrap-Up" and the "What's That Word?" sections in the "Taking It Home" section of the Student Workbook. They should also review the "Watch It!" questions to prepare for the next "Review Game."

Step 10 **Closing Prayer** (3 minutes)

As a way of building up community, ask if there are any prayer intentions. Write them down (or have candidates share them aloud) and after praying for those intentions, have the class read the "Closing Prayer" together (provided in the Student Workbook).

32 CHOSEN

Taking It Home

For next week's "Review Game,"
be sure to read over the following ...

1. **Watch It!** questions (page 27)
2. **Wrap-Up**
3. **"What's That Word?"**
4. **Memory Verse**

Don't forget to do your
Challenge of the Week (page 31)

Wrap-Up

"The probability of life originating from an accident is comparable to the probability of the unabridged dictionary resulting from an explosion in a print shop."
—Edwin Conklin[2]
(Princeton biologist and associate of Albert Einstein)

Think about it. A single strand of your DNA is more complex than a dictionary. While scientific theories all attempt to explain some aspect of Creation, from evolution to the Big Bang, believing the universe came into being without some intelligent "oversight" just doesn't make sense. If we see a book, we know there is an author. If we see a painting, we know there is a painter. And when we see an ordered universe, we know there was an ultimate "beginning" ... a Creator.

This is why all the philosophers of antiquity (some of the greatest minds that ever lived) believed in God and why most relativists believe in God. Nonetheless, as the *Catechism* points out, we must keep in mind that "Many ... of our contemporaries either do not at all perceive, or explicitly reject, this intimate and vital bond of man to God. Atheism must therefore be regarded as one of the most serious problems of our time" (CCC 2123).

In this lesson, we've talked about some of the ways God reveals himself through creation and through NATURAL REASON. These things are the starting points for something called "divine revelation," or how God reveals himself more intimately to the human race. The greatest divine revelation, of course, is Jesus Christ.

"What's That Word?"

FAITH

Faith refers to the gift that allows us to believe in God and what he has told us. As the Bible tells us, "Faith is the realization of what is hoped for and evidence of things not seen" (Hebrews 11:1, NAB). For example, we have faith that our friend will not let us down or betray us when we are not present.

Grace builds on a different kind of faith—the theological virtue that was infused in us at BAPTISM. Through the gift of faith, God grants us the ability to accept as true all he has revealed to us in Christ that we receive in the Church. "The faith," or "the Catholic faith," refers to the fullness of God's revelation that has been entrusted to the Church and which the Church faithfully hands on to each generation of believers in its doctrine, life, and worship. The living teaching office (the MAGISTERIUM) alone, under the guidance of the Holy Spirit, authentically interprets the Word of God that comes to us in Scripture and TRADITION. Scripture, Tradition, and the Magisterium are so closely connected that one cannot stand without the other two (see *Dei Verbum* 7, 8, 10).

On an individual level, the gift of faith must be exercised in virtue to grow strong and sustain us in difficult times. We pray for the gift of faith so that we will be able to believe, and we exercise and strengthen our faith when we try to understand what God has revealed and to live accordingly.

NATURAL REASON

Natural reason refers to the human power to think or figure something out, as opposed to "revelation," which is what we know because God has told us. We can know things by natural reason and by revelation. Using our reason, we are able to figure out that there must be a Creator of the world or that stealing from someone is unjust. There are some things we are not able to figure out by reason alone. We would not have known that God is a Trinity unless he had told us, unless it had been *revealed.*

REVELATION

God *reveals* himself to us, and what he reveals of himself is called *revelation.*

The authors of the Bible took this word from the Hebrew wedding RITUAL where it literally meant "unveiling." It is God's deepest desire to "unveil" himself to us and invite us to a new and wonderful life with him, a life characterized by a deep and lasting relationship more intimate than the one shared by a newly married couple.

The Church has carefully preserved and taught God's *revelation,* and we can find what God has revealed of himself in the Bible and in Sacred Tradition.

Memory Verse:

"Every one then who hears these words of mine and does them will be like a wise man who built his house upon the rock ..."

—Matthew 7:24

SACRED TRADITION

Jesus entrusted the "handing on" (*traditio* in Latin) of the Gospel message to his apostles, whom he commissioned to "make disciples of all nations, baptizing them in the name of the Father and of the Son and of the Holy Spirit" (Matthew 28:19). The Church, then, is founded upon the authority Christ gave to his apostles to teach the truths he gave them to hand on.

Jesus taught his apostles many things. Some of what Jesus taught was written down under the INSPIRATION of the Holy Spirit and comes to us in the form of the Bible (SACRED SCRIPTURE). Some of what he taught them was "handed on" through their teaching; we refer to these teachings as "Sacred Tradition." We have many "traditions" in the Church, just as we have "traditions" in our families and schools. However, Sacred Tradition refers to the handing on of the Gospel and the teaching of Jesus in the Holy Spirit by the Church in her doctrine, life, and worship.[3]

[3] CCC 75–83

Did You Know?

According to tradition, St. Helena discovered the true Cross of Christ in the fourth century. Enshrined in the Church of the Holy Sepulchre in Jerusalem, it was recaptured by Muslim forces in the seventh century. However, fragments have been restored, and the "Adoration of the Cross" is observed each Good Friday in Jerusalem.

Any questions?

Are Catholics the only ones who know God? Is everyone else flat-out wrong?

God made the human heart for himself, and he reveals himself to everyone through creation and in the circumstances of life. Because of that, other religions have beautiful and true glimpses of who God is and how we should live our lives, and the Church "rejects nothing that is true and holy in [other] religions."[4] But the FULLNESS of truth about God can only be found in Christ and in his Church. God became one of us to tell us in person who he is! So, while other faiths may provide glimpses of God, Jesus alone reveals the whole picture.

What's more important, the Church or the Bible?

They're *both* important! The two can't be pitted against each other. The Church Jesus founded (the "pillar and foundation of truth," 1 Timothy 3:15, NAB) authoritatively teaches us that the Bible is the Word of God. At the Council of Hippo (AD 393), the Catholic bishops declared that the seventy-three books of "the Bible" are the words of God himself in the words of men.[5] Catholics have been reading from those seventy-three books ever since. Every time the Sacred Scriptures are proclaimed, life-transforming grace is given, for "the word of God is living and effective, sharper than any two-edged sword" (Hebrews 4:12).

Notes

Lesson 5
Leader's Notes

Overview

"Who is Jesus?" This lesson answers this fundamental question, while also addressing basic questions such as "Was Jesus real?" and "Did he really claim to be God?" Christ is the model for how we are to live; he is the one who saves us from our sin and gives us the hope of eternal life. He is the fullness of revelation about God and is himself God in the flesh. Jesus, then, is the only way to find lasting peace and freedom. As the *Catechism* states, "'At the heart of catechesis we find, in essence, a Person, the Person of Jesus of Nazareth, the only Son from the Father ... who suffered and died for us and who now, after rising, is living with us forever.' To catechize is 'to reveal in the Person of Christ the whole of God's eternal design reaching fulfillment in that Person. It is to seek to understand the meaning of Christ's actions and words and of the signs worked by him'" (CCC 426).

Teenagers will have a variety of responses to the question, "Who is Jesus?" Living in a post-Christian society, surrounded by a dizzying panorama of creeds and worldviews, students need to be challenged to remember the words of the Lord: "I am the way, and the truth, and the life; no one comes to the Father, but by me" (John 14:6).

Objectives of this Lesson

1. *Who is Jesus Christ?* Have students respond to the question, "But who do you say that I am?" (Matthew 16:15; see CCC 436–442).

2. *Liar, lunatic, ... or Lord?* It is not possible that Jesus was just a "good person." He claimed to be the divine Son of the Father. This leaves only three possibilities: He made it up (liar); he was deluded (lunatic/crazy); or he really *is* God.

3. *Why did Jesus come to earth to be one of us?* The *Catechism* lists four reasons: (1) to remove sin and reconcile us to God, (2) to show us just how much God loves us, (3) to show us how to live, and (4) to fill us with his divine life (see CCC 456–460).

"Who is Jesus?"

(The Person and Mission of Christ)

Opening Prayer

"Our Father, who art in heaven,
hallowed be thy name;
thy kingdom come,
thy will be done, on earth as it is in heaven.
Give us this day our daily bread,
and forgive us our trespasses
as we forgive those who trespass against us;
and lead us not into temptation,
but deliver us from evil. Amen."

Lesson 5

Opening Prayer

Jesus, you have said, "I am the way and the truth and the life" (John 14:6, NAB). We ask you for the strength to follow you, the wisdom to know you, and the grace to live the life you wish to share with us. We want to know you. Open our hearts and minds to all that you want to show us about yourself in our time together.

Now let's pray the prayer that Jesus taught us. In the name of the Father …

Step 1 — Welcome/Review Game (5 minutes)

Begin by welcoming the class and telling them that you will be starting with a review of the previous lesson's material. On the DVD menu, click on Lesson 5; then on the sub-menu, click on "Review Game."

Have students answer the questions based on the previous lesson. For more information about how to adapt this game to meet the needs of your group, see the "Review Game" section in the Introduction to this Leader's Guide (page xvi).

Step 2 — Challenge of the Week Review (5 minutes)

Ask if anyone would like to share a "challenge experience" from the previous week. Try to draw students out by prompting them with basic questions regarding the challenges from last week (e.g., "Did anyone choose the first challenge?").

Step 3 — Opening Prayer (3 minutes)

Lead the class in the "Opening Prayer," which is included in the Student Workbook. Leader's Guide notes are provided above: Red text provides direction and guidance, and white text is for you to read aloud to the class.

36 | CHOSEN

Dive In:
Who Do YOU Think Jesus Is?

What do you think of when you hear the name "Jesus"?

- The stained-glass shepherd holding a sheep?
- That huge statue in your church of a man on a cross?
- "Hollywood Jesus": the skinny guy in the movies who apparently combed his hair for three hours every day before beginning his public ministry?
- The plastic man at the end of your ROSARY?

Or do you think of the gentle face on that holy card, with eyes filled with so much power and conviction that, with a look and a word, he could get people to drop everything and follow him?

Whatever image you have of Jesus, there's no doubt that this man—a man with no worldly wealth or standing—had more of an impact on human history than any other before or since.

But who was Jesus, really? What was he like? And what does he have to do with our lives here and now, nearly 2,000 years after his death? Let's find out.

"The sacred heart of Christ is an inexhaustible fountain and its sole desire is to pour itself out into the hearts of the humble so as to free them and prepare them to lead lives according to his good pleasure [his will]."
— St. Margaret Mary Alacoque

 Step 4 **Dive In** (5 minutes)

Read this story aloud, have a candidate read it aloud, or have the class read it silently before watching the video segments. This thought-provoking story ties in to the lesson's topic and serves to set up the video presentation.

Watch It!

Segment 1: "Who Do You Say That I Am?"

1. Which apostle said: "You are the Christ, the son of the living God?" __Peter__

2. Jesus is either a liar, a lunatic, or __Lord__.

Segment 2: Evidence for Jesus

1. According to St. Paul, at least how many witnesses saw the risen Christ with their own eyes?

   A) 12   B) 50   C) 100   (D) 500   (see 1 Cor 15:6)

2. Who was the only apostle to see the risen Lord who did not die a martyr? __John__

3. Sarah says that the most compelling evidence that Jesus rose from the dead is in the witness of the __apostles__.

Segment 3: Why Did Jesus Come to Us?

1. Jesus came to pay a _____ that we could never pay.

   A) commission   (B) debt   C) visit   D) lesson

2. Which of these is *not* one of the reasons Christ came into the world?

   A) to reconcile us to God   D) to show us how to live

   B) to show us the love of God   E) to give us divine life

   (C) to write the Gospels

Small-Group Discussion

Segment 1: "Who Do You Say That I Am?"

1. What words best describe the roles Jesus plays in your life? Can you give examples of how each role has played out for you?[1]

Segment 2: Evidence for Jesus

1. Who would you die for right now, if anyone? Why?[2]

2. Try to explain in your own words how Jesus is God and not just a prophet or a wise man.

Segment 3: Why Did Jesus Come to Us?

1. Explain why God became human and came into the world. Assume the person you are speaking to knows nothing about God or Jesus.

2. What are some ways we can respond to God's love in our daily lives?

Step 5 ## Watch It!/Small-Group Discussion (50 minutes)

On the video, click on Lesson 5, Segment 1. When Segment 1 ends, have students fill in the "Watch It!" questions (2 to 3 minutes). Run through them to be sure they wrote the correct answers so they will have them to prepare for the next "Review Game."

Next, lead students in a small-group discussion for Segment 1. You may begin by asking general questions like: "What part of the video spoke to you the most?" Discussion questions for each segment are provided in the blue box above.

Follow the same steps for Segments 2 and 3. (Allow for about 10 minutes of discussion time after each segment.)

Small-Group Discussion Leader's Notes

1. If they have nothing to say, suggest a few key words: "friend," "judge," "Savior," "helper," "nothing." There is no need to overcorrect here if the answer is "nothing." Let them be honest about where they are as these classes get started. You can challenge them to pray and ask Jesus what role he wants to have in their lives.

2. Connect this back to Jesus' unconditional willingness to die for them.

Question:
Have you ever known a "Jesus Freak"? Tell us about it.

38 | CHOSEN

> *... when I did give my whole life to Jesus, I experienced all that I had been missing.*

TO THE HEART with

When I was in high school, I went to a rock concert where the band dc Talk was performing. There was a guy with a T-shirt that said, "Jesus Freak" across the front. At one point in the concert, he stood up and I was able to read the back of his T-shirt, which said,

> *"What will people think when they hear that I'm a Jesus Freak?*
> *What will people do when they find that it's true?*
> *I don't really care if they label me a Jesus Freak.*
> *There ain't no disguising the truth."[1]*

It may sound strange, but that T-shirt had a major impact on my life. I felt like God asked me a question that night, "Who am I in your life, Sarah?" Until that night, I wouldn't have been caught dead in a T-shirt that said anything about Jesus on it. But after that guy stood right in front of me

at that concert, I started asking myself some hard questions about what I believed and how I acted, and it changed the way I lived.

My heart was opened to a new lifestyle, a new worldview. I didn't want God to be just someone I prayed to when things got tough or when I needed something. From that night on, I realized that Jesus Christ was as real to me, here and now, as he was to the apostles who walked with him 2,000 years ago. He was their Savior and Redeemer, but also their friend.

You might say the early disciples and martyrs were "Jesus Freaks." They went to the ends of the earth and to their deaths proclaiming the truth of Jesus Christ's love and forgiveness. They wanted everyone to have that intimate relationship with Jesus. The Jesus Freaks of today are doing the same

Step 6   **To the Heart** (10 minutes)

After the small-group discussions, read this story aloud, have a candidate read it aloud, or have the class read it silently. After the story (written by this week's video presenter), read the thought-provoking question(s) provided in the red "To the Heart" box above. Time permitting, ask follow-up questions and encourage discussion.

Lesson 5 | 39

thing, and I want it to be said of me as well, "I don't really care if they label me a Jesus Freak ... There ain't no disguising the truth."

When Jesus becomes Lord and King of our hearts, it affects every aspect of our lives—what we watch on TV, what music we listen to, who our friends are. When I gave my life to Jesus—wholly and entirely—it was scary; I thought I might lose myself. But what I found was that he gave me so much more in return. I feared that giving everything to Jesus might make me "miss out" on life; but when I did give my whole life to Jesus, I experienced all that I had been missing. All I can say is the "inch" I gave him is nothing compared to the "mile" he gave me. We just cannot outdo God in generosity.

Sarah Swafford

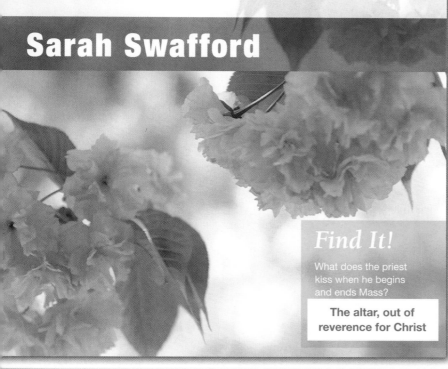

Find It!

What does the priest kiss when he begins and ends Mass?

The altar, out of reverence for Christ

40 | CHOSEN

Hero of the Week

Born:
March 28, 1515

Died:
October 4, 1582

Memorial:
October 15

Patron Saint of:
- headaches
- people in need of grace
- people ridiculed for piety

St. Teresa of Avila

Sometimes when we think of the saints, we wonder how we could ever be like them.

We think of them as heroic men and women who suffered terrible martyrdoms or who lived such lives of piety and **HOLINESS** that we could never follow in their footsteps.

Enter St. Teresa of Avila, a mystic and doctor of the Church who lived in the sixteenth century. She had a quick wit and a quicker tongue. Once, when she was rushing to the side of a sick friend, she got halfway across a river and fell off her horse. Shaken and soaking wet, she railed at God, "If this is the way you treat your friends, it's no wonder you have so few!"

Far from being a model of unattainable holiness, Teresa struggled with prayer and in her relationships with other people. Although she loved Jesus beyond measure, she just wasn't attracted to religious life as it was practiced in her day—the convents were full of spoiled young women who didn't want to be tied down by the demands of family life.

As a child, Teresa had looked for a quick way to holiness, running away from home with her little brother to fight the Moors so they could be martyred. Instead,

God called her to a "living martyrdom"—leading the reform of the Carmelite order. She endured great suffering both physically, with illness that struck her throughout her life, and emotionally, with resistance to her reforms from within her own community of sisters.

St. Teresa wrote several books on the spiritual life and about her mystical experiences. She taught her Carmelite sisters how to deepen their prayer lives in order to grow closer to the Savior. Her best-known work is *The Interior Castle*, a study of spirituality and contemplative prayer.

Although she lived a life of sacrifice and suffering, it was not without the joy of beautiful spiritual friendships, notably with another saint and doctor of the Church, St. John of the Cross. She valued friendship as a way for people to build each other up toward heaven and toward the true friendship, which is the friendship with Christ.

St. Teresa, pray for us. Help us to really know and love Jesus as you did.

Step 7

Hero of the Week (5 minutes)

This saint story will help to highlight and reinforce this lesson's topic. You may choose to read it aloud, have a candidate read it aloud, or have the class read it silently.

Challenge of the Week

☐ **Get your family thinking.** Next time your family is together, ask, "Who do you think Jesus was?" Share with them the three possibilities: liar, lunatic (crazy), or Lord. If you're feeling confident, try it with a friend. Write about what happened in the space below.

☐ **What do you think Jesus looked like?** Draw a picture, create an image, or describe in words (in the space below) what you think the Lord looked like. What does this picture say about who Jesus is to you?

☐ **What's your favorite song about Jesus?** It can be online, in a hymnal, or on a Gospel CD. Write your favorite line in the space below.

_____

_____

_____

_____

_____

_____

_____

_____

Closing Prayer

"I came that they may have life, and have it abundantly."
—John 10:10

O Divine Lord Jesus, we thank you for bringing us together to show us who you really are. You are our God, infinite and almighty, yet you humbly sacrificed yourself to save us from our sins and to teach us the best way to live.

We want to imitate the heroism of the saints, but sometimes we get discouraged by our own failings. Help us to receive the life you offer in abundance through your many gifts, especially through the sacraments of Reconciliation and Holy Communion. Amen.

Step 8 **Challenge of the Week** (2 minutes)

Ask your candidates to read the "challenges" above and choose one of the three to complete this week. Have them check the box next to the challenge they intend to complete. Encourage them to write about their experiences in the space provided.

Step 9 **Homework Instructions and Updates** (2 minutes)

Remind candidates to read the "Wrap-Up" and the "What's That Word?" sections in the "Taking It Home" section of the Student Workbook. They should also review the "Watch It!" questions to prepare for the next "Review Game."

Step 10 **Closing Prayer** (3 minutes)

As a way of building up community, ask if there are any prayer intentions. Write them down (or have candidates share them aloud) and after praying for those intentions, have the class read the "Closing Prayer" together (provided in the Student Workbook).

42 | 🔥CHOSEN

Taking It Home

For next week's "Review Game," be sure to read over the following …

1. **Watch It!** questions (page 37)
2. **Wrap-Up**
3. **"What's That Word?"**
4. **Memory Verse**

Don't forget to do your
Challenge of the Week (page 41)

Wrap-Up

Who was Jesus of Nazareth? This question has been debated ever since Jesus and his apostles walked the earth. In the Gospel of Mark, Jesus asks his followers, "Who do men say that I am?" (Mark 8:27). Here's how they responded:

"And they told him, 'John the Baptist; and others say, Elijah; and others one of the prophets.' And he asked them, 'But who do you say that I am?' Peter answered him, 'You are the Christ'" (Mark 8:28-29).

How would you have answered Jesus? Some people like to brush Jesus aside, saying he was a great prophet or a wise man. But what would you think if someone came up to you and claimed to

be God? Would you conclude he was the wisest person who ever lived? More likely, you'd think he was either kidding around or was delusional. A liar or a lunatic.

Jesus couldn't have been a liar. Liars lie to get something they want. No one dies a horrible death to perpetuate a falsehood. To teach with the wisdom and clarity that he did, Jesus couldn't have been crazy, either.

Jesus claimed to be God—and rose from the dead to prove it, something no other founder of a world religion has ever done. He was not a liar and not a lunatic … but Lord.[2]

Did You Know?

In the sixth century, many people said, "Good luck to you," if someone sneezed. Pope St. Gregory the Great began the practice of saying, "God bless you," as a protection from the plague ravaging Italy at the time.

"What's That Word?"

FIAT

Latin for "let it be done," this term refers to Mary's acceptance of the **ANGEL** Gabriel's words informing her that she would be the Mother of the Son of God. It is clear from the biblical account of the Annunciation in Luke 1:26-38 that Mary initially did not understand the angel Gabriel's words—"How can this be, since I have no husband?"—yet her unshakeable faith in God gave her the strength to say "yes" despite her lack of understanding. Mary's example of faith presents us with a model to follow in our own lives, showing us that we don't always need to understand God's will. We just need to follow it.

INCARNATION

If you like Mexican food, you've heard of *carne asada*. The Spanish word *carne* ("meat") comes from the Latin *caro/carnis,* meaning "flesh." So the *Incarnation* refers to God coming in the flesh when the second Person of the Trinity, the Son, took on a human nature (i.e., a human body and a human soul) when he was conceived by the Holy Spirit in the womb of the Blessed Virgin **MARY**. He became truly man, yet remained truly God.[3] He is 100 percent God and 100 percent human, not "part God and part human."

[3] CCC 464

Memory Verse:

"He said to them, 'But who do you say that I am?' Simon Peter replied, 'You are the Christ, the Son of the living God.'"

—Matthew 16:15-16

JESUS CHRIST

The second Person of the Trinity, Jesus Christ, is God incarnate. The name "Jesus" comes from the Hebrew *Yeshua*, meaning "God saves." The angel Gabriel told Joseph to give Jesus this name because "he will save his people from their sins" (Matthew 1:21). "Christ" was not Jesus' last name. It comes from *Christos* in ancient Greek, which means, "anointed one." (In Hebrew, the word is *Messiah*.)

In Scripture, to be anointed is to be empowered by God for a specific role and task. In Baptism and Confirmation, the Holy Spirit anoints us when our heads are marked with sacred chrism (holy oil). In union with Jesus, we are empowered to live as children who serve our heavenly Father.

PASCHAL MYSTERY

The PASCHAL MYSTERY is Jesus' Passion (suffering), Death, Resurrection from the dead, and Ascension into heaven. The word *paschal* comes from the Hebrew for Passover.

The Passover commemorates the Exodus, when God, through Moses, commanded the Hebrew people, then slaves of the Egyptians, to sacrifice a lamb and mark their doors with its blood. That night, the firstborn in every home in Egypt died—except those in homes with blood spattered on their doorways. This was the event that pushed Pharaoh to finally free God's people from slavery.

By the Paschal Mystery, Jesus, who is called the sacrificial "Lamb of God," is sacrificed for us all. He doesn't free us from an earthly ruler, but from our slavery to sin and death.

Any questions?

How do you know he really rose from the dead?

Nothing supports a case like an eyewitness. In the nineteenth century, Harvard law professor Dr. Simon Greenleaf set out to prove that Jesus' Resurrection would never hold up in a court of law. Instead, he became a Christian! He was convinced by the large number of eyewitnesses to Jesus' Resurrection (including most of the apostles), who were willing to die rather than recant their testimony.*

Why did Jesus come to us?

The *Catechism* lists four reasons:

1) To remove sin and reconcile us to God

2) To show us just how much God loves us

3) To show us how to live

4) To fill us with his divine life
   (see also CCC 456–460)

---

* While people of various beliefs have died for an *idea*, the apostles staked their lives on the truth of their *eyewitness testimony*.

Notes

Dive In:
A Time Machine

A time machine was recently put up for auction on eBay. It was (or will be, says the seller) built in the year 2239. He found it under his home while remodeling his bathroom. No need to run to the Internet, though. According to the ad, it's "in nonworking condition."

Too bad, huh? But think about it: How amazing would it be to *own* a time machine? When and where would you go to experience history firsthand? Would you go back in time or forward in time and then back to the present and then *back to the future?* You'd get to experience the most amazing people and events in history.

Maybe you would choose to travel back in time to witness a certain battle, attend an historic rock concert, or take a peek at the dinosaurs. Or maybe ... you'd witness the Resurrection or perhaps turn up with the shepherds to see the history-shaping event that transpired 2,000 years ago, when God was born. The maker of everything actually walked this earth, taught us how to live, and showed us his love by dying and rising for us.

And he didn't stop there. Jesus *could have* just let us read about all that in the history books, but he didn't. He wanted us to *experience* his love.

That's where the Catholic Church comes in. While the Church isn't a time machine, in a very real way, it helps us to experience the most significant part of history. We have direct access to the grace of the Last Supper, the cross, the empty tomb, PENTECOST Sunday, and more. ... And as part of the Church, we get to be part of bringing that grace to others, here and now.

Today, we're going to look at how being part of the Church gives us a front-row seat to God's saving works. And it's far more amazing than time travel ... and a whole lot more significant!

"The Church's vocation is to bring joy to the world, a joy that is authentic and enduring, the joy proclaimed by the angels to the shepherds on the night Jesus was born."
—*Pope Benedict XVI*

Step 4 — **Dive In** (5 minutes)

Read this story aloud, have a candidate read it aloud, or have the class read it silently before watching the video segments. This thought-provoking story ties in to the lesson's topic and serves to set up the video presentation.

Segment 1: The One True Church

1. Which is **not** one of the four "marks" of the Catholic Church?

   A) One   B) Holy   C) Catholic   (D) Roman)   E) Apostolic

2. Who was the "rock" to whom Jesus gave the "keys to the kingdom," appointing him to lead the Church?

   <u>**Peter (see Mt 16:19)**</u>

3. Which of the three Persons of the Blessed Trinity is considered the "guardian and protector" of the Church? <u>**the Holy Spirit**</u>

Segment 2: Apostolic and Catholic

1. The word "catholic" means <u>universal</u>.

2. The teaching authority of the Church is called the

   <u>   </u>.

   (A) Magisterium)   C) Divine Office
   B) Deposit of faith   D) Final Word

3. The word infallible means without _____.

   (A) error)   B) malice   C) confusion   D) sin

Segment 3: The Church Is Holy

1. The Church has both a visible and <u>invisible</u> reality.

2. The Church is often referred to as our _____, who is always there for us.

   A) brother   B) uncle   C) rock   (D) mother)

Small-Group Discussion

Segment 1: The One True Church

1. What does the term "cradle Catholic" mean to you?

2. Do you know anyone who was not born Catholic, but converted into the Church? Why do you think he or she converted? What are some other reasons people might want to become Catholic?

Segment 2: Apostolic and Catholic

1. If you started a club or a company, what are some reasons it would be important to establish an organized, visible, and structured leadership?[1]

2. What are some roles you have in the Church that priests do not have? What are some other things you can do to serve God and the Church?[2]

Segment 3: The Church Is Holy

1. What are some ways the Church makes Jesus Christ and his saving work a visible reality in the world today?

2. How would you respond to someone who questions the Church's holiness?

Step 5

Watch It!/Small-Group Discussion (50 minutes)

On the video, click on Lesson 6, Segment 1. When Segment 1 ends, have students fill in the "Watch It!" questions (2 to 3 minutes). Run through them to be sure they wrote the correct answers so they will have them to prepare for the next "Review Game."

Next, lead students in a small-group discussion for Segment 1. You may begin by asking general questions like: "What part of the video spoke to you the most?" Discussion questions for each segment are provided in the blue box above.

Follow the same steps for Segments 2 and 3. (Allow for about 10 minutes of discussion time after each segment.)

Small-Group Discussion Leader's Notes

1. Draw the connection for them. Jesus left us an organized religion for some of the same reasons.

2. Hint: If conversation lags, try reading 1 Corinthians 12:12-18 aloud. Ask them, "What part are you in the Body of Christ, and why?"

Question:

After being subjected to so much ugliness and racism from other Catholics, why do you think Fr. Tolton aspired to become a priest? What does his story say to us about how to respond to those who denounce the teachings of the Church because of the sinful actions of individual Catholics, including priests?[1]

---

1. Fr. Tolton understood that what the Catholic Church *actually teaches* is true, good, and beautiful, despite the hypocrisy of some Church members who do not *actually live* the faith they profess. He recognized that personal sin and human weakness are not greater or more powerful than the strength of objective truth found in the Church.

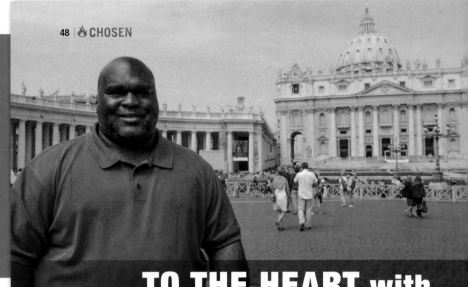

48 | 🔥 CHOSEN

TO THE HEART with

Have you ever felt out of place, like people wished you weren't there? Augustine Tolton knew that feeling well. When he was a child, Tolton, who was black, attended an all-white Catholic school where he was teased and insulted every day. The parents of some students were angry that a black student had been enrolled. One night, a rock was hurled through the pastor's window. Fearful for her son's safety, Augustine's mother withdrew him from the school after only a month.

Eventually, Tolton was accepted at another school. Once again, he was the only black student, but the pastor, Fr. McGirr, worked hard to win over the hardened hearts of those who couldn't see past race. Fr. McGirr became a mentor and inspiration to Augustine, who began to consider becoming a priest himself.

The question was, how?[1] Fr. McGirr helped Augustine apply to the Franciscan Order, where he met with the first of many rejections. With Fr. McGirr's help, the young man was accepted to the Vatican seminary in Rome and was later ordained to the priesthood in 1886 at age thirty-one.

As a young black priest in the nineteenth century, Fr. Tolton faced many challenges and fought against the racial prejudice that predominated in that day. He eventually moved to Chicago, where his awesome responsibilities and obligations to the Catholic community there took a toll on him. He died of heatstroke in 1897 at the age of forty-three.

Step 6

To the Heart (10 minutes)

After the small-group discussions, read this story aloud, have a candidate read it aloud, or have the class read it silently. After the story (written by this week's video presenter), read the thought-provoking question(s) provided in the red "To the Heart" box above. Time permitting, ask follow-up questions and encourage discussion.

Lesson 6 | 49

His story is a powerful testimony of persevering faith, even in the face of animosity and prejudice. His cause for canonization was opened in 2011.

Fr. Tolton was a visionary who saw far beyond issues of race and politics and far beyond the human imperfections we sometimes encounter in the Church (just as we do with any group of people). He looked inward—into the heart of the Church itself, where he saw the crucified Christ who, even as he was condemned and mocked, poured himself out with perfect love. "It was the priests of the Church who taught me to pray and to forgive my persecutors," said Fr. Tolton. "It was through their direction that I beheld for the first time the glimmering light of truth and the majesty of the Church."

The next time you feel out of place, unwanted, or attacked—or if you ever feel frustrated or angry with the Church—think of Fr. Tolton's patient endurance, his powerful witness, and his love for Christ and for the Catholic Church.

Deacon Harold Burke-Sivers

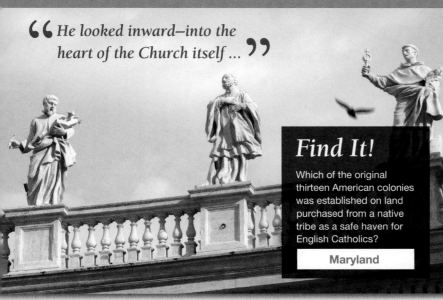

" He looked inward—into the heart of the Church itself ... "

Find It!

Which of the original thirteen American colonies was established on land purchased from a native tribe as a safe haven for English Catholics?

Maryland

50 | CHOSEN

Hero of the Week

Born:
October 12, 1891

Died:
August 9, 1942

Memorial:
August 9

Patron Saint of:
- Europe
- martyrs
- loss of parents
- World Youth Day

St. Teresa Benedicta
of the Cross (Edith Stein)

"My longing for truth was a single prayer." (Edith Stein)

The youngest daughter of a devout Jewish family with eleven children, nothing about Edith's earliest experiences suggested that she would one day die a Catholic martyr. Her father, a Jewish lumber merchant, died when Edith was a baby, and her devout Jewish mother labored tirelessly to feed and educate her family.

Edith soon distinguished herself at her schoolwork and became a top student at the Victoria School at Breslau. But at thirteen, she had a crisis of faith, left her Jewish roots, and declared herself an atheist. Yet, her interest in philosophy in college ultimately led her to convert to Catholicism as an adult: Having spent all night reading St. Teresa of Avila's autobiography, she exclaimed that she had found the truth.

Edith disappointed her mother with this CONVERSION, though Edith saw herself as uniquely qualified to bridge the gap between the Jewish and Christian communities, especially through her work entitled "Life in a Jewish Home." She didn't see her conversion as a break with her Judaism, but rather, a completion of it. She also wrote and spoke passionately about the dignity of the woman, rooted in her capacity for receptivity and motherhood. St. John Paul II called this the "feminine genius." Edith spoke of it as a unique power that could effect profound change in the world.

Edith remained proud of her Jewish roots and lived in Germany during the turbulent Nazi era. Eventually she was forced to quit teaching due to discriminatory laws against Jews—including those who converted to Christianity. She joined the Carmelite Sisters, taking the name Teresa Benedicta of the Cross. As Nazi persecution escalated, she fled to the Netherlands with her sister, Rosa, who had also converted. There, Teresa Benedicta wrote a letter to Pope Pius XI, asking him to denounce Nazism and put an end to "this abuse of Christ's name." Although there is no record of the pope responding to her plea, he issued an encyclical ("With Burning Anxiety") that denounced anti-Semitism and Nazism.

Teresa Benedicta and Rosa were arrested, imprisoned in Auschwitz, and eventually executed. This remarkable Carmelite sister serves as a great inspiration for all on the dignity of the human person, but especially for those who are seeking answers. She found the truth in Christ and went to her death knowing she was sharing in the sufferings of his cross.

St. Teresa Benedicta of the Cross, pray for us. Lead us to Christ, that we may receive the grace of God through the Holy Spirit.

Step 7 **Hero of the Week** (5 minutes)

This saint story will help to highlight and reinforce this lesson's topic. You may choose to read it aloud, have a candidate read it aloud, or have the class read it silently.

Challenge of the Week

 Ask your parents or another adult to tell you a story about a time they experienced the presence of God in their lives. Maybe they had an answer to prayer or heard a Scripture passage that spoke to them during a difficult time. Write about it in the space below.

 The Catholic Church is so *organized* that it is unmatched worldwide in reaching out to the poor, the sick, and those in need of disaster relief. Express your Catholic pride by posting a link on social media to a Catholic charity that interests you. Write the name of the group you chose in the space below.

 We are all members of the Body of Christ, each made for a purpose and all of equal dignity. Ask the Holy Spirit to be with you as you read 1 Corinthians 12. Which part of the "Body of Christ" do you think you represent, and why? Write about it in the space below.

_____

_____

_____

_____

_____

_____

_____

✝ Closing Prayer

"You are fellow citizens with the saints and members of the household of God, built upon the foundation of the apostles and prophets, Christ Jesus himself being the cornerstone ..."

—*Ephesians 2:19-20*

Oh, Blessed Trinity—Father, Son, and Holy Spirit—we are called to live in a community of love, as you do. Bless us with your love and protection, and help us to see the best in ourselves and in each other. Thank you for guiding and nourishing us here in class, and especially through the sacramental life, teaching, and mission we share in the one, holy, catholic, and APOSTOLIC Church. Amen.

 Challenge of the Week (2 minutes)

Ask your candidates to read the "challenges" above and choose one of the three to complete this week. Have them check the box next to the challenge they intend to complete. Encourage them to write about their experiences in the space provided.

 Homework Instructions and Updates (2 minutes)

Remind candidates to read the "Wrap-Up" and the "What's That Word?" sections in the "Taking It Home" section of the Student Workbook. They should also review the "Watch It!" questions to prepare for the next "Review Game."

 Closing Prayer (3 minutes)

As a way of building up community, ask if there are any prayer intentions. Write them down (or have candidates share them aloud) and after praying for those intentions, have the class read the "Closing Prayer" together (provided in the Student Workbook).

[2] Jn 17

[3] Jn 15:16, 20:21; Lk 22:29-30

[4] 1 Tm 3:1; Ti 1:5

[5] Mt 16:19

[6] Is 22:22

52 | CHOSEN

Taking It Home

For next week's "Review Game," be sure to read over the following …

1. **Watch It!** questions (page 47)
2. **Wrap-Up**
3. **"What's That Word?"**
4. **Memory Verse**

Don't forget to do your
Challenge of the Week (page 51)

Wrap-Up

Two thousand years ago, Jesus Christ founded a Church with a mission—to bring his presence and message to all generations until the end of time. That's quite a task! But, for a mission to be successful, it needs an organization behind it.

Structure is important in order for any group to stay unified and to get things done. Bill Gates would never have said, "I have a great idea, let's make programs for computers … OK … GO!" Instead, he structured an organization with sound business principles.

The Founding Fathers of the United States didn't just write the Constitution and tell everyone to go home and interpret it for themselves. They set up a structured government to represent the people and to interpret the Constitution.

Jesus is at least as smart as Bill Gates and the Founding Fathers! That's why he didn't just leave us a mission, but a structured Church to ensure that we, his people, would believe and work as one—the theme of his "high priestly prayer" on the night before his crucifixion.[2]

Right from the first days of Christianity, the Church has been organized. Jesus set aside twelve men as apostles to lead the Church.[3] Those apostles appointed other men to lead the Church in the same capacity as the Church grew. We call these successors "bishops."[4] Our bishops today trace their authority back to the twelve apostles. This is called APOSTOLIC SUCCESSION.

Adding further structure to his Church, Jesus established the papacy by making one of the apostles the head of the others. He gave Peter the "keys of the kingdom."[5] In biblical terms, "keys" = authority.[6] Peter was the bishop of Rome. Peter's God-given authority to govern the Church was passed down to our present-day bishop of Rome, the pope.

Why is this important? Why can't we simply read the Bible and interpret it for ourselves? Well, let's go back to the example of the government of the United States. Just as the Supreme Court is the final "voice of authority" on the Constitution, lest we fall into anarchy or civil war after every disagreement, the Magisterium guides the Church, but with more than man-made authority—with the authority of God.

That authority is necessary for us to remain one, as Jesus prayed we would. He gave us a mission, and we need to be united in carrying it out!

"What's That Word?"

APOSTOLIC

APOSTOLIC means "founded on the apostles." The apostles were the men that Jesus chose to lead his people and continue his work. The Church is "apostolic" because Jesus founded it on the apostles, because it keeps and follows the teachings that Jesus gave to the apostles, and because it is taught, sanctified, and guided by their successors, our bishops.[7]

CATHOLIC

The *Chosen* program is designed to prepare you to be confirmed in the Catholic Church. *Catholic* is not only the name of the Church but is one of its "marks," or characteristics (*see* CHURCH). One of the first bishops of the Church, St. Ignatius of Antioch, first referred to the Church as *catholic* and the name stuck.

The word *catholic* means "universal." The Church is catholic because God wants everyone to be members of the Church Jesus founded, to follow Jesus, and to be members of the kingdom of God. Christ is always and everywhere present in the world through the life and sacraments of the Church.[8]

CHURCH

The *Church* is made up of all the people who have responded to Jesus' call to follow him. Jesus started the Church and chose the apostles to lead it. Their successors, our bishops, continue to lead the Church today. Because God adopts us as his children in Baptism, the Church is often referred to as the "family of God."

The Catholic Church alone has the fullness of the means of salvation. The Church of Christ subsists in the Catholic Church, which means that every essential element that Christ intended his Church to have remains in the Catholic Church in a way that can never be lost.[9] The Church does not reject what is true and holy in other Christian communities and other faiths. There is a real, though imperfect, communion between the Catholic Church and other Christian communities. People of other faiths are also related in various ways to the Church.

We profess in the Creed that the Church is "one, holy, catholic, and apostolic." These characteristics, known as the *four* MARKS OF THE CHURCH, are the essential features of the Church that Jesus Christ established. The Church is *one* because of its source, soul, and founder—Jesus. The Church is *holy* because of the presence of Christ and the Holy Spirit in it. The Church is *catholic* (meaning "universal") because it possesses the fullness of the means of salvation. The Church is *apostolic* because it was built on the foundation of the apostles and continues to be governed by their successors, the bishops in union with the pope.

[7] CCC 857

[8] CCC 775, 830–831

[9] CCC 817–819

Memory Verse:

"So then, as we have opportunity, let us do good to all men, and especially to those who are of the household of faith."
—Galatians 6:10

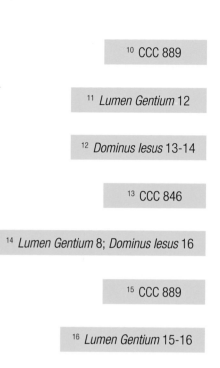

10 CCC 889

11 *Lumen Gentium* 12

12 *Dominus Iesus* 13-14

13 CCC 846

14 *Lumen Gentium* 8; *Dominus Iesus* 16

15 CCC 889

16 *Lumen Gentium* 15-16

17 *Ut Unum Sint* 3

18 *Gaudium et Spes* 22

INFALLIBILITY

Jesus gives the Church a share in his own INFALLIBILITY so that his disciples have the objective possibility of professing the true faith without error.[10] This charism is given to the entire People of God when, "from the bishops down to the last of the faithful they show universal agreement in matters of faith and morals."[11] The Church's Magisterium enjoys the gift of infallibility as the authentic teacher of the Gospel. The infallibility of the Magisterium is exercised when the pope and the bishops in union with him definitively proclaim a doctrine for belief by the faithful (e.g., solemn definitions of ecumenical councils). The pope also enjoys this gift by virtue of his office, when he proclaims by a definitive act (*ex cathedra*) a doctrine of faith or morals. The Church's Magisterium has no power to change what has been revealed to us by Christ. (*See also* TRADITION.)

KERYGMA

KERYGMA (Greek): A proclamation of the Gospel, distilled into its most essential elements: God the Father, Son, and Holy Spirit created us to be in loving communion with him for all eternity. But sin alienated us from God, so God sent his Son, Jesus, to fix the "sin problem." Jesus suffered and died to pay the penalty for our sin and restore us to right relationship with God, and he gave his apostles the power to build the Church he founded. Through the Church, we are invited to conversion and to be changed by the power of the Holy Spirit, beginning at Baptism. Through the sacraments of the Church, we receive a share in the very life of God.

Any questions?

Is the Catholic religion the only correct religion?

We believe that Jesus Christ, the eternal Son of God, is the unique and only Savior of the world. Anyone who is saved—no matter what faith they profess—is saved by Jesus.[12] The Church is God's plan for reconciling all of humanity in the body of his Son. All salvation comes from Christ the Head through the Church he founded, which is his body.[13] We believe that the Church Christ founded and entrusted to his apostles to govern is present and active in the world today and that this Church of Christ continues to exist fully only in the Catholic Church.[14]

The Catholic Church alone has the fullness of the means of salvation. Jesus has given the Church a share in his own infallibility so that his apostles could profess the truths he revealed without error.[15] The Catholic Church does not reject what is true and holy in other Christian communities and other faiths. People of other faiths are related in various ways to the Church.[16] There is a real, though imperfect, communion between the Church and other Christian communities, and the Church is committed to participating in the ecumenical movement and promoting the unity of all Christians, a unity firmly rooted in our common Baptism in Christ. The Church also engages in dialogue with members of non-Christian faiths because it sees "all goodness and truth found in these religions as 'a preparation for the Gospel and given by him who enlightens all men that they may at length have life'" (CCC 843).[17]

The Catholic Church teaches that God offers the possibility of being saved to all people because the Holy Spirit can associate all with the saving Paschal Mystery of Christ.[18] Each one of us is called to spread this "good news" to all the world, that is, that all are called to be one in Christ, and that all of humanity is called into communion with the Church. (See CCC 836-383, 1398.)

Notes

**Lesson 7
Leader's Notes**

Overview

The purpose of this lesson is to convey the truth about what happens after death, sometimes called the "four last things": death, judgment, heaven, and hell (see CCC 1021–1041). We will consider the destiny of not only the individual, but of the whole human race, which will be revealed at the Second Coming of Christ—the resurrection of the dead, the Last Judgment, and the triumph of the kingdom of God in a new heaven and a new earth.

While the subject of life after death makes some people uncomfortable, God in his great mercy reveals these truths to us for two reasons: First, to give us a chance to prepare ourselves for that final journey, and second, so that each day we will "remember death" (*memento mori*)—full of the hope that each day brings us closer to attaining the end for which we were created: lifelong union with God. We also focus on this because, much like the end of a physical journey dictates the direction we should drive, the glory to which every person on earth is called reveals how we should live our lives here and now.

Objectives of this Lesson

1. *Death is a part of life.* It is not a cheery subject, but we cannot avoid it because it is the doorway to our ultimate end and, for the faithful, our ultimate happiness (see CCC 1006–1007).

2. *Eternity is real.* Whether we end up in heaven or hell is the result of what we choose while we are here on earth. God does not force himself on anyone. The choices we make today have serious and lasting consequences (see CCC 1021–1022).

3. *Purgatory is a state of purification.* It is not pleasant, but neither is it permanent. All those in Purgatory will one day see heaven (see CCC 1030–1032). Because of this, it is a state of great hope where souls experience the mercy of God. We can help the people there through our prayers and sacrifices, and they will help us by their prayers once they are in heaven. This is a beautiful way to express our love for those who have gone before us (see CCC 1032).

4. *Every human being who has ever lived will stand before God.* When Christ returns, he will establish a new heaven and a new earth, where there will be perfect love, peace, justice, and freedom from all death and pain. God is love and wants us all to be with him in paradise forever. But he will not force himself on anyone. Those who willingly reject him will get what they choose: eternal separation from God (see CCC 1033).

"Where am I going?"

(A Look at the Four Last Things)

✝

Opening Prayer

"Eternal rest grant unto them, O Lord,
and may perpetual light shine upon them.
May the souls of the faithful departed,
through the mercy of God,
rest in peace. Amen."

Opening Prayer

Today we are going to talk about the "four last things": death, judgment, heaven, and hell. We will also discuss Purgatory and the very last thing: Jesus coming again at the end of time. To start, close your eyes for one minute and remember someone in your life, a friend or family member, who has died.

> *Pause for 30 to 60 seconds.*
>
> *Invite the students to say the name of the person they are thinking of aloud. After a minute continue with ...*

Let's begin today by saying the simple and traditional Catholic prayer that is often prayed for those who have died. In the name of the Father ...

 Welcome/Review Game (5 minutes)

Begin by welcoming the class and telling them that you will be starting with a review of the previous lesson's material. On the DVD menu, click on Lesson 7; then on the sub-menu, click on "Review Game."

Have students answer the questions based on the previous lesson. For more information about how to adapt this game to meet the needs of your group, see the "Review Game" section in the Introduction to this Leader's Guide (page xvi).

 Challenge of the Week Review (5 minutes)

Ask if anyone would like to share a "challenge experience" from the previous week. Try to draw students out by prompting them with basic questions regarding the challenges from last week (e.g.,"Did anyone choose the first challenge?").

Opening Prayer (3 minutes)

Lead the class in the "Opening Prayer," which is included in the Student Workbook. Leader's Guide notes are provided above: Red text provides direction and guidance, and white text is for you to read aloud to the class.

56 | 🔥 CHOSEN

Dive In:
The Way of the Bow

Kyudo ("the way of the bow") is Japan's oldest martial art form. Long before the samurai met in fields of battle with their swords, and before ninjas loaded themselves with spikes and stars to scale castle walls, Japanese warriors regarded this eastern form of archery as their "weapon of choice."

Through the centuries, as the gun replaced the bow-and-arrow on the battlefield, kyudo evolved into a highly ritualized art form that can be summarized in a single word: "focus."

From the beginning to the end of the kyudo ritual, the archer's eyes never leave his target. Birds fly, children cry, squirrels jump in the way, yet his concentration is absolute. Everything from the costume he wears to the way he draws the bow is designed to attain excellence in truth, goodness, and beauty.*

This emphasis on focus as a means to attain excellence extends not only to martial arts and to all sports, but to life as well. The cheering crowds, aching muscles, and trash-talking opponents—any or all of these things can cause a person to get distracted. Your attention has to remain on that basket, goal, end zone, or target. If you're not focused there, you have no chance of winning the game!

Life has a goal. It has an end zone. It has a target. And, in life, as in kyudo, the only way to attain our goal—to be with God forever in heaven—is to stay focused on our target and to pursue truth, beauty, and goodness (which are glimpses of heaven ... and of God) here and now. Otherwise, we end up meandering through life from one activity to the next, aiming our hearts at one wrong target after another. And, if we live for all the wrong things, we might end up losing at the "game" of life itself.

We're going to talk today about what the end goal of life is, how to stay focused on it in a healthy way, and how that end goal impacts us in the here and now.

---

* This is an example of how we, as Catholics, affirm that which is good and true in other traditions, while holding fast to the revealed faith given by God through Christ and the Church. (See *Nostra Aetate* ["In Our Age"], 2.)

"Do not lose courage in considering your own imperfections, but instantly set about remedying them."
– St. Francis de Sales

Dive In (5 minutes)

Step 4

Read this story aloud, have a candidate read it aloud, or have the class read it silently before watching the video segments. This thought-provoking story ties in to the lesson's topic and serves to set up the video presentation.

Watch It!

Segment 1: Death and Judgment

1. **(T) or F?** It was due to man's sin that death entered the world.

2. What aggressive animal did Chris claim to have to kill and turn into a pelt?

   A) Lion   B) Camel   C) Squirrel   **(D) Panda)**

3. Chris says that justice necessitates _____.

   A) revenge   **(B) judgment)**   C) a trial   D) anger

Segment 2: Heaven and Hell

1. **(T) or F?** Jesus taught about the reality of hell.[1]

2. The *Catechism* calls heaven the state of "supreme, definitive _____**happiness**_____." **(see CCC 1024)**

Segment 3: Purgatory

1. **(T) or F?** Purgatory is a state for those who need to be purified before they enter heaven.

2. What was the penance that the priest gave Chris?

   _____**one Hail Mary**_____

---

[1] See Mt 5:22, 8:12, 10:28; Mk 9:43-48; Lk 16:19-31.

Small-Group Discussion

Segment 1: Death and Judgment

1. If you knew you were going to die tomorrow, what would be the first thing on your "to-do" list? What other things would be on the list?

2. Have you ever experienced the death of a friend or family member? What about the experience made the strongest impression on you? Did it make you think about what happens after death?

Segment 2: Heaven and Hell

1. How would you answer someone who asks why a loving God would allow people to go to hell?

2. What do you imagine heaven to be like? What types of experiences here on earth do you think most closely resemble what you will experience in heaven?

Segment 3: Purgatory

1. How is Purgatory a sign of God's mercy?

2. How does believing in (and wanting to get to) heaven make a difference in how you live your life, here and now?

Step 5

Watch It!/Small-Group Discussion (50 minutes)

On the video, click on Lesson 7, Segment 1. When Segment 1 ends, have students fill in the "Watch It!" questions (2 to 3 minutes). Run through them to be sure they wrote the correct answers so they will have them to prepare for the next "Review Game."

Next, lead students in a small-group discussion for Segment 1. You may begin by asking general questions like: "What part of the video spoke to you the most?" Discussion questions for each segment are provided in the blue box above.

Follow the same steps for Segments 2 and 3. (Allow for about 10 minutes of discussion time after each segment.)

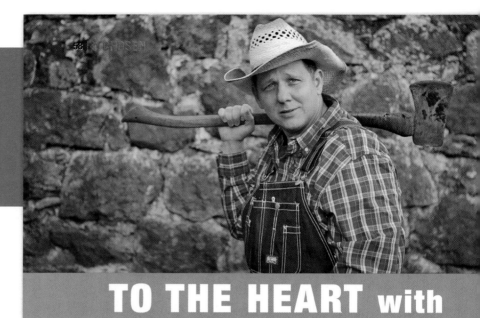

Question:

If you found out you had only a week to live, what are some things you would do with that time? Who would you talk to, and what would you want to say?

TO THE HEART with

About ten years ago, on Christmas Day, I had just opened my wife's gift to me—my own little incense burner (I love the smell!)—when a bad feeling hit me. I wondered if I was having a heart attack. "I think I need to go to the hospital," I said.

We arrived at the hospital within minutes. As I gave my symptoms to the nursing staff, part of me wondered if I was overreacting. Did I really need a doctor? The other part of me already knew that the moment I had been dreading had finally arrived.

I was born with a partially closed aortic valve, and the doctors had told me that one day it would give out. I had annual checkups, and I didn't play competitive sports (since it might mean "sudden death"). Eventually, death would come for me—of that I was certain.

After a few hours in the hospital, I started to feel a bit better, so my wife, Linda, went home, since we were having guests for Christmas dinner. I was napping when the doctor walked into my room and told me I had to have surgery. My valve had shrunk and was leaking. "If we don't operate, within three months to a year, you'll be dead."

A priest gave me the ANOINTING OF THE SICK. Linda stayed with me until they rolled me into surgery. I remember thinking: *I have put my whole life in your hands, Jesus. I trust in you, and I trust you will take care of my family.* As the drugs caused me to start slipping away, I thought: *Well, this is it, God. I believe in you!*

It was a sobering moment. It made me sad to think that my life might be over, that I might not be able

---

Step 6 **To the Heart** (10 minutes)

After the small-group discussions, read this story aloud, have a candidate read it aloud, or have the class read it silently. After the story (written by this week's video presenter), read the thought-provoking question(s) provided in the red "To the Heart" box above. Time permitting, ask follow-up questions and encourage discussion.

to watch the kids grow up and get married. But I knew I was in the hands of Jesus.

You probably have already guessed that I didn't die on the operating table. More than ten years have passed. I don't know how much time I have left, or whether the new heart valve will ever give out. What I *do* know is that every day is a gift to embrace.

Not everyone goes through life with a faulty heart valve, but we all are going to die at some point, possibly without any warning. And I didn't share this to encourage you to live your life in fear, but the opposite ... to encourage you to live with the freedom that comes from knowing you're right with God and with the knowledge that he loves you more than you can imagine. So, live your life in a way that will allow you to have no regrets in your relationships with others and no regrets when you finally see your Father in heaven. That's a life lived to the full, every day!

Chris Padgett

Find It!

Who is the patron saint of priests?

St. John Vianney, the Curé of Ars

... live with the freedom that comes from knowing you're right with God and ... that he loves you more than you can imagine.

60 | CHOSEN

Hero of the Week

Born:
circa 256

Died:
circa 288

Memorial:
January 20

Patron Saint of:
- soldiers
- archers
- holy Christian death
- athletes

St. Sebastian
Martyr

St. Sebastian is a model of a saintly superhero.

He had joined the ranks of the Roman army in order to assist Christians without arousing suspicion. He served as a captain of the Praetorian Guard for Emperor Diocletian ... until he was exposed as a Christian due to a number of miracles involving two brothers, Marcellian and Marcus, and the healing of a mute woman, Zoe, a convert to Christianity.

When Sebastian's faith was discovered, he was sentenced to die by being shot full of arrows. It was a horrible way to die! But when St. Irene of Rome, the widow of St. Castulus, went to collect Sebastian's body, she discovered that he was still alive. She nursed him back to health, only to have Sebastian publicly denounce the emperor for his cruelty to Christians. This time, the emperor had him beaten to death.

St. Sebastian is considered the patron saint of archers, as well as the patron saint for a holy death. He is also associated with sufferers of the plague because many sufferers of the disease were cured after praying for his INTERCESSION.

When athletes seek a patron saint, many look to St. Sebastian for inspiration.

Saint Sebastian Interceding for the Plague Stricken, by Josse Lieferinxe

His incredible physical strength and endurance in the face of his terrible ordeal exemplify the excellent conditioning athletes aspire to attain. St. Sebastian's conviction and persistence in bringing others to the faith are qualities that not only athletes, but all of us, should find appealing and worth imitating.

St. Sebastian, pray for us. Give us strength on our journey as we see it to God's good end.

Step 7 — Hero of the Week (5 minutes)

This saint story will help to highlight and reinforce this lesson's topic. You may choose to read it aloud, have a candidate read it aloud, or have the class read it silently.

Challenge of the Week

Lesson 7 | 61

 This week, pray for the release of souls from PURGATORY. Copy this powerful prayer into the space below, and offer it on behalf of those who have died. If you've recently lost someone dear to you, remember that person in particular:

"Eternal Father, I offer you the most precious blood of your divine Son, Jesus, in union with the Masses said throughout the world today, for all the holy souls in Purgatory, for sinners everywhere, for sinners in the universal church, for those in my own home and within my family. Amen." (Prayer of St. Gertrude the Great)

 Go to Confession this week.

Invite your family or friends to go with you. Plan something fun to do afterward to celebrate your fresh start. Write about it in the space below.

☐ **Just say it!** Is there someone with whom you need to be reconciled, someone who needs your apology or forgiveness? What are you waiting for? Talk to them or write them a letter if that would be easier. Write about your experience in the space below.

_____

_____

_____

_____

_____

✝ Closing Prayer

"For the wages of sin is death, but the free gift of God is eternal life in Christ Jesus our Lord."
—*Romans 6:23*

Lord Jesus, we sin and we know it. We'd like to pretend it doesn't matter, and that we're not hurting anyone, but in this lesson we have learned that we damage our own souls and often the souls of others when we turn away from you.

Give us the grace to live each day with our eyes on heaven. Help us to recognize and repent of any habits or attitudes that keep us from loving you with all our hearts. Amen.

 Challenge of the Week (2 minutes)

Ask your candidates to read the "challenges" above and choose one of the three to complete this week. Have them check the box next to the challenge they intend to complete. Encourage them to write about their experiences in the space provided.

Step 9 **Homework Instructions and Updates** (2 minutes)

Remind candidates to read the "Wrap-Up" and the "What's That Word?" sections in the "Taking It Home" section of the Student Workbook. They should also review the "Watch It!" questions to prepare for the next "Review Game."

Step 10 **Closing Prayer** (3 minutes)

As a way of building up community, ask if there are any prayer intentions. Write them down (or have candidates share them aloud) and after praying for those intentions, have the class read the "Closing Prayer" together (provided in the Student Workbook).

62 | CHOSEN

Taking It Home

For next week's "Review Game," be sure to read over the following …

1. **Watch It!** questions (page 57)
2. **Wrap-Up**
3. **"What's That Word?"**
4. **Memory Verse**

Don't forget to do your **Challenge of the Week** (page 61)

Wrap-Up

The walls of the Capuchin Crypt in Rome are adorned with a most distinctive motif: human bones. From the earliest days of the Church, *memento mori* ("remember death") was a phrase used to describe the attitude of believers toward every aspect of life: They always lived with their final destiny in view.

In this phase of our *Chosen* journey, we move from facts about God and the Church to a deeper examination of what the Church teaches and how that affects us. As we do, it is helpful for us to keep our "end goal" in mind. The Church refers to this end goal as the "four last things": death, JUDGMENT, heaven, and hell. (This includes Purgatory, which is understood to be like heaven's "mudroom," where we go to get cleaned up before entering our Father's house.)

At one time or another, someone has probably asked you if you are "saved," or if you know you are going to heaven when you die. This question reminds us that, while many Christian groups embrace certain Catholic teachings, the application of those teachings in daily practice can vary significantly. Jesus was *very* clear that hell is a real state and that it is a real possibility for one's eternal destiny.[1] Although God wants *everyone* in heaven,[2] he will not force himself on anyone. He gave us free will so we could choose *freely* to live in eternal union with him.

In an effort to reconcile the idea of a loving, merciful God with the reality of hell, some deny that God will hold us accountable for our choices—so long as we "have faith." But this is simply not what God has revealed to us through his Word or what has been handed down through the apostles. Catholics believe that we become children of God at Baptism,[3] and that we must persevere in faith to the end, by the grace of God, to reach eternal life.[4]

We must choose God by the way we live our lives. We must always *memento mori*—remember we will die. This lesson reminds us to take our choices seriously, to love and serve others diligently, and to seek reconciliation urgently when we mess up. Remember that no matter how "messy" we get, God wants to save us, never gives up on us, and has promised to be with us "to the end" (Matthew 24:13).

1. Mt 5:29, 25:41-46; Lk 16:23

2. 2 Pt 3:9

3. Mk 16:16; Jn 3:3-5

4. 2 Tm 2:12-13; Rom 11:22; 1 Pt 1:15-17

"What's That Word?"

HEAVEN

Heaven is "the state of supreme, definitive happiness" (CCC 1024). Every true joy we experience in this life comes from God like rays of sunlight reflecting off things and shining on us.[5] We get a glimpse of the joyful COMMUNION OF SAINTS through our family and friends. We get a taste of the love of the Trinity by loving one another. We get a glimpse of the vastness of God by looking up at the stars. In heaven, we get the fullness of the "sun" as we "soak up" God directly for all eternity. In heaven, we directly experience the source of all joy forever.

HELL

We have been created to love God and our neighbor as ourselves. But love, by its very nature, must be freely given. "Forced love" is a contradiction in terms. This is why God created us with free will—so that we might love. Because we are free to choose good and act in love, we are also free to choose evil and make unloving, sinful choices. If we freely choose to do something we know is mortally sinful, we lose SANCTIFYING GRACE (which is necessary for salvation).

Those who willfully persist in a state of MORTAL SIN until death—that is, those who freely choose to reject God—cannot be saved. God cannot force us to love him and be with him forever in heaven against our will. So there must be a place for those who reject him. This place is *hell*.[6] In hell, people are separated from the source of every joy.

JUDGMENT

A *judgment* is made when one thing is compared to another, such as when we get a report card. Our teacher compares our academic performance against the expectations he or she outlined at the beginning of the class. We are sometimes surprised by the grade we receive, but we usually have a good sense of how our performance compares to what was expected.

At the end of our lives, we will experience the *particular judgment* of God, and we will know how our actions and life compared to what he made us to be. This judgment will determine how we spend eternity, either with God in heaven or separated from him in hell.[7] When Jesus returns at the end of time "to judge the living and the dead" (see CCC 1040), all will experience the *Last Judgment,* when at last justice, love, and truth will triumph over evil. After that Last Judgment and the resurrection of the body, people will be whole, body and soul, again, either in heaven or in hell.

PURGATORY

Purgatory is the state of preparation and purification for those who die in the state of grace but are not yet ready for heaven due to remaining imperfections in their souls.[8] Life with God in heaven will be more exciting and intense than anything we have ever done or can even imagine. If we are not yet able to love perfectly, we will find the experience of heaven more painful than happy. So God, in his mercy, created a place where we can be purified so that we enter heaven prepared to experience its blessings. We are called to pray and "offer up" our sufferings for the souls in Purgatory, so that their sufferings might be lessened and their entry into heaven may occur more quickly. It is a beautiful way to express our love for family and friends who have died and to extend forgiveness to those who have hurt us and who we were unable to forgive while they were living. Once they enter heaven ahead of us, they will become our biggest prayer support!

[5] Jas 1:17

[6] CCC 1033

[7] CCC 1022

[8] CCC 1030–1032

64 | CHOSEN

⁹ Rv 21:27

¹⁰ Cor 3:13; 1 Pt 1:7; CCC 1030–1032

¹¹ 1 Pt 3:21

¹² Jn 6:51-55

¹³ Gal 6:9, Jas 1:2-4

Any questions?

What about Purgatory? Where is it in Scripture?

The word "Purgatory"—like the words "Trinity," "Bible," and "Incarnation"—is not found explicitly in Scripture. However, like all of the above, belief in Purgatory is found in Sacred Tradition and *implied* in Scripture.

Scripture passages such as 1 Corinthians 3:13 and 1 Peter 1:7 and the *Catechism* tell us of getting to heaven through a "purifying fire." From the start, the early Christians took up the Jewish tradition of praying for the dead who are still being purified. The Church teaches that, if we die in a state of grace (i.e., free from mortal sin), we will go to heaven. Because nothing unclean can enter the kingdom of heaven,[9] many of us leave this world needing to be purified of any remaining traces or attachments to sin. This process of purification is called "Purgatory," which purifies us of venial sins and temporal punishment due to the sins we have committed.[10]

Memory Verse:

"Draw near to God and he will draw near to you" —James 4:8

Did You Know?

St. Catherine of Siena, a trusted advisor to Pope Gregory XI and a great "doctor of the Church," had difficulty learning to read.

So ... what should I say when my Protestant friends ask if I'm "saved"?

The short answer is, "Yes."

The longer answer is:

"I believe that Jesus' death on the cross and Resurrection from the dead *made it possible for all* people to be saved.

"I believe that even though Jesus died and rose for all of us, everyone is not automatically saved as a result. I believe it is God's plan to apply the fruits of Jesus' saving work to individuals through Baptism.[11]

"I believe that salvation is not just a one-time event, but a share in God's very life that can increase, diminish, and end just like any relationship; it begins in Baptism as a birth into new life.

"I believe that the 'saved' are guided by the Church and strengthened for the journey by receiving him in the EUCHARIST.[12] I believe that *those who persevere* in faith will one day be united with God in heaven.[13]

"I believe that, in redeeming me, *God has not taken away my freedom to reject him,* and thus I can jeopardize my salvation if I want to. I also believe that my relationship with God can suffer if I simply neglect him in daily choices that fall short of outright rejection.

"I believe that my life with God—my salvation—necessarily begins, is nourished, and is restored when lost, within his family, which is the Church that Christ established, the 'pillar and foundation of truth'" (1 Timothy 3:15, NAB).

Notes

**Lesson 8
Leader's Notes**

Overview

The purpose of this lesson is to review the place of the sacraments in the Christian life. Each of the sacraments has a physical or tangible component, but unlike other signs and symbols we encounter in life, that which is signified by the sacraments actually occurs (see CCC 774). For example, in Baptism, the water signifies the "washing away" of Original Sin and of being born into God's family. The person goes into the water to show that he or she is "dying" with Christ and rises from the water as a sign of "rising to new life." In Baptism (as in all the sacraments), the physical sign also confers the grace of all these spiritual realities. "The saving work of [Christ's] holy and sanctifying humanity is the sacrament of salvation, which is revealed and active in the Church's sacraments (which the Eastern Churches also call 'the holy mysteries')" (CCC 774).

Human beings are the culmination and crown of God's creation: We differ from animals, which do not have rational souls (see CCC 363, 1703, 2258); we also differ from the angels, which are pure spirits. And because we possess both bodies and rational souls, God reveals himself to us and encounters us through the physical world—beginning with the Incarnation and continuing today by the imparting of his divine life to us through the sacraments of the Church. In this lesson, students will be encouraged to consider the importance of the sacraments in their own lives, including how Confirmation will affect their lives and how they will continue to "grow in grace" even after they have received that sacrament.

Objectives of this Lesson

1. *God created us to share in his divine life and gave us the sacraments to impart that grace to us* (see Philippians 4:13; CCC 1131, 1992). Sacraments are actions of God in our lives—giving us the power to live "life to the full" (John 10:10, NIV). But like any gift or grace, we need to receive the sacraments with "well-disposed hearts" (CCC 1133) in order for them to impact our lives.

2. *"The sacraments are efficacious signs of grace, instituted by Christ and entrusted to the Church, by which divine life is dispensed to us"* (CCC 1131). They remind us that we are part of something much bigger than ourselves—the universal Church and Body of Christ. Each of us has a job to do, and each of us has a gift to share (see CCC 791).

3. *Give students an overview of the seven sacraments.* There are three Sacraments of Initiation (Baptism, Confirmation, and the Eucharist); two of healing (Confession and the Anointing of the Sick); and two of service (Matrimony and Holy Orders), which the *Catechism* refers to as "sacraments at the service of communion" (CCC 1211). The Sacraments of Service are also sometimes called "sacraments of vocation."

"How do I get there?"

(The Power and Purpose of the Sacraments)

✝

Opening Prayer

"He entered Jericho and was passing through. And there was a man named Zacchaeus; he was a chief tax collector, and rich. And he sought to see who Jesus was, but could not, on account of the crowd, because he was small of stature. So he ran on ahead and climbed up into a sycamore tree to see him, for he was to pass that way. And when Jesus came to the place, he looked up and said to him, 'Zacchaeus, make haste and come down; for I must stay at your house today.' So he made haste and came down, and received him joyfully. And when they saw it they all murmured, 'He has gone in to be the guest of a man who is a sinner.' And Zacchaeus stood and said to the Lord, 'Behold, Lord, the half of my goods I give to the poor; and if I have defrauded any one of anything, I restore it fourfold.' And Jesus said to him, 'Today salvation has come to this house, since he also is a son of Abraham. For the Son of man came to seek and to save the lost.'"

—*Luke 19:1-10*

Opening Prayer

This week we are going to meditate on the story about Jesus and Zacchaeus, a despised tax collector. He collected money from his own people for the Romans and stole a bit for himself. Note how Jesus approached this man. He could have shouted, "Repent, you sinner!" Instead he said, "I want to come over for dinner." And that changed Zacchaeus' life.

> *Have the teens take a deep breath and be silent for about 10 seconds before you start reading Luke 19:1-10. After reading, say:*

Think about what it must have been like for Zacchaeus to encounter Jesus. Imagine Jesus' expression, finding him up in that tree. That is how Jesus looks at us, comes to us, and invites us.

Now, in the silence of your heart, thank him for his love in your own words.

> *Wait 30 seconds more.*

Today, we will see how Jesus comes to each of us in that same loving manner through the sacraments of the Catholic Church.

Step 1 — Welcome/Review Game (5 minutes)

Begin by welcoming the class and telling them that you will be starting with a review of the previous lesson's material. On the DVD menu, click on Lesson 8; then on the sub-menu, click on "Review Game."

Have students answer the questions based on the previous lesson. For more information about how to adapt this game to meet the needs of your group, see the "Review Game" section in the Introduction to this Leader's Guide (page xvi).

Step 2 — Challenge of the Week Review (5 minutes)

Ask if anyone would like to share a "challenge experience" from the previous week. Try to draw students out by prompting them with basic questions regarding the challenges from last week (e.g., "Did anyone choose the first challenge?").

Step 3 — Opening Prayer (3 minutes)

Lead the class in the "Opening Prayer," which is included in the Student Workbook. Leader's Guide notes are provided above: Red text provides direction and guidance, and white text is for you to read aloud to the class.

66 | CHOSEN

Dive In:
The Doldrums

For hundreds of years, the world was connected by sailboats. Sailing (or rowing) was the most efficient way to cross the large expanses of sea for travel, trade, or war. Sailboats have one fatal flaw, however, that led to their replacement by motorboats. If there was no wind, there was no movement.

The doldrums is a region stretching around the world's equator that, due to low air pressure, has very calm winds. Sometimes winds disappear entirely, trapping sailors for weeks at a time in the blistering heat.

The doldrums could be a sailor's worst nightmare! In the famous poem, "The Rime of the Ancient Mariner," Samuel Taylor Coleridge described what it was like.

> *Day after day, day after day,*
> *We stuck, nor breath nor motion;*
> *As idle as a painted ship*
> *Upon a painted ocean.*
> *Water, water, every where,*
> *And all the boards did shrink;*
> *Water, water, every where,*
> *Nor any drop to drink.*

Doldrums could kill a crew if it held them long enough. You could have a million-dollar sailboat and the best-trained crew in the world, but without wind, that sailboat would sit and bob like a buoy.

There are many things that depend on something else to function properly. Cars need gas. No matter how cool its rims are or how high its spoiler, a car without gas is a useless heap of metal. Computers need power. A $3,000 Mac with all the best software is nothing but an overpriced Frisbee if its battery won't work.

We're like that, too. We need an external "power source" to become who we are meant to be and to fulfill our purpose in life. We need fuel! We need God. We need grace. Grace doesn't just help us to become "religious"; it helps us to function the way God intended.

Today we're going to talk about what grace is and how God gives it to us.

> *"Totally love him, who gave himself totally for your love."*
> —St. Clare of Assisi

Step 4 **Dive In** (5 minutes)

Read this story aloud, have a candidate read it aloud, or have the class read it silently before watching the video segments. This thought-provoking story ties in to the lesson's topic and serves to set up the video presentation.

Segment 1: The Gift of Grace

1. The word "grace" comes from the Latin word for _____.

   A) power   (B) gift)   C) salvation   D) holy

2. Through our _____ Baptism _____ we become adopted sons and daughters of God.

Segment 2: What Is a Sacrament?

1. The sacraments are efficacious signs, instituted by Christ, entrusted to __ his Church __.

2. Like the manna given to the Israelites, Christ gives us the _____ Eucharist _____.

Segment 3: The Seven Sacraments

1. The three Sacraments of Initiation are Baptism, Confirmation, and the _____ Eucharist _____.

2. The two Sacraments of Healing are the Anointing of the Sick and _____ Confession (Reconciliation) _____

3. The two Sacraments of Service are _____ Matrimony _____ and Holy Orders.

Small-Group Discussion

Segment 1: The Gift of Grace

1. Pretend I have never heard of grace. Tell me what it is in your own words.

2. What does it mean when we read in the "Opening Prayer" that Jesus "came to seek and to save the lost?" Can you think of a time you experienced this in your own life or heard about it in someone else's?

Segment 2: What Is a Sacrament?

1. Why do people need the sacraments? Why do you think God gave them to us?[1]

2. Why do you think God entrusted the sacraments to the Catholic Church?

Segment 3: The Seven Sacraments

1. How do the sacraments help you fulfill your purpose in life?

2. Why do you think it is important to take advantage of the grace Jesus offers in the sacraments? What can happen if we do not?

Step 5 — Watch It!/Small-Group Discussion (50 minutes)

On the video, click on Lesson 8, Segment 1. When Segment 1 ends, have students fill in the "Watch It!" questions (2 to 3 minutes). Run through them to be sure they wrote the correct answers so they will have them to prepare for the next "Review Game."

Next, lead students in a small-group discussion for Segment 1. You may begin by asking general questions like: "What part of the video spoke to you the most?" Discussion questions for each segment are provided in the blue box above.

Follow the same steps for Segments 2 and 3. (Allow for about 10 minutes of discussion time after each segment.)

Small-Group Discussion Leader's Notes

1. We have bodies. We need tangible encounters with God. Also, without tangible reminders of God's presence, faith is too easily reduced to what we "feel" about God. Especially in the Eucharist, we encounter the risen Lord.

68 | CHOSEN

TO THE HEART with

Questions:

In this story, Sr. Amelia tells of how God "bridged the gap" that was between them, making it possible for her to become Catholic. How does God reach out to you?

I took a left and began the drive up the steep hill toward the cathedral. The sky seemed to be higher up than normal. It had been four months since I had last seriously thought about joining the Catholic Church. I wanted to believe; I wanted to be a part of the Church. The problem was that I just didn't believe ... yet.

As I continued the drive up the hill, the dome of the cathedral loomed ahead. A majestic gold cross crowned it and seemed to pull it up higher into the blue sky. "I don't know how to climb up to you!

> **The sacraments are signs that not only point us where to go, but that bring God directly to us.**

How do I get to you?" I found myself unexpectedly screaming this prayer inside, quietly, without audible words. My eyes began to water, and for some unknown reason, I pulled into the parking lot and went inside the cathedral.

Not long after this day, I began the formal steps to become a Catholic. This experience of being unable to reach God, however, stayed with me. By our own powers, we cannot even grasp at God. And yet, I wanted to do so much more than grasp; I wanted to tell God "thank you" for the gift of life; I wanted to ask him how I could give my life back to him. I wanted to know God intimately.

In my simplicity and ignorance, I had stumbled upon the reality that without God coming to us, we truly cannot get to him. The sacraments are signs that not only point us where to go, but that bring God directly to us. The sacraments flood us with his

Step 6 **To the Heart** (10 minutes)

After the small-group discussions, read this story aloud, have a candidate read it aloud, or have the class read it silently. After the story (written by this week's video presenter), read the thought-provoking question(s) provided in the red "To the Heart" box above. Time permitting, ask follow-up questions and encourage discussion.

life and grace and make tangible and accessible a God who, despite his majesty, or precisely because of it, will not stay away from his children.

I didn't have to find a way to climb up to God; I had to let him climb down to me. I received Baptism, Confirmation, and First Holy Communion in one night. By the grace of the sacraments, I was made a child of God. And yet, the climb and struggle of faith does not just go away in an instant. God knows that we need him physically present to us. This is why in Baptism, veiled in the minister's triple pouring of (or immersion in) water as he says, "I baptize you in the name of the Father, and of the Son, and of the Holy Spirit," God enters our souls. This is why in Confirmation, veiled in the sacred chrism oil and the bishop's blessing, the GIFTS OF THE HOLY SPIRIT are flamed into action in our very souls. And while all the sacraments communicate God's grace, it is in the Eucharist, veiled in bread and wine, that Jesus physically and substantially enters into our bodies and feeds us.

I had longed to know God, to find him, to be with him. The beauty and gift of being a Catholic is that I have come to realize that his longing is greater than my own. He comes down to us in the sacraments so that we may come to him.

Sister Amelia, O.P.

Find It!

What famous painting by Jean-Francois Millet depicts two workers in a field pausing to reflect on the Annunciation—inspiring Vincent van Gogh to portray a similar work decades later?

The Angelus, 1859

70 | CHOSEN

Hero of the Week

Born:
January 2, 1873

Died:
September 30, 1897

Memorial:
October 1

Patron Saint of:
- missions
- pilots
- AIDS patients
- florists

St. Thérèse of Lisieux

"After my death, I will let fall a shower of roses. I will spend my heaven doing good upon earth. I will raise up a mighty host of little saints. My mission is to make God loved …"

—*St. Thérèse of Lisieux*

The last words of this young nun, who died of tuberculosis at the age of twenty-three, were prophetic. Today, the "Little Flower" is regarded as both the patron saint of missions and as one of the four women doctors of the Church.

Even as a child, young Thérèse loved roses, plucking them and scattering their petals before the Blessed Sacrament. When she told her dad that she wanted to join the Discalced Carmelites (a community of nuns who devote their entire lives to prayer and who live physically separated from the outside world), he plucked a little flower from the ground and gave it to her. She took it to mean she was going to be replanted somewhere else to grow and thrive.

Convent life was never going to be a source of dramatic adventure for the young woman who wanted to be a saint. Nothing extraordinary was going to happen to her, but she did small things with great love. She saw God's love and care everywhere in nature and recorded her thoughts in simple yet profound prose. In her autobiography, *The Story of a Soul*, she writes:

"If all flowers wanted to be roses, nature would lose her springtime beauty, and the fields would no longer be decked out with little wild flowers. So it is in the world of souls, Jesus' garden. He has created smaller ones and those must be content to be daisies or violets destined to give joy to God's glances when he looks down at his feet. Perfection consists in doing his will, in being what he wills us to be."[1]

St. Thérèse of Lisieux believed that simple acts of love and sacrifice not only paved her "little way" of holiness, they helped to save the world! Every slight was an opportunity for humble sacrifice—a smile instead of a scowl, an apology instead of an explanation. She lived every moment, every act, all for the love of God. She knew that God loved her not because she was accomplishing great deeds, but because her small deeds were accomplished with great love.

Her autobiography, *The Story of a Soul*, not only shares the story of her life; it explains in detail her approach to living a sacramental life. The book became a worldwide hit. The young woman who wanted to do small things with great love became a saint who accomplished great things for God along her "little" way.

St. Thérèse of Lisieux, pray for us. Teach us your little way, that we may show our love daily to God who loves us.

Step 7

Hero of the Week (5 minutes)

This saint story will help to highlight and reinforce this lesson's topic. You may choose to read it aloud, have a candidate read it aloud, or have the class read it silently.

Lesson 8 | 71

Challenge of the Week

☐ **Do something small for God.** Read a child a story from the Bible. Pick up trash around your school or neighborhood. Do an extra chore. (This one works best if you're just a little "sneaky" so no one else notices!) In the space below, describe what you did ... and how it felt.

☐ **Ask God to help you to sincerely forgive someone who has hurt you.** Offer something to God as a spiritual gift for this person's well-being (i.e., extra effort at school and chores, your next Eucharist, or avoiding sweets for the week). In the space below, describe what you did and how you felt.

☐ **Take advantage of the sacraments!** In addition to Sunday Mass, try going to Mass during the week, and take note of the impact this has on your day. Write about it in the space below.

_____

_____

_____

_____

_____

_____

_____

_____

_____

✝ Closing Prayer

"I can do all things in him who strengthens me."

—*Philippians 4:13*

Lord, you strengthen us with your grace through the sacramental life of the Church. In the sacraments, we encounter you in a personal and intimate way and receive a share in your divine life.

Walking with you in this way changes everything, as we begin to see ourselves and our lives more clearly, with greater hope and with a holy joy. Give us the grace to cling to the sacraments all the days of our lives and to become the best people we can be. Amen.

 Step 8 **Challenge of the Week** (2 minutes)

Ask your candidates to read the "challenges" above and choose one of the three to complete this week. Have them check the box next to the challenge they intend to complete. Encourage them to write about their experiences in the space provided.

 Step 9 **Homework Instructions and Updates** (2 minutes)

Remind candidates to read the "Wrap-Up" and the "What's That Word?" sections in the "Taking It Home" section of the Student Workbook. They should also review the "Watch It!" questions to prepare for the next "Review Game."

 Step 10 **Closing Prayer** (3 minutes)

As a way of building up community, ask if there are any prayer intentions. Write them down (or have candidates share them aloud) and after praying for those intentions, have the class read the "Closing Prayer" together (provided in the Student Workbook).

72 | CHOSEN

Taking It Home

For next week's "Review Game," be sure to read over the following ...

1. **Watch It!** questions (page 67)
2. **Wrap-Up**
3. **"What's That Word?"**
4. **Memory Verse**

Don't forget to do your **Challenge of the Week** (page 71)

Wrap-Up

When Adam and Eve sinned, the connection they had shared with God was broken. And just as they hid when God wanted to walk in the garden with them,[2] we often try to hide our brokenness from God and resist his efforts to reach out to us.

God sent Jesus to walk here on earth, proclaiming the kingdom of God and shedding his blood to restore our connection with God. Jesus also established seven sacraments, transforming channels of grace that fill us with his divine life.[3] The seven sacraments are Baptism, Confirmation, Eucharist, PENANCE (Confession), Anointing of the Sick, HOLY ORDERS, and MATRIMONY.

Now, Jesus didn't establish the sacraments of the Church because God needs rituals, but because we do. Every culture throughout history—from the jungles of South America to the urban centers of Europe—has had rituals, with ceremonies ranging from burial rites to birthday cakes to social greetings. Something inside us longs for meaningful ritual, which provides a sense of identity and order.

Religious rituals serve a similar purpose in the spiritual world. If, like the angels, we were pure spirits, we would simply worship God with our intellects and wills. However, since we are SPIRIT and matter, soul and body, we need to encounter and express unseen realities in tangible, external ways. Our Creator recognizes this, and he meets us where we are through the sacraments he entrusted to the Church.

[2] Gn 3:8

[3] CCC 1129, 1131

"What's That Word?"

GRACE

Grace is God's gift of his life to us. Without grace, we are spiritually dead and unable to share in the eternal life of heaven. Grace makes it possible to live in the heroic, holy way that God calls us to live; to believe, hope, and love in ways that would otherwise not be available to us. Though we cannot "see" or "feel" grace, we can observe its effects in the lives of holy people, and it is often associated with our own sense of being "really alive."

The word *grace* comes from the Latin for "gift." Because grace is a gift, we do not deserve it. God generously bestows his grace on us for our benefit. Anyone who has given a gift only to have it rejected knows that gifts must be received. Grace is not magic; it does not automatically make us holy, but needs to be accepted and cooperated with in order to become effective. (*See also* ACTUAL GRACE *and* SANCTIFYING GRACE.)

SACRAMENT

A *sacrament* is a "sacred sign" that Christ gave to the Church to deliver grace to us, share his divine life with us, and make us holy.[4] A sacrament includes *matter,* a physical part (for example, water, bread, or oil), and *form,* the accompanying words or prayers that make it effective (for example, "I baptize you in the name of the Father, and of the Son, and of the Holy Spirit"). The physical sign points to a spiritual presence of grace and its effects. For example, in Baptism, through the triple pouring of (or immersion in) water as the minister says the words, "I baptize you in the name of the Father, and of the Son, and of the Holy Spirit," we are really washed clean from sin and God really pours SUPERNATURAL life into our souls.

The seven sacraments are Baptism, Confirmation, Eucharist, Penance (Confession), Anointing of the Sick, Holy Orders, and Matrimony. (*See also* SACRAMENTS OF INITIATION, SACRAMENTS OF HEALING, *and* SACRAMENTS OF SERVICE.)

[4] CCC 1131

Memory Verse:

"I am the true vine, and my Father is the vinedresser. Every branch of mine that bears no fruit, he takes away, and every branch that does bear fruit he prunes, that it may bear more fruit."

— John 15:1-2

> 5   CCC 1129

> 6   (see footnote below)

> 7   Mt 26:17-30; Mk 14:12-25; Lk 22:7-30

This week's "Did You Know?" feature provides an opportunity for you to explain to students the difference between private and public revelation. The Catholic Church has a rich tradition of pious belief and devotion based on private revelation. We can find many examples of private revelation when we study the lives of the saints (e.g., St. Catherine Labouré and the Miraculous Medal devotion). However, Catholics are not required to believe in private revelation. See the footnote to this weeks "Did You Know?" to learn more.

---

74 CHOSEN

SALVATION

Salvation is the restoration of our relationship with God. It can be understood in two ways because we are always saved *from* something and saved *for* something. Salvation includes the forgiveness of sin—we are saved from sin and its result, eternal death—and we are saved for life with God here on earth and forever with him in heaven. "Whoever believes and is baptized will be saved" (Mark 16:16, NAB).

God saves us by sharing his life with us, something we call sanctifying grace, when we receive him reverently and worthily in the sacraments.[5] For this reason, Confirmation is not an ending, but the beginning of a deeper life of faith.

Did You Know?

There are many documented Eucharistic miracles. For example, consecrated hosts stolen in 1730 from a church in Siena, Italy, and later returned, have not decayed for nearly 300 years.[6]

Any questions?

Where are the seven sacraments in the Bible?

The sacraments are gifts from Jesus Christ to his Church. All seven sacraments can be found throughout the Bible. Here are just a few examples.

Anointing of the Sick: The scriptural roots of this sacrament can be traced to James 5:14-15, in which the apostle describes the "prayer of faith" that brings healing and forgiveness.

Baptism: Jesus told his apostles to "make disciples of all nations, baptizing them ..." (Matthew 28:19-20).

Confession (*Penance*): Jesus says to the apostles, "Receive the Holy Spirit. If you forgive the sins of any, they are forgiven; if you retain the sins of any, they are retained" (John 20:22-23).

Confirmation: Confirmation is described when the apostles laid hands on those who had been baptized, "and they received the Holy Spirit" (Acts 8:14-17).

Eucharist: Jesus instituted this sacrament at the Last Supper.[7] Evidence that the Eucharist was celebrated from the beginning of the Church is found in 1 Corinthians 11:23-26.

Holy Orders: We find the election of bishops when Matthias is "enrolled with the eleven apostles" (Acts 1:24-26). The ordination of clergy (including deacons) is found in Acts 6:2-6 and 2 Timothy 1:6.

Matrimony: Ephesians 5:25-32 speaks of the "great mystery" (*sacramentum*) of the relationship between Christ and the Church, revealed through MARRIAGE.

---

6   The Catholic Church makes a distinction between public revelation and private revelation. Public revelation pertains to what is contained in the deposit of faith and must be believed by Catholics. Private revelation, in contrast, are the revelations made in the course of history that do not add to or form the deposit of faith. Some private revelations have been recognized by the authority of the Church; however, strictly speaking, Catholics are not required to believe in private revelation (see CCC 67).

Notes

**Lesson 9
Leader's Notes**

Overview

The purpose of this lesson is to help students appreciate the significance and importance of their Baptism. Through washing and regeneration, the waters of Baptism make us children of God and mark the first step in our journey toward our final home in the kingdom of God.

The imagery of Baptism is found in Creation; in Noah's ark (where eight souls are saved "through water"); in the escape of the Hebrews under Moses from captivity by crossing the Red Sea; and in the crossing of the Jordan River by God's chosen people in order to enter into the "Promised Land" (see CCC 1217–1222). By understanding the symbolism and significance of this rite in their lives, students will be encouraged to think of the salvation story more definitively as *their* story.

Objectives of this Lesson

1. *Review the sign of water in the salvation story.* From Creation to the Baptism of Jesus and the miracle at Cana, water appears again and again in the salvation story. Each instance points to another important truth about Baptism (see CCC 1220–1222).

2. *Describe what the "form and matter" of Baptism teach us about its effects.* Consider the significance of all the signs: the water, candle, oil, garment, and Trinitarian formula (see CCC 1234–1245). Discuss what it means that Baptism is necessary for salvation, that though we are obliged to follow God's plan for us to be baptized, we also recognize that God himself is not "bound" by the sacraments and may save people by means unknown to us (see CCC 1257–1261).

3. *Review what happens at Baptism.* The two primary effects (fruits) of Baptism are washing away sins and being raised up to new life in the Holy Spirit (see CCC 1262). However, Baptism has other effects as well, including the imprint of an indelible mark on the soul that makes Baptism unrepeatable (see CCC 1279–1280).

This week you will need …

A small bottle of holy water (for the opening prayer)

Lesson 9

"When did my journey begin?"

(Baptism, Your Initiation into God's Family)

✝ Opening Prayer

Do you believe in God, the Father almighty, Creator of heaven and earth?

All: I do!

Do you believe in Jesus Christ, his only Son, our Lord, who was born of the Virgin Mary, was crucified, died, and was buried, rose from the dead, and is now seated at the right hand of the Father?

All: I do!

Do you believe in the Holy Spirit, the holy catholic Church, the communion of saints, the forgiveness of sins, the resurrection of the body, and life everlasting?

All: I do!

This is our faith. This is the faith of the Church. We are proud to profess it, in Christ Jesus our Lord.

All: Amen.

Opening Prayer

Hold up a bottle of holy water, then bless yourself with the water and explain that one of the reasons we bless ourselves with holy water is to remind us of our Baptism. Then say:

This week we are going to pray a short "Q&A" form of the "Renewal of Baptismal Promises" that is sometimes used at Easter, Baptisms, and Confirmations. This Creed sums up the key points of our faith. I will ask a question and your response will be a loud, "I do!" In the name of the Father …

Pass the holy water around the room for the teens to use to bless themselves with after you pray.

 Welcome/Review Game (5 minutes)

Begin by welcoming the class and telling them that you will be starting with a review of the previous lesson's material. On the DVD menu, click on Lesson 9; then on the sub-menu, click on "Review Game."

Have students answer the questions based on the previous lesson. For more information about how to adapt this game to meet the needs of your group, see the "Review Game" section in the Introduction to this Leader's Guide (page xvi).

 Challenge of the Week Review (5 minutes)

Ask if anyone would like to share a "challenge experience" from the previous week. Try to draw students out by prompting them with basic questions regarding the challenges from last week (e.g., "Did anyone choose the first challenge?").

Step 3 Opening Prayer (3 minutes)

Lead the class in the "Opening Prayer," which is included in the Student Workbook. Leader's Guide notes are provided above: Red text provides direction and guidance, and white text is for you to read aloud to the class.

76 | CHOSEN

Dive In:
Encountering the Mountain

For as long as he could remember, Zach had been fascinated with Mauna Kea, an iconic mountain of his Hawaiian ancestry. Mauna Kea is the largest mountain in the world. The now-dormant volcano punched its way out of the sea with volcanic explosions over the course of millions of years.

This volcanic mountain is even bigger than Mount Everest—if you measure the part that's under the ocean. While Everest beats it in height above sea level, Mauna Kea's base is at the bottom of the ocean floor, rising a total of 33,474 feet (13,803 feet above sea level). From top to bottom, it towers over Everest by 4,445 feet.

Even though it's on the tropical island of Hawaii, you can ski or snowboard at the top. Mauna Kea's name means "white mountain" because its peak is often snow-covered all winter. Traveling from the coast of the island to the top of Mauna Kea brings you through ten climate zones! Its environment is so unique that some plants and animals that thrive on Mauna Kea are found almost nowhere else on earth.

The clean, dry mountain air high above the Pacific makes it so ideal for astronomical observation that it's the home of thirteen telescopes funded by eleven countries.

Zach knew all this. He even wrote his college thesis on it. But he had never been to Hawaii. He had never actually *seen* Mauna Kea. Until now. As a graduation gift to himself, he climbed the great mountain. When he arrived at the summit, looking down at the clouds, his eyes filled with tears. "I knew all *about* this mountain." He said. "Now I *know* this mountain."

There's a difference between knowing *about* something and actually *knowing* it. No matter how many facts you hear, you can't really know something until you've encountered it firsthand!

That's why God gave us sacraments. He didn't want us merely to hear about salvation history and about his dying and rising. He left us sacraments, starting with Baptism and the other SACRAMENTS OF INITIATION, so we could encounter all he did for us in a direct way, here and now.

> *"The Lord was baptized, not to be cleansed himself but to cleanse the waters, so that those waters, cleansed by the flesh of Christ which knew no sin, might have the power of Baptism."*
> —St. Ambrose of Milan

Step 4 — **Dive In** (5 minutes)

Read this story aloud, have a candidate read it aloud, or have the class read it silently before watching the video segments. This thought-provoking story ties in to the lesson's topic and serves to set up the video presentation.

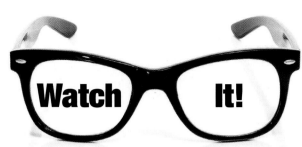

Watch It!

Lesson 9 | 77

Segment 1: Actions Have Consequences

1. Through the Fall of Adam and Eve, we have inherited Original _____Sin_____.

2. Before the Fall, Adam and Eve lived in a graced state the Church calls _____.

   A) original peace   (C) original holiness) **(see CCC 399)**

   B) original righteousness   D) A, B, and C

3. God wants to restore you as his rightful heir so that you may have _____eternal life_____ with him forever.

Segment 2: What Is Baptism?

1. When you were baptized, the sacrament left a permanent, or _____, mark on your soul.

   (A) indelible)   B) unifying   C) biblical   D) graced

2. (**T** or **F?**) Baptism is the necessary first step toward eternal life.

Segment 3: The Symbols of Baptism

1. At a Baptism, the white garment represents _____purity_____.

2. The oil used at both Baptism and Confirmation is _____.

   (A) sacred chrism)   B) sacred myrrh   C) holy frankincense

---

Small-Group Discussion

Segment 1: Actions Have Consequences

1. What is the difference between thinking of yourself as an heir—that is, as a son or daughter of God—versus as a "subject" or "member" of a kingdom?

2. What are some ways that people hurt others when exercising their free will in a selfish manner?

Segment 2: What Is Baptism?

1. What does Baptism do for us?[1]

2. Matthew 28:19 says, "Go, therefore, make disciples of all nations; baptizing them in the name of the Father and of the Son and of the Holy Spirit." What does this teach us about Baptism?

Segment 3: The Symbols of Baptism

1. What are some of the symbols used in Baptism?[2]

2. What do these symbols mean?[3]

3. What can you do this week to live more fully and publicly as a child of God?

Step 5

Watch It!/Small-Group Discussion (50 minutes)

On the video, click on Lesson 9, Segment 1. When Segment 1 ends, have students fill in the "Watch It!" questions (2 to 3 minutes). Run through them to be sure they wrote the correct answers so they will have them to prepare for the next "Review Game."

Next, lead students in a small-group discussion for Segment 1. You may begin by asking general questions like: "What part of the video spoke to you the most?" Discussion questions for each segment are provided in the blue box above.

Follow the same steps for Segments 2 and 3. (Allow for about 10 minutes of discussion time after each segment.)

Small-Group Discussion Leader's Notes

1. Two principal effects of this sacrament are (a) the removal of both Original Sin and personal sin, and (b) sealing with the Holy Spirit. At your Baptism, when God saved you and marked you as his, you became a "new creature" in Christ. Through Baptism, you became part of the Church, the Body of Christ (see CCC 1262, 1265).

2. See CCC 1234–1245.

3. Water (washing); oil (anointing/sealing with the Holy Spirit); candles (light of Christ); white gown (purity); going in and out of the water (dying and rising).

78 | CHOSEN

Questions:

What are some ways you could try to reconnect with your Baptism? (Ask your parents if they have pictures or videos of the event. Also ask them and other family and friends who were there what they remember from the day.)

Do you know anyone who needs the faith "handed on" to him or her? How might you go about doing that?

TO THE HEART with

The other day, my friend Heidi was looking through her scrapbooks from a mission trip to Senegal, West Africa. She came across a photograph of her much younger self spending Christmas at a resort town called Ziguinchor, seated on what looked like a surf board with two large sails attached. Oliver, a French college student, had invited Heidi to go sailing with him.

As we got onto the boat, I asked Oliver if he was sure he knew what he was doing. "Sure, no problem," he said, playing with the lines. A group of young men pushed us off the shoreline … and we began sailing rapidly out into the ocean. I had to duck as the sail came swinging around.

The next thing I knew, we were both in the water. The boat had capsized, and the sails were too full of water to get the boat back upright. My ankle stung, and when I lifted my foot, I could see a gash in my ankle. "Better keep that

out of the water," Oliver shouted. "There could be sharks nearby." We made it back safely—but we never spoke again. He was too embarrassed!

Looking back, it was one of the highlights of the trip. But at the time, all I could think about was the sharks.

Some water encounters are more memorable than others. You may not remember the most important one of all … your Baptism! If you take down your family scrapbooks and dust them off, you might come across a picture of your Baptism day—maybe a smiling photograph of your family and godparents or even an image of the priest pouring a dipper of water over your head. If you were a baby at the time, it's unlikely you remember it. Your parents will—I'll never forget seeing my children baptized. That day is precious to me; it marks the day they became citizens of heaven.

Step 6

To the Heart (10 minutes)

After the small-group discussions, read this story aloud, have a candidate read it aloud, or have the class read it silently. After the story (written by this week's video presenter), read the thought-provoking question(s) provided in the red "To the Heart" box above. Time permitting, ask follow-up questions and encourage discussion.

Lesson 9 | 79

When we see our Baptism this way, as our birthday in the Church as a member of the Body of Christ, it's easier to grasp what Confirmation is all about. Confirmation is a continuation of the journey we began at Baptism.

Through the sacraments, we experience the living handing on of the faith. We see the power of God, not just locked in the past, but encountering us in the present. In Confirmation, you will receive the powerful gifts of grace you will need to continue your journey of faith. And it all began at Baptism, when you became a new creation: a child of God, an heir to the kingdom.

> ❝ *Confirmation is a continuation of the journey we began at Baptism.* ❞

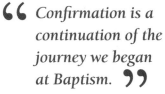

Sarah Swafford

Find It!

How is holy chrism (oil) made, and what gives it that wonderful smell?

Sacred chrism is pure olive oil mixed with the fragrant resin of balsam trees, and it must be blessed by a bishop.

80 | CHOSEN

Hero of the Week

Born:
circa 1869

Died:
February 8, 1947

Memorial:
February 8

Patron Saint of:
• Sudan

St. Josephine Bakhita

One moment, the young Sudanese girl was a beloved child of her family, playing with her brothers and sisters.

The next, she was kidnapped and sold as a slave. Humiliated, shackled, and suffering, she was forced to walk barefoot over 900 miles, away from her family and her homeland.

The shock of the kidnapping, forced march, and ill treatment caused her to forget her own name. She no longer knew who she was. But she was alive, so the slave traders called her *Bakhita*, an Arab word that means "lucky." For ten years Bakhita, served various masters, until the day she found herself working for the Michieli family, whose father was an Italian diplomat. When political upheaval occurred, they returned to Italy and brought Bakhita with them. In time, the couple returned to Sudan, but, for safety's sake, they left their daughter and Bakhita in a Canossian convent in Venice.

When the Michieli family returned for them, Bakhita refused to leave the convent. Within those walls she had discovered who she was, a child of God. Although the Michieli family tried to take her with them, the superior intervened on her behalf, pointing out changing laws regarding slavery, and that Bakhita was, in fact, a free woman and always had been.

Shortly after that, she was baptized and took the name Josephine. She couldn't resist kissing the baptismal font when she entered a Church. "Here is where I became a child of God," she'd say. Soon after her Baptism, she entered the novitiate to become a Canossian sister. St. Josephine was known for her gentle smile, and it was often said of her, *"Her mind was always on God, and her heart in Africa."* She spent the next years of her life working to prepare missionaries for Africa. Asked what she would say to her captors, if she were to return to Sudan, she replied that she would kiss their hands for leading her to a place where she discovered God.

Though her journey took her along a path filled with pain and loss, St. Josephine Bakhita did not allow her crosses to make her bitter. She found her true identity as a daughter of God and united her pain to the suffering of Jesus' cross—and he empowered her to love everyone, even her enemies.

Despite all her suffering, she summed up her life with these words: "I am definitively loved and, whatever happens to me, I am awaited by this Love. And so my life is good." Her life was not the story of some sad tragedy. She knew that her Baptism had inserted her into a story that began with the creation of the world and that will end in eternal glory!

St. Josephine Bakhita, pray for us. Just as you found freedom from slavery, lead us out of our own spiritual slavery.

Step 7

Hero of the Week (5 minutes)

This saint story will help to highlight and reinforce this lesson's topic. You may choose to read it aloud, have a candidate read it aloud, or have the class read it silently.

Challenge of the Week

 What have you inherited? Think of something you or someone in your family inherited. It could be an object, a photo, or property. Write about it below, and explain why it is considered valuable and what steps you would take to be sure it is passed on to future generations.

Buy or create a bottle for storing holy water in your home, and then stop in at your parish to fill it. Write about what you did with the bottle in the space below.

Priest, prophet, king! A priest intercedes and offers spiritual sacrifice. A prophet shares the word of God with people. A king is given power so he might serve and at the same time has a dignity he needs to uphold. Think of a specific way to live one of those roles this week and do it. Write about your experience below.

_____
_____
_____
_____
_____
_____
_____
_____
_____

✝ Closing Prayer

"When we cry, 'Abba! Father!' it is the Spirit himself bearing witness with our spirit that we are children of God, and if children, then heirs ..."

—Romans 8:15-17

Heavenly Father, thank you for restoring our inheritance! We are beginning to understand the beauty and power of our Baptism. We know it's not only a treasured Catholic tradition, but a holy initiation into your royal family, and that it changes our souls forever. Help us to stand tall as children of God, anointed, sealed, and blessed in the name of the Father, the Son, and the Holy Spirit. Amen.

 Step 8 Challenge of the Week (2 minutes)

Ask your candidates to read the "challenges" above and choose one of the three to complete this week. Have them check the box next to the challenge they intend to complete. Encourage them to write about their experiences in the space provided.

Step 9 Homework Instructions and Updates (2 minutes)

Remind candidates to read the "Wrap-Up" and the "What's That Word?" sections in the "Taking It Home" section of the Student Workbook. They should also review the "Watch It!" questions to prepare for the next "Review Game."

 Step 10 Closing Prayer (3 minutes)

As a way of building up community, ask if there are any prayer intentions. Write them down (or have candidates share them aloud) and after praying for those intentions, have the class read the "Closing Prayer" together (provided in the Student Workbook).

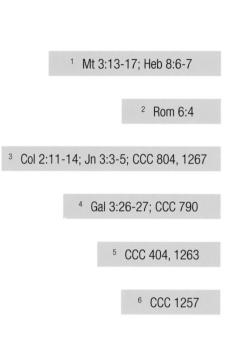

¹ Mt 3:13-17; Heb 8:6-7

² Rom 6:4

³ Col 2:11-14; Jn 3:3-5; CCC 804, 1267

⁴ Gal 3:26-27; CCC 790

⁵ CCC 404, 1263

⁶ CCC 1257

---

82 | CHOSEN

Taking It Home

For next week's "Review Game,"
be sure to read over the following …

1. **Watch It!** questions (page 77)
2. **Wrap-Up**
3. **"What's That Word?"**
4. **Memory Verse**

Don't forget to do your
Challenge of the Week (page 81)

Wrap-Up

In the Old Testament, God's people circumcised their baby boys as a sign that they belonged to God. When Jesus came, he allowed himself to be baptized by John the Baptist, and he commanded his apostles to baptize the entire world, thereby establishing Baptism as the sign of the new covenant.[1]

Through his death and Resurrection, Jesus renews all things in himself. He said, "I have come that they may have life, and have it to the full" (John 10:10, NIV). In Baptism, we are made new by entering his death[2] and receiving his resurrected life!

In Baptism, we become "partakers of the divine nature" (2 Peter 1:4) and are made *children of God*.[3] Baptism initiates a person into the Church—the Body of Christ. Baptism unites us to Jesus,[4] infuses sanctifying grace (divine life) and removes Original and personal sins.[5] Because Baptism is the ordinary means for our salvation,[6] and because, like Confirmation, it is more about God's choice of us than our choice of him, Catholic parents are strongly urged to have their children baptized as infants.

The spiritual life is a journey, and we who were baptized as infants were "carried" by our parents for the first part of this journey. As we grow, we continue walking with God on our own, living out the truths we have learned from our parents and faith community. Confirmation is an important step along this journey because it completes and perfects the grace given to us in Baptism and deepens in us the Gifts of the Holy Spirit that we need to serve God and the Church as mature Christians. (*See also* SPIRITUAL MATURITY.)

"What's That Word?"

BAPTISM

Baptism is the first of the seven sacraments. Its symbols of water and washing remind us of a kind of "birth." Through Baptism, God adopts us as his children, sharing his life with us by the gift of sanctifying grace so that we can live supernaturally, now and forever, in heaven with him.[7]

The share in God's life that we receive in Baptism frees us from ORIGINAL SIN, the absence of grace in us at birth that was a result of our first parents' disobedience. Baptism is God's "remedy" for both Original and PERSONAL SIN.[8] The Trinitarian formula for Baptism, "I baptize you in the name of the Father, and of the Son, and of the Holy Spirit," reminds us that this sacrament makes us members of God's family, the Church.

"The ordinary ministers of Baptism are the bishop and priest and, in the Latin Church, also the deacon. In case of necessity, anyone, even a non-baptized person, with the required intention, can baptize, by using the Trinitarian baptismal formula" (CCC 1256).

CONVERSION

In its most fundamental sense, the word *conversion* means a radical reorientation of one's entire life away from sin and evil and a turning toward God. This change of heart is a central element of Christ's preaching, of the Church's ministry of EVANGELIZATION, and of the Sacrament of Reconciliation.[9] The word *conversion* can also refer to the ongoing process of growing in holiness and living a deeper Christian life, with the help of God's grace. Conversion, like salvation, is not a "once-and-done" thing; it is a lifelong journey.

[7] CCC 1213

[8] CCC 1263

[9] CCC 1423, 1427, 1431

Memory Verse:

"'I baptize you with water; but he who is mightier than I is coming ... he will baptize you with the Holy Spirit and with fire.'"

– Luke 3:16

84 | **CHOSEN**

ORIGINAL SIN

Original Sin was the sin of Adam and Eve's disobedience of God's command not to eat of the fruit of the Tree of Knowledge of Good and Evil in the Garden of Eden.[10] Original Sin also refers to the way in which we are born without the original justice and holiness that Adam and Eve lost through their sin. For us descendants of Adam and Eve, it is not a personal sin, but rather a sin of human nature that is transmitted to all the descendants of Adam by propagation. As a result of Jesus' saving work, God gives us a share in his life through Baptism, where Original Sin is "forgiven" or "washed away" and God's life is "poured in" to us.

[10] Gn 3

[11] CCC 1261

[12] CCC 1258

[13] CCC 1260; *Lumen Gentium* 16

Did You Know?

In the sixteenth century, Pope Clement VIII was urged to ban coffee as "the devil's drink," because it was beloved by Muslims. After tasting it, Clement found it delicious and blessed it, making it popular the world over.

Any questions?

What happens to those who die before they are baptized, either because their parents don't believe in infant Baptism or because they are part of another religion?

The short answer is: We trust in the mercy of God. Jesus is the only way into heaven, and he has made the sacraments (starting with Baptism as the foundation) the ordinary way that we receive the salvation he offers.

God can work outside of the ordinary way he established for us to be saved. The Church teaches that we should trust in the mercy of God for the salvation of infants who have died without being baptized,[11] and the *Catechism* refers to a BAPTISM OF BLOOD for those people martyred before Baptism.[12]

Finally, the Church acknowledges that people who are completely unaware of the Gospel and of Jesus, but who seek the truth and try to follow God's will as they understand it, have the possibility of being saved through Jesus in a way that only he knows.[13]

We base these teachings on the fact that Jesus made the necessity of Baptism clear, but he also made it clear that he is mercy and love itself, and that he wants our salvation more than we do. So, while we follow his commands and don't take his mercy for granted, we always have reason to trust.

Notes

Lesson 10
Leader's Notes

Overview

The purpose of this lesson is to convey the reality of sin and its consequences, to instill an aversion to personal sin, and to cultivate a desire to seek the healing power of Christ in Confession in order to achieve deeper conversion (see CCC 1428) and a more intimate walk with God.

The *Catechism* teaches us that Catholics who have reached the "age of discretion" (CCC 1457) must go to Confession at least once a year or whenever they have committed mortal sin. Confessing venial sin on a regular basis is also recommended by the Church (see CCC 1458).[7] A regular examination of conscience and sacramental Confession are important to personal conversion. It is important to recall that *reconciliation* is not primarily about punishment, but about re-establishing the unity and intimacy that sin disrupts in our relationships with God and other people.

Objectives of this Lesson

1. *Spell out what sin does to us, and point out that only God's laws make us free.* Deliberately choosing to turn away from God and disobey his laws is sin (see CCC 1849–1855). Though laws often seem to limit our freedom, it is only by embracing God's plan for us, by following his laws, that we can experience true freedom and happiness (see CCC 1972; 2 Corinthians 3:2-6).

2. *Impart an understanding of the difference between mortal and venial sin and the three conditions required for a sin to be mortal.* Mortal sin breaks the connection between God and us; venial sin weakens it (see CCC 1855). For a sin to be mortal, it must meet these three conditions: It must involve a grave matter, be done with full knowledge, and include deliberate consent (see CCC 1857).

3. *Clarify that sin has both a personal and a corporate nature.* It offends God, weakens the Body of Christ, and breaks "fraternal communion" (CCC 1469). This is one of the reasons why the Sacrament of Reconciliation is needed.

4. *Outline the steps to a good confession.* The essential acts of the penitent are contrition (or sorrow for one's sins), confession, and making satisfaction (or doing penance). Explain making an examination of conscience, confessing mortal sins by kind and number (as well as any venial sins), and the difference between regret and repentance (see CCC 1454–1456).

This week, we recommend you hand out the "Examination of Conscience," available as a free download at ConfirmationStudy.com. This can be done at the end of class during Step 9, "Homework Instructions and Updates."

"Why tell my sins to a priest?"

(The Healing Power of Confession)

Opening Prayer

"I confess to Almighty God and to you, my brothers and sisters, that I have greatly sinned, in my thoughts and in my words, in what I have done and in what I have failed to do, through my fault, through my fault, through my most grievous fault; therefore I ask Blessed Mary ever-Virgin, all the angels and saints, and you, my brothers and sisters, to pray for me to the Lord our God. Amen."

Lesson 10

Opening Prayer

If you do not think about your "problem areas," spiritual and personal growth are simply impossible. An examination of conscience is when you think about your life—your attitudes and actions—to determine whether you have sinned and how you need to change and grow. One way to do this is to think about each of the Ten Commandments and consider how you have (or have not) lived up to God's law.

Read the Ten Commandments aloud slowly.

The Ten Commandments
(adapted from Exodus 20:2-17)

1. "I am the LORD your God, you shall have no other gods before me."
2. "You shall not take the name of the LORD your God in vain."
3. "Remember the Sabbath day, to keep it holy."
4. "Honor your father and your mother."
5. "You shall not kill."
6. "You shall not commit adultery."
7. "You shall not steal."
8. "You shall not bear false witness against your neighbor."
9. "You shall not covet your neighbor's house."
10. "You shall not covet your neighbor's wife."

Now let's pray the prayer asking for forgiveness that we say at Mass every week. In the name of the Father …

Step 1 — Welcome/Review Game (5 minutes)

Begin by welcoming the class and telling them that you will be starting with a review of the previous lesson's material. On the DVD menu, click on Lesson 10; then on the sub-menu, click on "Review Game."

Have students answer the questions based on the previous lesson. For more information about how to adapt this game to meet the needs of your group, see the "Review Game" section in the Introduction to this Leader's Guide (page xvi).

Step 2 — Challenge of the Week Review (5 minutes)

Ask if anyone would like to share a "challenge experience" from the previous week. Try to draw students out by prompting them with basic questions regarding the challenges from last week (e.g., "Did anyone choose the first challenge?").

Step 3 — Opening Prayer (3 minutes)

Lead the class in the "Opening Prayer," which is included in the Student Workbook. Leader's Guide notes are provided above: Red text provides direction and guidance, and white text is for you to read aloud to the class.

86 | 🔥 CHOSEN

Dive In:
William Portillo:
A Gangster Transformed

In 1988, sixteen-year-old William Portillo was initiated (or "jumped") into an El Salvadorian gang called *Mara Salvatrucha*. He was given the gang name *Maniaco* (Maniac). He was the kind of guy you didn't want to meet in a dark alley. His favorite hobby was robbing people at gunpoint so he could see the fear in their eyes.

Two years after being initiated into the gang, William was sentenced to sixteen years in prison. Armed with steel shanks and connections to the Mexican Mafia, he and other gangsters were soon running the show—until a prison riot landed William in solitary confinement, where he encountered God for the first time.

While he was in solitary, a chaplain gave William a copy of the New Testament. With nothing else to do, he began to read the Gospels for the first time. The pages came alive as he read about God's redeeming love for his people: the Prodigal Son, the woman at the well, and the story of Mary Magdalene. The power of those stories gave him hope and made him decide to turn his life around.

When he was released, William took to the streets with a new mission: preaching to gang members. At one point, another *Mara Salvatrucha* gangster reminded William that the penalty for leaving the gang was death. William responded simply, "You do what you have to do; I'll do what I have to do."

William is still with us. He started a ministry called *Prevención y Rescate* (Prevention and Rescue), a nonprofit ministry that reaches out to and rehabilitates gang members and assists their families. William is a new person.

William's story has been repeated countless times throughout history. God doesn't just forgive us when we ask him. He has the power to change us—to totally and completely remake us. We encounter that transforming power every time we meet God in Confession.

> "Let us throw ourselves into the ocean of his goodness, where every failing will be canceled and anxiety turned into love."
>
> — St. Paul of the Cross

Step 4   **Dive In** (5 minutes)

Read this story aloud, have a candidate read it aloud, or have the class read it silently before watching the video segments. This thought-provoking story ties in to the lesson's topic and serves to set up the video presentation.

Segment 1: Hitting the Goal

1. Which of his relatives did Father Schmitz say were "insanely good" at sports?

   A) his brothers   C) his cousins

   B) his grandparents   D) his nieces

2. The _____Commandments_____ are God's "rules" that allow us to be truly free.

Segment 2: What Is Sin?

1. Which of these is a condition of mortal sin?

   A) grave matter   C) full consent

   B) full knowledge   D) A, B, and C

2. T or **F?** The Church distinguishes between private and public sin because some sin only affects us personally. *

Segment 3: The Power of Confession

1. The "_____ of Confession" assures us that a priest would never reveal confessed sins.

   A) trust   B) wisdom   C) memory   D) seal

2. **T** or F? In confessing our sins, we don't need to regret them, but we do need to repent of them.

3. Father Schmitz explains that we should confess our sins in _____ and kind.

   A) number   B) humility   C) total   D) fact

*All sin affects our relationships with others and with the whole Church.

Small-Group Discussion

Segment 1: Hitting the Goal

1. Do you think God intends for his rules to oppress us or to give us a freer, fuller life? How so?

2. Name the Ten Commandments and what each one means to you.

Segment 2: What Is Sin?

1. Father Schmitz says no sins are private. What do you think he means?

2. What does the following passage teach us about Confession?

   [Jesus] said to them again, "Peace be with you. As the Father has sent me, so I send you." And when he had said this, he breathed on them and said to them, "Receive the Holy Spirit. Whose sins you forgive are forgiven them, and whose sins you retain are retained."   —John 20:21-23

Segment 3: The Power of Confession

1. How do you feel going into Confession? How do you feel leaving?

2. What are some reasons God gives us the Sacrament of Reconciliation, instead of having us say "sorry" in a purely private way?[1]

3. How can we get ready to go to Confession, especially if we have not gone in awhile?[2]

 Step 5 **Watch It!/Small-Group Discussion** (50 minutes)

On the video, click on Lesson 10, Segment 1. When Segment 1 ends, have students fill in the "Watch It!" questions (2 to 3 minutes). Run through them to be sure they wrote the correct answers so they will have them to prepare for the next "Review Game."

Next, lead students in a small-group discussion for Segment 1. You may begin by asking general questions like: "What part of the video spoke to you the most?" Discussion questions for each segment are provided in the blue box above.

Follow the same steps for Segments 2 and 3. (Allow for about 10 minutes of discussion time after each segment.)

Small-Group Discussion Leader's Notes

1. See the "Wrap-Up" in the Student Workbook.

2. Examination of conscience, pray, make a list.

Question:

What advice would you give a friend who said he was too embarrassed to let the priest at his church hear his confession about a particular sin?

88 | CHOSEN

❝ *I don't remember the sin ... I remember the win.* ❞

TO THE HEART with

I was once riding in an airport shuttle with a number of older folks. They noticed my collar and started asking questions. "Do you do all of the priest stuff?" "Yep," I replied. "Even the Confession thing?" one asked. "Yeah ... all the time." An older lady exclaimed, "Well, I think that would be so depressing; hearing all about people's sin!"

For me, it's just the opposite: There is almost no greater place to be than in the confessional. *It's a place where God's love wins.* Every time a priest celebrates this sacrament, he gets to see the costly mercy of God in action and be reminded of how good God is. And sometimes priests get to share a bit of that goodness.

I was a missionary teacher the year after I graduated from college. At that time, I was doing all of the "good kid" things on the surface, but my life was very, *very* far from Christ. When I finally returned

to Confession, the priest simply gave me something like "one Hail Mary" as my penance.

I stopped. "Um, Father? Did you hear everything I said?"

"Yes, I did."

"Don't you think I should get a bigger penance than that?" He looked at me with great love and said, "No. That small penance is all that I'm asking of you." He hesitated and then continued, "But you should know ... I will be FASTING for you for the next thirty days."

I was stunned. I didn't know what to do. He told me that the *Catechism* teaches that the priest must do penance for all those who come to him for Confession.[1] And here he was, embracing a severe penance for all of my sins. I never forgot it.

[1] CCC 1466, 1589

 Step 6   **To the Heart** (10 minutes)

After the small-group discussions, read this story aloud, have a candidate read it aloud, or have the class read it silently. After the story (written by this week's video presenter), read the thought-provoking question(s) provided in the red "To the Heart" box above. Time permitting, ask follow-up questions and encourage discussion.

Priests get to see firsthand how the Cross of Christ can break into people's lives and melt the hardest hearts. We offer consolation to those devastated by their sins and strength to those who want to give up on God or on life. People who have been abandoned, abused, and rejected, even by their own friends and family, encounter the Christ who reminds them that they are worth dying for ... so they can go out and start living.

As a priest, I get to see this kind of thing happen every day.

So often, people will ask if I remember people's confessions. People think that sins are *so* exciting or interesting. They're not. Honestly, once you realize that the Sacrament of Reconciliation is about Christ's death and Resurrection having victory in a person's life, sin loses its luster as Jesus' victory takes center stage. When the person leaves the confessional, I don't remember the sin ... I remember the *win*.

Whenever someone comes to Confession, I see a person who is deeply loved by God telling God that they love him back. That's it, and that's all.

The priest stands in judgment of no one. In the confessional, the *only thing* I have to offer is mercy. Whether you have confessed a particular sin for the first time or if this is the twelve thousandth time, every Confession is a win for Jesus. And I get to be there, standing in for Jesus. *That's* what it's like ... I get to sit and watch Jesus win his children back all day. It's actually pretty awesome, if you think about it.

Father Mike Schmitz

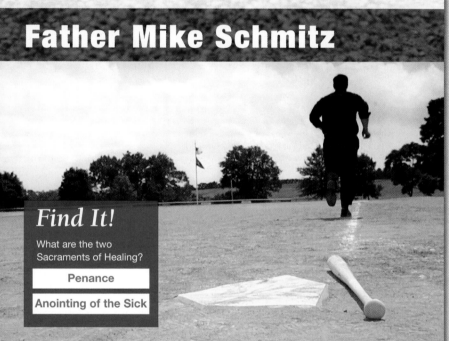

Find It!

What are the two Sacraments of Healing?

Penance

Anointing of the Sick

90 | CHOSEN

Hero of the Week

St. Augustine of Hippo

Do you like going to Confession?

Some people avoid Confession because they're too embarrassed or ashamed to tell their sins to a priest. And yet, when we reject this opportunity for the Sacrament of Reconciliation, we also reject the opportunity for healing and continue to be drawn to "being bad," even though, in our hearts, we want to be good!

St. Augustine of Hippo understood this struggle only too well. His early life was filled with parties, drinking, and a lifestyle that led to sins of impurity as well as false ideas and pride.

Augustine was raised a Christian, but fell deeply into sinful ways. He lived with a woman and had a son out of wedlock. Once, his own mother threw him out of the house because he offended her so much. Augustine felt unworthy of being a Christian; he failed to realize that God loves us, warts and all.

Sometimes shame and regret make us feel unworthy of God's love, but this is not true! There is no sin that God will not forgive if we come before him truly repentant. God doesn't love us because we're good; God wants us to be good because it is *good for us*. Mortal sin destroys us in big ways, and even smaller sins can chip away at us slowly, causing us to lose hope, as Augustine did.

One day, fed up with his own despair, Augustine tearfully pleaded with God to free him from his desire to sin. He knew in his heart that he was hurting God, hurting himself, and hurting others. Everything he thought made him happy was actually the source of his unhappiness. He begged the Lord to heal him. In that moment he opened himself up to God's love. Suddenly, he heard children singing, "Take up and read."

Augustine thought he was hearing things, but he obeyed the voices and opened St. Paul's letter to the Romans. He read a little bit before being converted on the spot.

"Let us conduct ourselves properly as in the day, not in orgies and drunkenness, not in promiscuity and licentiousness, not in rivalry and jealousy. But put on the Lord Jesus Christ, and make no provision for the desires of the flesh" (Romans 13:13-14, NAB).

From that point on, St. Augustine had the strength to set aside his sinful ways and "put on the Lord Jesus Christ." He became one of the most influential theologians and spiritual writers in the history of the Church. His life shows us the transforming power of God's grace.

St. Augustine, pray for us. Help us seek God's healing forgiveness.

Born:
November 13, AD 354

Died:
August 28, 430

Memorial:
August 28

Patron Saint of:
- sore eyes
- brewers
- printers
- theologians

Step 7 **Hero of the Week** (5 minutes)

This saint story will help to highlight and reinforce this lesson's topic. You may choose to read it aloud, have a candidate read it aloud, or have the class read it silently.

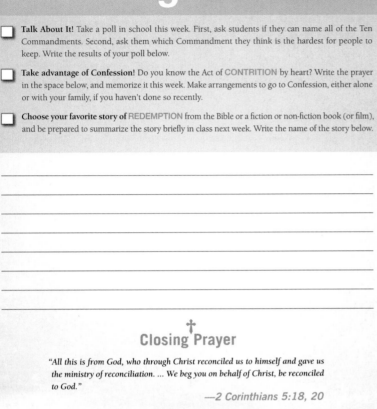

Lesson 10 | 91

Challenge of the Week

 Talk About It! Take a poll in school this week. First, ask students if they can name all of the Ten Commandments. Second, ask them which Commandment they think is the hardest for people to keep. Write the results of your poll below.

☐ **Take advantage of Confession!** Do you know the Act of CONTRITION by heart? Write the prayer in the space below, and memorize it this week. Make arrangements to go to Confession, either alone or with your family, if you haven't done so recently.

☐ **Choose your favorite story of** REDEMPTION from the Bible or a fiction or non-fiction book (or film), and be prepared to summarize the story briefly in class next week. Write the name of the story below.

_____

_____

_____

_____

_____

_____

_____

_____

✝ Closing Prayer

"All this is from God, who through Christ reconciled us to himself and gave us the ministry of reconciliation. ... We beg you on behalf of Christ, be reconciled to God."

—*2 Corinthians 5:18, 20*

Lord Jesus, you are waiting to forgive us in the Sacrament of Reconciliation. Help us to get to Confession regularly, to stay positive, and to never give up on ourselves, no matter how many times we fail. Thank you for refreshing and strengthening us to live out our purpose with joy and enthusiasm. Amen.

 Challenge of the Week (2 minutes)

Ask your candidates to read the "challenges" above and choose one of the three to complete this week. Have them check the box next to the challenge they intend to complete. Encourage them to write about their experiences in the space provided.

Step 9 **Homework Instructions and Updates** (2 minutes)

Remind candidates to read the "Wrap-Up" and the "What's That Word?" sections in the "Taking It Home" section of the Student Workbook. They should also review the "Watch It!" questions to prepare for the next "Review Game."

 Closing Prayer (3 minutes)

As a way of building up community, ask if there are any prayer intentions. Write them down (or have candidates share them aloud) and after praying for those intentions, have the class read the "Closing Prayer" together (provided in the Student Workbook).

92 | CHOSEN

Taking It Home

For next week's "Review Game," be sure to read over the following …

1. **Watch It!** questions (page 87)
2. **Wrap-Up**
3. **"What's That Word?"**
4. **Memory Verse**

Don't forget to do your **Challenge of the Week** (page 91)

Wrap-Up

"There are people who believe they are righteous, follow the catechism well enough and abide by the Christian faith, but they don't have the experience of having been saved.

"It's one thing to hear about a boy who was drowning in a river and the person who jumped in to save him; it's another to have personally been at the scene and lent a hand; and even another for it to have actually been you who was drowning while someone jumps in the water to save you. Only we big sinners have this grace … [to understand what salvation really means]."

—Pope Francis[2]

Have you ever done something wrong and tried to cover it up—even avoiding Confession—because of what others might think of you if they knew? Guilt can drive us crazy. When we try to cover up or "hide" that we've done something wrong, sin molds, festers, and rots. It makes us sick on the inside. It's human nature to want to "unload" a guilty CONSCIENCE—it makes us feel better!

But wait! Can't we just tell God we're sorry when we mess up? Why go to a priest?

Private prayer is important—and it's a good thing to be honest with God. But private prayer can never take the place of the sacraments. Jesus gave us the Sacrament of Reconciliation (or "Confession") for four important reasons:

It gives us a direct encounter with God. Sacraments are our deepest encounters with God this side of eternity. When we go to Confession, we are going *straight to God* in a *deeper* way than we could by praying in private.

It gives us power to stop sinning. The Church classifies some sins as mortal (serious or "deadly") and some as venial (less serious[3]). Confession is required for mortal sins; however, it's good to confess smaller, VENIAL SINS, as well. Jesus understands it's hard for us to break sinful habits, and so he gives us that sacramental help.

It reconciles us with God and the Church. Whenever we commit mortal (serious or "grave") sins, we *need* to go to Confession to get right with God.* (When we offend someone, we need to reconcile on their terms, not ours.) Reconciliation with God is inseparable from reconciling with the whole Church, the Body of Christ. So it makes sense to go to God's representative in the Church (the priest) for the reconciliation we seek.

---

* You can't commit a mortal sin without knowing it (full knowledge is a requirement). If you're not sure whether a certain sin is mortal, ask a priest.

[3] CCC 1456–1458

It eliminates any confusion about whether we're forgiven. Perfect contrition (repenting not out of fear of hell but out of love for God) sets us right with God even if we've committed mortal sin–provided we have a firm resolution to go to confession as soon as possible (see CCC 1452). However, the Church teaches that we must go to Confession at least once a year, during Lent, in part because we don't always judge our own actions accurately.[4]

("Am I really in mortal sin? Was I really sorry?") In confession, the priest has the authority by virtue of the Sacrament of Holy Orders to forgive sins. Think about how powerful this is the next time you go to Confession and hear the words, "I absolve you from your sins, in the name of the Father, and of the Son, and of the Holy Spirit." This assurance is a great gift!

"What's That Word?"

CULPABILITY

CULPABILITY refers to the responsibility a person has for acts, thoughts, and omissions. For an action to be sinful, the sinner must (1) be aware that what he is doing is wrong and (2) freely choose to act. If he doesn't know it is wrong, or if he is coerced into doing what he knows is wrong, his culpability is reduced. However, even if a person has reduced culpability for a particular action, the action can remain a venial sin. So while the circumstances of an act may limit one's culpability, this does not change the moral quality of the act or prevent us from experiencing its consequences (see CCC 1754). For example, being unaware that getting drunk is a sin will not prevent the body from experiencing the harmful physical effects of

alcohol or prevent the harm that could come to oneself or others from driving while intoxicated. Some actions, such as murder and adultery, are always *objectively* gravely sinful, regardless of the circumstances or one's intentions (see CCC 1756).

We have a duty to form our consciences according to the teachings of the Church. Otherwise, we can fall into *culpable ignorance,* which occurs "when a man 'takes little trouble to find out what is true and good, or when conscience is by degrees almost blinded through the habit of committing sin.' In such cases, the person is culpable for the evil he commits" (CCC 1791).

[4] CCC 1790–1793

Memory Verse:

"This is the message we have heard from him and proclaim to you, that God is light and in him is no darkness at all."

—1 John 1:5

MORTAL SIN

To be a mortal sin, three conditions must be met: (1) the sin must be objectively mortal, i.e., consist of "serious" or "grave" matter; (2) one must have full knowledge that such an act is gravely sinful; and (3) one must fully and willfully **CONSENT** to committing the sin. If any one of these three conditions is not present, then the culpability for the sin—though it might be a "big" or seriously immoral act—would be lessened. Even if one is not *subjectively* guilty of committing a mortal sin, he or she will still be harmed by it. Just as one who unknowingly drinks poisoned water will still be harmed by the poison, one who sins—even if he or she is not aware that the act is sinful—will suffer negative consequences.

RECONCILIATION (CONFESSION)

The *Sacrament of Reconciliation* is the primary way that God has arranged for people to take care of their "sin problem" and to be reconciled with him for sins committed after Baptism. Sin harms our relationships with God and others. Because the healing of any relationship begins with a recognition that one has done something wrong, it is important to regularly consider "what I have done or failed to do"—to examine our consciences.

Sorrow for sin (or *contrition*) leads to a genuine apology. This sacrament is often called *Confession* because it provides the opportunity to confess sins and apologize for them so that they may be forgiven. God longs for us to return to him, and, therefore, he is always ready to forgive us when we are sorry. The priest who hears our confession acts *in persona Christi Capitis* "in ... the person of Christ himself" (CCC 1548)[5] and can help us in our battle against sin. Although he isn't perfect—every priest has a confessor to whom he confesses his own sins—the priest has been chosen by God to listen to our sins, to forgive us in God's name, and to welcome us back to life in his family. (*See also* SIN, EXAMINATION OF CONSCIENCE, *and* SEAL OF CONFESSION.)

[6] CCC 1466

Any questions?

Where is Confession found in Scripture?

We can find a scriptural basis for Confession in John 20:21-23:

"Jesus said to them again, 'Peace be with you. As the Father has sent me, even so I send you.' And when he had said this, he breathed on them, and said to them, 'Receive the Holy Spirit. If you forgive the sins of any, they are forgiven; if you retain the sins of any, they are retained.'"

Did You Know?

Before hearing confessions, the priest kisses a cross that is embroidered in the center of his purple stole and then places the stole around his neck, symbolically "putting on Christ." When he takes it off again, the burden of our sins remains in Christ, not with the priest—though in his office, he does penance for others in the name of Christ.[6]

Notes

Overview

The purpose of this lesson is to address the mystery of suffering and the Sacrament of the Anointing of the Sick. In this sacrament, God gives us grace to deal with suffering heroically; he also uses the sacrament to bring spiritual healing and, when it is God's will, physical healing as well.

We call suffering a "mystery" because the most painful tragedy of human history—the killing of the Son of God on the cross—became the source of infinite blessing, our salvation. So we have faith that God can bring great good out of great pain and that he allows suffering in order to perfect us.

Through the Sacrament of the Anointing of the Sick, God provides spiritual and sometimes even physical healing. He gives the sick person the grace to face serious illness and death. Through the mystery of redemptive suffering, we can offer our earthly sufferings back to God where, joined to the sufferings of Christ, we participate in the redemption of the world (see CCC 1505; Colossians 1:24; 1 Peter 2:21).

Although the concept of "redemptive" suffering may be new to many of your students, most of them will have experienced some kind of significant suffering or loss. The death of a grandparent or other relative, a beloved pet, or even one of their own peers will color the students' reactions to this subject, and so it is important to be sensitive to any underlying concerns they may have.

Objectives of this Lesson

1. *Discuss what suffering is, why God allows it, and, most importantly, where God is in the midst of suffering.* It can be said that man suffers whenever he experiences any kind of evil. In allowing free will, God allows the possibility, and therefore the existence, of suffering. Jesus knows suffering and is with us: Emmanuel= "God is with us" (see CCC 1503; Hebrews 4:15).

2. *Explain the Sacrament of the Anointing of the Sick.* This sacrament is depicted throughout Scripture and especially in the public ministry of Christ (see CCC 1506–1510). Explain who can receive the sacrament (see CCC 1514–1515) and describe what happens in the celebration of the rite (see CCC 1517–1519).

3. *Describe how redemptive suffering can help us ... and other people.* "I make up in my body what was lacking in the sufferings of Christ," writes St. Paul (Colossians 1:24). This "making up" by joining our sufferings with those of Christ, rather than allowing these experiences to turn us away from God, makes those sufferings *redemptive* in our lives and in those of other people (see CCC 307, 618).

4. *Explain why understanding suffering requires an "eternal perspective."* Temporal suffering can bring about spiritual health. Earthly losses lead to heavenly rewards (see CCC 544, 272–273; 2 Corinthians 12:9-10).

"How does God help when it hurts?"

(Anointing of the Sick and Redemptive Suffering)

✝

Opening Prayer

"The Lord is my shepherd, I shall not want. ... I fear no evil; for you are with me."
—*Psalm 23:1, 4*

"Come to me, all who labor and are heavy laden, and I will give you rest."
—*Matthew 11:28*

"Let not your hearts be troubled; believe in God, believe also in me."
—*John 14:1*

"And they cast out many demons, and anointed with oil many that were sick and healed them."
—*Mark 6:13*

"I have said this to you, that in me you may have peace.
In the world you have tribulation; but be of good cheer, I have overcome the world."
—*John 16:33*

Opening Prayer

Today we are talking about the Anointing of the Sick and how God is with us in our sufferings. We are going to start by praying and meditating on a few Scriptures.

Ask for volunteers, or assign a teen to read each passage.

In the name of the Father …

Step 1 — Welcome/Review Game (5 minutes)

Begin by welcoming the class and telling them that you will be starting with a review of the previous lesson's material. On the DVD menu, click on Lesson 11; then on the sub-menu, click on "Review Game."

Have students answer the questions based on the previous lesson. For more information about how to adapt this game to meet the needs of your group, see the "Review Game" section in the Introduction to this Leader's Guide (page xvi).

Step 2 — Challenge of the Week Review (5 minutes)

Ask if anyone would like to share a "challenge experience" from the previous week. Try to draw students out by prompting them with basic questions regarding the challenges from last week (e.g.,"Did anyone choose the first challenge?").

Step 3 — Opening Prayer (3 minutes)

Lead the class in the "Opening Prayer," which is included in the Student Workbook. Leader's Guide notes are provided above: Red text provides direction and guidance, and white text is for you to read aloud to the class.

96 | CHOSEN

Dive In:
The Woman Who
Wanted to Say Good-Bye

"Come fast. She's at the end." Father Jim Crismin, a priest of the Archdiocese of Denver, put on his collar and rushed to the hospital. There in the ICU lay a sixty-year-old woman on a respirator with her sisters at her side. She had been brain dead for ten days. All that remained was to give her the Anointing of the Sick and allow her family to say their good-byes. The end of her journey on earth had arrived.

As he had done many times, Fr. Jim took out his oils for the ANOINTING and opened his prayer book. He read the prayers, anointing her head and hands: "Through this holy anointing may the Lord in his love and mercy help you with the grace of the Holy Spirit. May the Lord who frees you from sin save you and raise you up." As he finished tracing the Sign of the Cross on her hand, her eyes opened. She tried to sit up, rip the tubes out, and talk!

He had been prepared for this kind of thing in seminary, and he knew what to do. He turned to the woman's sisters and explained that the primary effect of this sacrament is spiritual healing and the grace to face death, but that sometimes a temporary physical healing is needed to make that possible. This woman, he gently suggested, might need to give or receive forgiveness from someone before she died. He asked, "Do you know who that might be?" Eyes wide, they slowly nodded. "She needs to be reconciled with her daughter."

"Then get her here. Right away," he said.

The daughter was already on her way to the hospital. She walked into the room expecting to find her mother unconscious or dead. She was amazed to find her mother sitting there, waiting for her. They reconciled with one another in tears and with great joy. Then the mother said good-bye, lay back down on the hospital bed, and died.

This is the power we find in the Anointing of the Sick, a sacrament where Jesus Christ himself comes to us to strengthen us, comfort us, and give us the healing we need—whether that healing be physical or spiritual.

Step 4 **Dive In** (5 minutes)

Read this story aloud, have a candidate read it aloud, or have the class read it silently before watching the video segments. This thought-provoking story ties in to the lesson's topic and serves to set up the video presentation.

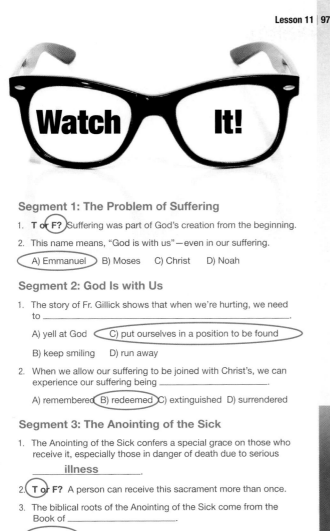

Segment 1: The Problem of Suffering

1. **T or F?** Suffering was part of God's creation from the beginning.

2. This name means, "God is with us"—even in our suffering.

   A) Emmanuel   B) Moses   C) Christ   D) Noah

Segment 2: God Is with Us

1. The story of Fr. Gillick shows that when we're hurting, we need to _____.

   A) yell at God   C) put ourselves in a position to be found

   B) keep smiling   D) run away

2. When we allow our suffering to be joined with Christ's, we can experience our suffering being _____.

   A) remembered   B) redeemed   C) extinguished   D) surrendered

Segment 3: The Anointing of the Sick

1. The Anointing of the Sick confers a special grace on those who receive it, especially those in danger of death due to serious _____ illness _____.

2. **T or F?** A person can receive this sacrament more than once.

3. The biblical roots of the Anointing of the Sick come from the Book of _____.

   A) James   B) John   C) Jeremiah   D) Revelation

Small-Group Discussion

Segment 1: The Problem of Suffering

1. Have you ever known someone who experienced great suffering? What about you?

2. Is it possible for God's gift of free will to cause suffering? How?

3. Have you ever experienced suffering bringing out the best in someone else or in you?

Segment 2: God Is with Us

1. As Fr. Toups says, we often are tempted to avoid suffering, but what are some ways we can allow God into our suffering?

2. How does the Cross of Christ change the meaning of suffering?[1]

3. What are some ways we can put ourselves into a position to be found by God?

4. Can you think of a saint who suffered?

Segment 3: The Anointing of the Sick

1. Have you ever known someone who received the Anointing of the Sick? Or, have you been present for an anointing? Share your experience.

2. What would be some examples of appropriate times to call a priest for the Anointing of the Sick?

3. Even without a physical healing, what are some ways the Anointing of the Sick may help someone who is in danger of despair or is losing hope due to their illness?[2]

Step 5 Watch It!/Small-Group Discussion (50 minutes)

On the video, click on Lesson 11, Segment 1. When Segment 1 ends, have students fill in the "Watch It!" questions (2 to 3 minutes). Run through them to be sure they wrote the correct answers so they will have them to prepare for the next "Review Game."

Next, lead students in a small-group discussion for Segment 1. You may begin by asking general questions like: "What part of the video spoke to you the most?" Discussion questions for each segment are provided in the blue box above.

Follow the same steps for Segments 2 and 3. (Allow for about 10 minutes of discussion time after each segment.)

Small-Group Discussion Leader's Notes

1. See CCC 307.

2. Hint: It gives spiritual strength and hope.

Question:

How does God enter into the "messy" parts of your life? What have you learned through those hard times?

"God never promised us freedom from 'messiness,' but his presence with us in it, strengthening us."

TO THE HEART with

My favorite time of the year is Christmas. I loved it as a kid, and I still get excited about it as an adult. When I was a kid, I used to anticipate Santa, time with my family, and, of course, all those presents. Growing up I longed to hear two words: "Merry Christmas."

Now that I am a priest, I still yearn for Christmas, but for very different reasons. I love hearing the story of Mary and Joseph's journey to Bethlehem. I love the motley crew of visitors—from shepherds to Magi. And I love that manger ... I *really* love that manger. On the outskirts of Bethlehem, rocky caves had been used as stables since ancient times. Jesus was probably born in a cave like these, a resting place for sheep when they were sleeping. Jesus was born in a poor cave ... crowded with sheep ... in the cold night outside Bethlehem. There was no hospital, no nurse, no one to care for them.

You see, the Christmas story is more messy than merry. It's about people like you and me, who live our lives in homes that, for most of the year, are not decorated like they are in December. It's about people like you and me, who live in a world where bad things sometimes happen to good people. It's about people like you and me, who live with tough questions and real problems. You see, life is messy. I am messy. You are messy. Christmas— the real Christmas story—reveals God's desire to enter into a messy world. God loves us ... and all of our messiness. It's easier for me to say, "Messy Christmas" than "Merry Christmas."

God made a statement at Christmas. When he entered the world as a man, God chose to enter all of humanity. God still desires to enter *everything* human. God wants to enter human suffering. God wants to enter human sickness. God never

---

Step 6 To the Heart (10 minutes)

After the small-group discussions, read this story aloud, have a candidate read it aloud, or have the class read it silently. After the story (written by this week's video presenter), read the thought-provoking question(s) provided in the red "To the Heart" box above. Time permitting, ask follow-up questions and encourage discussion.

promised us freedom from "messiness," but his presence with us in it, strengthening us. It might seem weird to think that God could be a part of things that are messy, but then again, God can enter anything he wants.

There are a few things in life that we can expect. We will experience highs and lows. We will experience good times and tough times. And, at some point in our lives, we will come face to face with suffering and sickness. The good news is that we are not alone. In fact, Christ has entrusted the Church with the Sacrament of the Anointing of the Sick so that we might know that God is with us, even when we are sick. That's an awesome gift—God entering every part of our lives.

Father Mark Toups

Find It!

What is the Catholic meaning of the word *lavabo*, and what is it used for?

This word refers to the ceremonial washing of the priest's hands during Mass, as well as the bowl he uses to perform this purification rite.

100 | CHOSEN

Hero of the Week

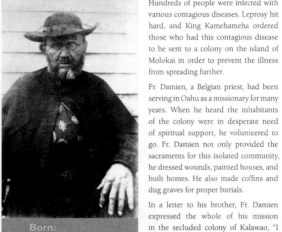

Born:
January 3, 1840

Died:
April 15, 1889

Memorial:
May 10

Patron Saint of:
• people with leprosy

St. Damien of Molokai, Martyr of Charity

Getting assigned to Hawaii for work sounds like a great adventure in paradise, doesn't it?

Would you still be enthusiastic if you found out it was to live in a leper colony?

In the 1870s, when Hawaii was still a kingdom, a health crisis hit the islands. Hundreds of people were infected with various contagious diseases. Leprosy hit hard, and King Kamehameha ordered those who had this contagious disease to be sent to a colony on the island of Molokai in order to prevent the illness from spreading further.

Fr. Damien, a Belgian priest, had been serving in Oahu as a missionary for many years. When he heard the inhabitants of the colony were in desperate need of spiritual support, he volunteered to go. Fr. Damien not only provided the sacraments for this isolated community, he dressed wounds, painted houses, and built homes. He also made coffins and dug graves for proper burials.

In a letter to his brother, Fr. Damien expressed the whole of his mission in the secluded colony of Kalawao, "I make myself a leper with the lepers to gain all to Jesus Christ." It became an opportunity for **REDEMPTIVE SUFFERING**, offered simply and in accordance with Christ's call to take up our crosses and follow his example.

He chose to stay with the community although the original plan was to cycle through four priests in order to limit their exposure and provide periods of respite. Fr. Damien embraced the work

he had before him, to make the colony more than just habitable. It was home. He had plans to enlarge the orphanage, build new community buildings, and continue to add construction projects.

Eventually he contracted leprosy, and it redoubled his efforts to complete as many of his projects as possible. By this time, the story of his courageous holiness had begun to spread around the world, and he was joined by four unlikely heroes: another Belgian priest, Fr. Louis-Lambert Conrardy; Mother Marianne Cope, who ran a hospital in New York (she was recently declared a saint); Joseph Dutton, a Civil War soldier; and James Sinnett, a nurse from Chicago.

It took these four people to take over the tasks Fr. Damien had been doing by himself.

When Fr. Damien died, he was laid to rest under the same tree where he napped upon his arrival. This gentle and sweet closure to a life dedicated to the ailing people in Molokai demonstrates that we can achieve great grace, Christ-like love, and heroism in the midst of pain and suffering—perhaps even because of it.

St. Damien, pray for us. Help us discover Christ's presence in our brokenness and pain.

Step 7

Hero of the Week (5 minutes)

This saint story will help to highlight and reinforce this lesson's topic. You may choose to read it aloud, have a candidate read it aloud, or have the class read it silently.

Challenge of the Week

 Invite friends or family to come with you to visit a hospital, nursing home, or someone who is elderly or homebound, and pick an activity to share with them. Read or play cards or a board game, help them write letters, or play them some music and perhaps sing. Write about it in the space below, and come prepared to talk about it next week.

 Evaluate your physical health, and make a new commitment to improve your diet or get more exercise. Offer the extra effort as a sacrifice for someone who is chronically ill or disabled. Commit to what you are going to do by writing it in the space below.

 Spend five minutes in prayer, looking closely at an image of Jesus Christ crucified or carrying his cross. Write a prayer or reflection in the space below, and consider sharing it next week.

_____

_____

_____

_____

_____

☦ Closing Prayer

"Is any among you sick? Let him call for the elders of the church, and let them pray over him, anointing him with oil in the name of the Lord ..."

—James 5:14

Lord, you suffered, and you felt alone on the cross. You are very close to us when we suffer, especially when we feel completely alone.

You always accept us just as we are, wounded by sadness and sin. But you love us too much to leave us that way. Thank you for the powerful graces we receive through anointing and for teaching us to accept our sufferings willingly, knowing that they bring us closer to you and help us to become the authentic and heroically loving people that you call us to be. Amen.

 Step 8 **Challenge of the Week** (2 minutes)

Ask your candidates to read the "challenges" above and choose one of the three to complete this week. Have them check the box next to the challenge they intend to complete. Encourage them to write about their experiences in the space provided.

 Step 9 **Homework Instructions and Updates** (2 minutes)

Remind candidates to read the "Wrap-Up" and the "What's That Word?" sections in the "Taking It Home" section of the Student Workbook. They should also review the "Watch It!" questions to prepare for the next "Review Game."

Step 10 **Closing Prayer** (3 minutes)

As a way of building up community, ask if there are any prayer intentions. Write them down (or have candidates share them aloud) and after praying for those intentions, have the class read the "Closing Prayer" together (provided in the Student Workbook).

102 | CHOSEN

Taking It Home

For next week's "Review Game," be sure to read over the following …

1. **Watch It!** questions (page 97)
2. **Wrap-Up**
3. **"What's That Word?"**
4. **Memory Verse**

Don't forget to do your **Challenge of the Week** (page 101)

Wrap-Up

It's one of the most mind-boggling mysteries of the Christian faith: If God is all-loving and all-powerful … why does suffering exist?

To answer that question, we have to go all the way back to the Garden of Eden, to the sin of our first parents, whose actions brought very real consequences into the world, including ignorance, concupiscence, sickness, and death.[1] And just as God did not prevent the first man from sinning, he does not prevent all suffering. But the good news is that, "God permits evil in order to draw forth some greater good" (Thomas Aquinas).[2]

Here's the thing: God never promised us that life would be easy. What God promises is that he's with us when it's tough. He never leaves us. When we are tempted to doubt that God loves us because of what we are suffering, we need to look at the cross. The crucifix reminds us that God did not abandon us in our suffering, but allowed himself to experience the worst of it with us and for us. So, we never need to feel alone. Even when we feel like God has forgotten us, he never does. He loves us.

God doesn't take away the pain of this life; instead, he transforms it. As we offer our pain back to God, our sufferings unite with his and become a single offering of prayer for the world and an opportunity for us to be purified and to practice heroic virtue. United with him, we get to do what Jesus did on the cross: suffer for the redemption of the world.

Anointing of the Sick is the sacrament where God shows his transforming and life-giving presence in our pain. In the book of James, we see that this sacrament has changed very little in 2,000 years:

"Is any among you sick? Let him call for the elders of the Church, and let them pray over him, anointing him with oil in the name of the Lord; and the prayer of faith will save the sick man, and the Lord will raise him up; and if he has committed sins, he will be forgiven" (James 5:14-15).

In this sacrament, God gives us strength and courage, spiritual healing, and cleansing from sin; and sometimes he even works a physical healing. Vatican II restored the more ancient understanding that the sacrament of anointing is not only for those who are about to die but also for those who are seriously ill.

[1] CCC 405

"What's That Word?"

ANOINTING OF THE SICK

Anointing of the Sick is one of the SACRAMENTS OF HEALING, given to those who are seriously ill, in danger of death, or are already dying. In the past, it was given only to those who were about to die, but today, the elderly and people who are suffering from long illnesses are able to receive the sacrament, as are people about to undergo serious surgery.

While some receive physical healing from anointing, the focus of the sacrament is spiritual healing, the forgiveness of sins, and the strength to endure the suffering that often accompanies illness. The prayers of the sacrament are a beautiful invitation to accept suffering, which unites us to Jesus who willingly suffered to save us from sin and death. (*See also* VIATICUM.)

REDEMPTIVE SUFFERING

God did not create people to suffer. When our first parents sinned, they introduced suffering into their lives and the lives of others. We do the same when *we* sin. The good news is that by his passion and death on the cross, Jesus showed that suffering can lead to new and eternal life—for us and for others. In other words, suffering can be *redemptive*.

Just as Jesus suffered for us, he invites us to offer our sufferings back to him, to bring life back to ourselves and to others. Many of the saints took Jesus up on his invitation. When we accept suffering without complaint, we participate in Jesus' saving work. Praying in front of a crucifix or placing a crucifix nearby can help us to keep our own suffering in perspective and remember how powerful suffering can be. (*See also* PENANCE.)

Memory Verse:

"... *upon him was the chastisement that made us whole, and with his stripes we are healed.*"

– Isaiah 53:5

104 | CHOSEN

Any questions ?

When should I call a priest for Anointing of the Sick?

Definitely call if someone is in danger of dying. Parishes usually have an emergency line for that. But you don't have to wait that long! This sacrament is not just for people on the verge of death. If someone is about to have surgery, has a terminal or persistent illness, or is very old,[3] he or she is a candidate for anointing.

---

[3] CCC 1514

Did You Know?

St. Francis of Assisi, a rich and generous Italian nobleman, was captured in a military battle and spent a year praying in a filthy dungeon, ill with fever. Later, he left all his riches behind to start the Franciscan Order, known for its service to the poor and sick.

Notes

**Lesson 12
Leader's Notes**

Overview

The purpose of this lesson is to encourage students to understand who the Holy Spirit is and to cultivate a relationship with the Holy Spirit, the third Person of the Blessed Trinity.

At Pentecost, the Holy Spirit descended to lead them "to all truth" (John 16:13) as the apostles built up the Church all over the world. However, the Holy Spirit (like God the Father and God the Son) has no beginning or end; he was present at Creation, has worked throughout salvation history, enters us at Baptism, and seals each person at Confirmation with an indelible mark, empowering him or her with all that is necessary to accomplish the task God has in store.

Objectives of this Lesson

1. *Detail the images of the Holy Spirit in the Bible.* From "hovering over the waters" at Creation, to rushing upon David as he took on Goliath, to the dove descending from heaven upon Christ at his Baptism, to wind rushing through the house and tongues of fire coming to rest on the apostles at Pentecost, many images of the Holy Spirit throughout salvation history give us a glimpse into who he is (see CCC 694–701).

2. *Explain that the Holy Spirit is the soul of the Church.* As a soul animates and directs the activity of a body, so the Holy Spirit animates, unites, and leads the Church (see CCC 737–741).

3. *Discuss the Holy Spirit and the Blessed Trinity: "consubstantial" with the Father and the Son.* The Holy Spirit is the love that emanates from the first two Persons of the Trinity, like the child who comes into being from the love of his or her parents. The Holy Spirit is also one with and equal to the Father and the Son. The third Person of the Trinity, the Holy Spirit is not an "it" but a "he" (see CCC 685–686).

4. *Convey that the Holy Spirit is the one who connects us to God in a bond of love.* From this love flows the strength, grace, and courage we need to live our faith (see CCC 687–688).

"Who is the Holy Spirit?"

(Meeting the Third Person of the Trinity)

Opening Prayer

Litany of the Holy Spirit

"Promise of God the Father, *have mercy on us.*
Ray of heavenly light, *have mercy on us.*
Author of all good, *have mercy on us.*
Source of heavenly water, *have mercy on us.*
Consuming Fire, *have mercy on us.*
Ardent Charity, *have mercy on us.*
Spirit of love and truth, *have mercy on us.*
Spirit of wisdom and understanding,
have mercy on us.
Spirit of counsel and fortitude, *have mercy on us.*
Spirit of knowledge and piety, *have mercy on us.*
Spirit of the fear of the Lord, *have mercy on us.*

Spirit of grace and prayer, *have mercy on us.*
Spirit of peace and meekness, *have mercy on us.*
Spirit of modesty and innocence, *have mercy on us.*
Holy Spirit, the Comforter, *have mercy on us.*
Holy Spirit, the Sanctifier, *have mercy on us.*
Holy Spirit, who governs the Church,
have mercy on us.
Gift of God the Most High, *have mercy on us.*
Spirit who fills the universe, *have mercy on us.*
Spirit of the adoption of the children of God,
have mercy on us. Amen."

Opening Prayer

A litany is a type of prayer used to meditate on a particular theme, such as the names of Christ or the saints. A leader says a line, and the people respond, usually with, "Have mercy on us" or, "Pray for us."

In this Litany to the Holy Spirit, we will contemplate the various names for the Holy Spirit in order to help us think about who he is. I will lead, and you simply respond to each prayer by saying, "Have mercy on us." In the name of the Father …

Step 1 — Welcome/Review Game (5 minutes)

Begin by welcoming the class and telling them that you will be starting with a review of the previous lesson's material. On the DVD menu, click on Lesson 12; then on the sub-menu, click on "Review Game."

Have students answer the questions based on the previous lesson. For more information about how to adapt this game to meet the needs of your group, see the "Review Game" section in the Introduction to this Leader's Guide (page xvi).

Step 2 — Challenge of the Week Review (5 minutes)

Ask if anyone would like to share a "challenge experience" from the previous week. Try to draw students out by prompting them with basic questions regarding the challenges from last week (e.g.,"Did anyone choose the first challenge?").

Step 3 — Opening Prayer (3 minutes)

Lead the class in the "Opening Prayer," which is included in the Student Workbook. Leader's Guide notes are provided above: Red text provides direction and guidance, and white text is for you to read aloud to the class.

106 | CHOSEN

Dive In:
A Place in the Sun

Indonesia is a nation of thousands of islands dotted like pearls across countless miles of ocean. People travel from every corner of the globe to enjoy the tropical waters of Indonesia, but the locals are rarely seen in the water. The country has great waves, but the locals seldom surf. It has world-class snorkeling and diving, but the locals don't snorkel or dive. It has warm beaches year-round—yet the locals don't often sunbathe.

So why don't Indonesian families spend more time at the beach? There could be cultural factors, including the strict dress code observed by the predominantly Muslim population. Two of the indigenous cultures (the Balinese and the Javanese) are rice farmers. For thousands of years, their lives have been about working the land. Since they don't have much experience navigating the ocean, it has always been something they've seen as dangerous and certainly not "fun." And so the country has 50,000 miles of stunning tropical coastline, with no locals jumping in!

So ... what does that have to do with the Holy Spirit? Well, as Catholics, we have full access to the "gift of God," the third Person of the Blessed Trinity.[1] We are called to be people with life-giving waters[2] flowing from within us to a thirsty world. We have an Advocate (or Counselor)[3] to support us on our journey toward heaven. We have all the gifts we could possibly need to become who we're meant to be and do what we're called to do in this world.

Are we eager to use those gifts? And if not ... why not?

We're going to talk today about who (not "what") "the gift of God" is and how to begin jumping into the life and the power he has in store for us.

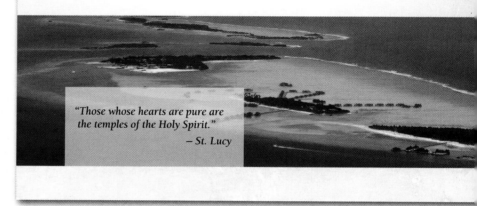

"Those whose hearts are pure are the temples of the Holy Spirit."
— St. Lucy

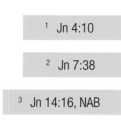

[1] Jn 4:10

[2] Jn 7:38

[3] Jn 14:16, NAB

Step 4 **Dive In** (5 minutes)

Read this story aloud, have a candidate read it aloud, or have the class read it silently before watching the video segments. This thought-provoking story ties in to the lesson's topic and serves to set up the video presentation.

Segment 1: Symbols of the Holy Spirit

1. In the Creed, we say that the Holy Spirit proceeds from the ___Father___ and the ___Son___.

2. Which of these does the *Catechism* **not** list as a symbol of the Holy Spirit?

   (A) Earth   B) Wind   C) Fire   D) Water

Segment 2: Our Guide and Map

1. Who is the principal author of the Bible? ___Holy Spirit___

2. The Holy Spirit is the ___soul___ of the Church.

Segment 3: The Holy Spirit in Your Life

1. (T) or **F?** The Holy Spirit is a pipeline or conduit to God's grace.

2. Deacon Burke-Sivers says that the Holy Spirit is the anchor and _____ of the Church.

   A) motor   B) sail   (C) defender   D) promoter

Small-Group Discussion

Segment 1: Symbols of the Holy Spirit

1. What are some images (or "symbols") traditionally related to the Holy Spirit? What do they teach us about him?[1]

2. Deacon Burke-Sivers says the Holy Spirit can come in powerful or subtle ways. What are some of the quiet ways we can experience him in our lives?

Segment 2: Our Guide and Map

1. What are some ways that you think the Holy Spirit "animates" the Church?

2. How does the Holy Spirit act as our "map"? What are some ways we can "access" that map?

3. What is one thing you can do to open your heart more fully to the grace of the Holy Spirit every day?

Segment 3: The Holy Spirit in Your Life

1. Which Person of the Blessed Trinity do you find it easiest to talk to?[2]

2. When might you choose to pray directly to the Holy Spirit?[3]

Step 5 **Watch It!/Small-Group Discussion** (50 minutes)

On the video, click on Lesson 12, Segment 1. When Segment 1 ends, have students fill in the "Watch It!" questions (2 to 3 minutes). Run through them to be sure they wrote the correct answers so they will have them to prepare for the next "Review Game."

Next, lead students in a small-group discussion for Segment 1. You may begin by asking general questions like: "What part of the video spoke to you the most?" Discussion questions for each segment are provided in the blue box above.

Follow the same steps for Segments 2 and 3. (Allow for about 10 minutes of discussion time after each segment.)

Small-Group Discussion Leader's Notes

1. See CCC 694–701.

2. Remember, God is "one," so any time we pray to God, all three Persons—Father, Son, and Holy Spirit—hear our prayers.

3. Hint: What does the Holy Spirit do for us?

Question:

What kinds of decisions, other than where to go to college, are you facing right now that you could bring to God in Adoration to help you make the right choice?

108 | ⚜ CHOSEN

"God the Father sends the Holy Spirit to awaken and ignite the fire of faith within us."

TO THE HEART with

At a reception following a presentation I gave in Idaho, a high-school senior wanted to talk to me about college choices. She explained in great detail the process she had been using to narrow down the list of schools to consider, but it was clear to me that one major element was missing from her decision-making process. I commended her diligence and thoughtfulness in approaching the task, then asked her, "Have you ever thought about where God wants you to go to college?"

"I don't know," she said. "I guess I never really thought about it."

"Part of the reason you're trying to figure out where to go to college is that you want to be happy. God loves you and wants you to be happy and fulfilled as well. He wants you to unite your mind, heart, and will with his. When you do that, then you will be filled with great joy and peace."

"How do I do that?"

"Here's what you do. Take the information from all the schools you are considering with you to ADORATION. Kneel down in front of the tabernacle or the monstrance where the Eucharist is exposed. Look at Jesus, there in the Eucharist. Thank him for the opportunity you've received to go to college. Then say, 'Lord, I love you, and I know you love me. I know you want what's best for me. I have so many choices. Where do you want me to be?' Then sit there in silence with Jesus and let the Holy Spirit speak to you."

"How will I know what God wants?"

"Keep going to Adoration. If you can stay for an hour, great! If not, stay for as long as you can. Do the same thing each time. As you're sitting there in silence and listening with your heart to the Holy

Step 6   **To the Heart** (10 minutes)

After the small-group discussions, read this story aloud, have a candidate read it aloud, or have the class read it silently. After the story (written by this week's video presenter), read the thought-provoking question(s) provided in the red "To the Heart" box above. Time permitting, ask follow-up questions and encourage discussion.

Spirit, look through the packets from each school. For some reason that you may not be able to explain in words, some schools will seem to leap off the page, while others will not. When you've narrowed it down to three or four choices, ask your parents to arrange a visit to each school. After visiting the colleges and talking with your parents, go back to Adoration. If you open yourself completely to God's love and life through the Holy Spirit, you will know where you are supposed to be."

"That's so cool! Thank you!"

God the Father sends the Holy Spirit to awaken and ignite the fire of faith within us. This knowledge of faith is possible only in the Holy Spirit. To be in touch with Christ, we must first have been touched by the Holy Spirit. The Holy Spirit is the Lord and giver of life, and if we cooperate with the grace that the Spirit freely gives us, if we say "yes" to God's invitation to life-giving love, our lives will be transformed. The more we seek to know and to do God's holy will in our lives, the more we will grow in holiness.

Deacon Harold Burke-Sivers

Find It!

What does *ruah* mean in ancient Hebrew?

Hint: Read Genesis 1:2.

Wind or breath, specifically the breath of God, the Holy Spirit (CCC 691)

110 | CHOSEN

Hero of the Week

Born:
circa 1412

Died:
May 30, 1431

Memorial:
May 30

Patron Saint of:
- France
- soldiers
- martyrs
- women in the military

St. Joan of Arc

The military standard caught the breeze and snapped open, displaying its colors and inspiring the countless soldiers.

The standard bearer, a teenaged girl dressed as a knight, led the charge against the English.

Joan of Arc was a peasant—illiterate, uneducated, and unworldly—who had managed to defeat the English with a victory at Orleans. The unlikely circumstances that placed her in the midst of professional soldiers can only be attributed to the Holy Spirit.

Joan came from a humble background, the daughter of a poor farmer. Her parents were devout, so she was raised in an environment of pious understanding. Even so, when, as a young teenager, she started having visions of saints, she was hesitant to share these experiences too openly because she feared her father's response.

The visions continued for years. By the time she was sixteen years old, the saints began *appearing* to Joan, urging her to drive out the English from France and to help Charles ascend to the throne of France.

Although Joan believed these messages were from God, she did not know how she might convince those with political power to listen to her, and it was outright dangerous to make such claims before Church officials—heresy was considered a capital crime.

Investigations resulted, especially as she triumphed on the battlegrounds.

Brandishing a twelve-foot banner emblazoned with "Party of the Kingdom of Heaven," the virgin warrior turned the course of the Hundred Years War by fearlessly leading the French troops, not according to the counsel of seasoned generals, but by following the voice of God.

Joan took an arrow in the neck and another in the leg (something that would have taken down a grown man), and yet this young woman survived, increasing in esteem among the soldiers and fueling the claims of supernatural intervention.

After a series of victories, she was betrayed and handed over to the British—an event she had prophesied about in detail. For more than a year, she was held on trumped-up charges of heresy, despite the lack of any credible evidence against her. Nevertheless, Joan was burned at the stake, a horrific death.

Admired for her tenacity and unwavering trust in God, Joan was exonerated twenty-five years after her death. She was canonized in 1920. In the words of Pope Pius X, "Joan has shone like a new star destined to be the glory not only of France but of the universal Church as well."

St. Joan of Arc, pray for us. Your trust in the Holy Spirit inspires us to do the same.

Step 7

Hero of the Week (5 minutes)

This saint story will help to highlight and reinforce this lesson's topic. You may choose to read it aloud, have a candidate read it aloud, or have the class read it silently.

Challenge of the Week

 Do an online search for "Catholic teen saints," and read up on some of our youngest heroes. Write about one of them in the space below, and come prepared to talk about this saint at the next class.

☐ **Memorize this "Holy Spirit prayer."** Copy it in the space below, and read it aloud every day this week: "Come, Holy Spirit, fill the hearts of your faithful and enkindle in them the fire of your love. Send forth your Spirit and they shall be created. And you shall renew the face of the earth" (CCC 2671).[4]

 Prepare a meal for someone you love, while meditating on the Holy Spirit's power to sustain each human life. Write about it in the space below.

Closing Prayer

"The spirit of God has made me, and the breath of the Almighty gives me life."

—Job 33:4

Holy Spirit, you breathed life into every person here, and you make us strong when we trust in you. Inspire us to look more deeply into our lives for signs of your life-giving presence. Give us the words we need this week to inspire and comfort the people you have placed in our lives. Help us to know you better, so we can be more open to your guidance and more aware of our need for you in everything we do. Amen.

Step 8 — Challenge of the Week (2 minutes)

Ask your candidates to read the "challenges" above and choose one of the three to complete this week. Have them check the box next to the challenge they intend to complete. Encourage them to write about their experiences in the space provided.

Step 9 — Homework Instructions and Updates (2 minutes)

Remind candidates to read the "Wrap-Up" and the "What's That Word?" sections in the "Taking It Home" section of the Student Workbook. They should also review the "Watch It!" questions to prepare for the next "Review Game."

Step 10 — Closing Prayer (3 minutes)

As a way of building up community, ask if there are any prayer intentions. Write them down (or have candidates share them aloud) and after praying for those intentions, have the class read the "Closing Prayer" together (provided in the Student Workbook).

112 | 🔥 CHOSEN

Taking It Home

For next week's "Review Game,"
be sure to read over the following ...

1. **Watch It!** questions (page 107)
2. **Wrap-Up**
3. **"What's That Word?"**
4. **Memory Verse**

Don't forget to do your
Challenge of the Week (page 111)

Wrap-Up

The Holy Spirit is sometimes known as the "hidden" Person of the Blessed Trinity.[5] He completes Jesus' work on earth in our lives here and now. He brings us the sacraments, is the primary author of Sacred Scripture, gives us the grace to become saints, guides the Church, and makes us one with the Father and the Son.[6]

When we talk about the distinctions between the three Persons of the Trinity, we first have to remember their UNITY as God. The *Catechism* reminds us that, "We do not confess three Gods, but one God in three Persons" (CCC 253). They are one in their divine *nature*, and the life and work of the Trinity is "inseparable," that is, common to all three Persons. They are also distinct in their relationship to one another. The Nicene Creed declares that it is the Son who is "begotten, not made, consubstantial with the Father," and it is the Holy Spirit "who proceeds from the Father and the Son." As we proclaim in the Creed, the Holy Spirit is "the Lord, the giver of life."

This week, we talked about who the Holy Spirit is and how he works in the Church and the world. For the next two weeks, we will talk more specifically about all the ways the Holy Spirit works in each of our lives. In the next lesson, we will explore the Gifts of the Holy Spirit and how they are used in the life of the believer. Finally, in lesson fourteen, we will take a closer look at the role of the Holy Spirit in the Sacrament of Confirmation.

[5] CCC 687, 702

[6] CCC 683–684, 2818

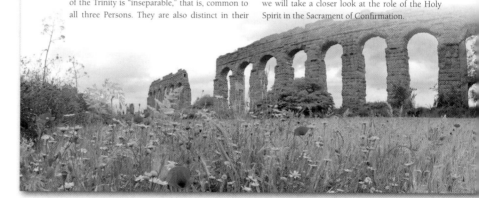

"What's That Word?"

HOLY SPIRIT

The *Holy Spirit* is God, the third Person of the Trinity. Because he is pure spirit, he has no body, and we often use things like breath, wind, fire, water, and a dove to represent him. However, the *Holy Spirit* is a Person, and he desires a relationship with each of us. In the Nicene Creed, we profess him to be "the Lord, the giver of life" because just as our own spirit makes us alive, the *Holy Spirit* who comes to live within us at Baptism gives us a supernatural life that will never end. Alive with the *Holy Spirit*, we are empowered to do the great things that God has planned for us—to love heroically and to bring others into God's family. *(See also* **PARACLETE**.)

SPIRIT/SOUL

Spirit is used in the Bible to translate a word that means "breath" because we associate our ability to breathe with being alive. While all living creatures have a life principle, or soul, only human beings have a spiritual soul,[7] a soul that is a spirit. As the *Catechism* states, "By virtue of his soul and his spiritual powers of intellect and will, man is endowed with freedom, an 'outstanding manifestation of the divine image'" (CCC 1705).

Angels are pure, immortal spirits. They do not have bodies, but they do have intellects and wills (see CCC 330). Though our soul is separated from our body when we die, our body will rise at the end of time in a glorified state and be reunited with our soul. So contrary to popular myth, we do not become angels when we die.

[7] CCC 363

Memory Verse:

"... for we do not know how to pray as we ought, but the Spirit himself intercedes for us with sighs too deep for words."

— Romans 8:26

114 | CHOSEN

PARACLETE/ADVOCATE

Jesus promised to send his disciples the PARACLETE, which is one of the titles of the Holy Spirit. *Paraclete* (or *Advocate*) literally means "he who is called to one's side" (CCC 692) and is a term often used in a courtroom setting when referring to the lawyer who stands with the defendant and argues his or her case before the judge. The Holy Spirit "stands with us" in our everyday lives, making it possible for us to act courageously in the service of God and others and, in a special way, when we are suffering or persecuted. He also "comes to the aid of our weakness" and helps us to pray when we are unable to help ourselves.

8 Ex 13:21

9 Ex 31:18

10 Lk 1:35

11 Mt 3:16

12 Acts 2:3

13 Jn 16:13; CCC 696–701

14 Jn 14:16, 15:26, 16:7

15 CCC 688

Did You Know?

During the Nazi occupation of Italy during World War II, Padre Pio appeared in the sky over his village, San Giovanni Rotondo, as American bombers were about to attack. None of the planes were able to release their bombs, and the village was protected. One pilot later saw the saint in person and confirmed his identity.

Any questions?

Jesus promised to send the Holy Spirit to the apostles after the Ascension—but wasn't the Holy Spirit already active in the world?

The Holy Spirit has worked throughout salvation history. To list just a few examples of this: In the Old Testament, the Holy Spirit led the Israelites through the desert in pillars of cloud and fire[8] and wrote the Ten Commandments upon stone tablets.[9] In the New Testament, the Holy Spirit caused Mary to conceive Jesus[10] and descended upon Jesus like a dove at his Baptism.[11] At Pentecost, the same Spirit rested upon the disciples as "tongues as of fire,"[12] to lead them "into all the truth."[13]

We can see how the Holy Spirit has been active throughout the history of the Church and remains active in it today. When Christ sent the Paraclete (the Holy Spirit) at Pentecost, he initiated an even more intimate relationship between God and the human race.[14] The Holy Spirit inspired the writing of Sacred Scripture and guided the bishops of the early Church, who decided which books were Spirit-inspired and belonged in the Bible. He guides the leaders of the Church, brings us into communion with Christ through the sacraments, intercedes for us through our prayer, and is at work in the ministries and missionary life of the Church. By virtue of our Baptism, the Spirit dwells within each of us, inviting us to grow in holiness. He transforms us through sanctifying grace and empowers us with gifts. He is our "Advocate" and strengthens us on our journey toward heaven.[15] Today, the "pillar of fire" that is the third Person of the Trinity is burning within every Christian living in the state of grace.

Notes

**Lesson 13
Leader's Notes**

Overview

The purpose of this lesson is to introduce students to the Gifts of the Holy Spirit, which are "permanent dispositions" (CCC 1830) that allow us to follow the promptings of the Holy Spirit. These gifts, which are strengthened in us at Confirmation, are intended to help us grow in holiness—and to empower us to help others grow as well.

In this lesson, we talk about the two types of Gifts of the Holy Spirit—the seven gifts listed in Isaiah 11, which help us to grow in holiness and produce in us the Fruits of the Holy Spirit—and the *charismatic* gifts, which the Holy Spirit gives us to empower us to lead others to holiness and to build up the kingdom of God on earth.

The Gifts of the Holy Spirit, received at Baptism and strengthened through Confirmation, help us to live the Christian life. As with any gift, however, we must be willing to *open* the gift in order to use it. The more we cooperate with and exercise a particular gift, the stronger we grow in using it.

Objectives of this Lesson

1. *The gifts of the Holy Spirit equip us for the journey of faith.* We receive these gifts at Baptism, and they are "increased" in us (see CCC 1303) at Confirmation.

2. *Scripture identifies two types of gifts:* The first set of Gifts of the Holy Spirit is listed in Isaiah—wisdom, understanding, counsel, fortitude (courage), knowledge, piety, and fear of the Lord (see Isaiah 11:1-2; CCC 1831).

3. *In addition, there are charisms,* or charismatic gifts, that help individuals serve the Church for the common good (see 1 Corinthians 12; Romans 12:6-8; CCC 799, 2003–2004).

4. *The Fruits of the Spirit,* the "first fruits of eternal glory," are twelve "perfections" or qualities that prove the Holy Spirit is at work in our lives as we grow in virtue. These fruits are: charity (love), joy, peace, patience, kindness, goodness, generosity, gentleness, faithfulness, modesty, self-control, and chastity (see CCC 1832; Galatians 5:22-23).

"What does the Holy Spirit do for me?"

(Gifts for the Journey)

✝

Opening Prayer

Veni Sancte Spiritus (Come Holy Spirit)

"Come, Holy Spirit, send forth the heavenly radiance of your light.
Come, Father of the poor.
Come, giver of gifts.
Come, light of the heart.
Greatest comforter, sweet guest of the soul, sweet consolation: in labor, rest; in heat, temperance; in tears, solace.
O most blessed light, fill the inmost heart of your faithful.
Without your grace, there is nothing in us, nothing that is not harmful.

Cleanse what is unclean,
Water what is dry.
Heal what has been wounded.
Flex what is inflexible.
Warm what is chilled.
Correct what has gone astray.
Give to your faithful, those who trust in you, the sevenfold gifts.
Grant the reward of virtue, the deliverance of salvation, and our eternal joy. Amen."

Opening Prayer

Search online for Veni Sancte Spiritus Gregorian sequence," and you will find several YouTube renditions of this beautiful chant. Consider playing it in the background as class begins and introducing it to your class with the following:

Since the eleventh century, *"Veni Sancte Spiritus"* (Come Holy Spirit) has been chanted before the Gospel on Pentecost Sunday. The prayer beautifully shows our need for the Holy Spirit in our lives and how helpless we are without him. Let's read it together now. In the name of the Father …

 Welcome/Review Game (5 minutes)

Begin by welcoming the class and telling them that you will be starting with a review of the previous lesson's material. On the DVD menu, click on Lesson 13; then on the sub-menu, click on "Review Game."

Have students answer the questions based on the previous lesson. For more information about how to adapt this game to meet the needs of your group, see the "Review Game" section in the Introduction to this Leader's Guide (page xvi).

 Challenge of the Week Review (5 minutes)

Ask if anyone would like to share a "challenge experience" from the previous week. Try to draw students out by prompting them with basic questions regarding the challenges from last week (e.g.,"Did anyone choose the first challenge?").

Step 3 **Opening Prayer** (3 minutes)

Lead the class in the "Opening Prayer," which is included in the Student Workbook. Leader's Guide notes are provided above: Red text provides direction and guidance, and white text is for you to read aloud to the class.

116 | CHOSEN

Dive In:
Horvath's Violin

When the aging farmer discovered an unexpected gift under the roof space of his family's ancient farmhouse, he had no idea that his life was about to change. Sixty-eight-year-old Imre Horvath had spent his entire life scratching out an existence by selling poultry and eggs as a chicken farmer on the farm his father had built.

When Imre was young, his father, Zoltan, was called off to war. His father never returned, and the priceless gift he had hidden in the attic of the family farm lay, undiscovered, for decades. When at last Imre uncovered his father's violin, he knew it was a beautiful instrument. But when he took it to the city to have the violin appraised, Imre received astounding news: The violin was a Stradivarius!

Stradivarius violins are among the most highly valued in the world. Antonio Stradivari (1644–1737) is believed to have crafted about 1,100 instruments; only about 650 survive. A Stradivarius can sell at auction for up to $16 million. All those years, Imre had an AMAZING gift that could have changed his life … but he never "cashed in" on it or used it. He simply didn't know it was there.

That's us with the Holy Spirit!

The Holy Spirit is called "the gift of God" because he lavishly pours out his gifts on us! The gifts you've been given in Baptism, which will be strengthened in you in Confirmation, *probably* won't make you a millionaire, but they are valuable currency in the kingdom of God.

The Holy Spirit comes to give us everything we need to become the people he made us to be and to fulfill the mission he has called us to accomplish in this world.

Are you cooperating with those gifts? Are you asking for them? Are you cashing in?

> *"Here lies the difference between those who are good Christians but remain until death in mediocrity and those who strive for, and reach, sanctity. It is up to us! And, strange as it may seem, when God sees we appreciate the grace we have by using it, he gives us more."*
>
> *– Servant of God,*
> *Fr. John A. Hardon, S.J.*

Step 4 **Dive In** (5 minutes)

Read this story aloud, have a candidate read it aloud, or have the class read it silently before watching the video segments. This thought-provoking story ties in to the lesson's topic and serves to set up the video presentation.

Watch It!

Segment 1: Gifts of the Spirit (Part 1)

1. Which gift of the Holy Spirit helps us put "first things first and second things second" (that is, love of God first, love of neighbor second, and fitting in the other details of life with those two priorities in mind)? **Wisdom**

2. **T** or F? The gift of counsel is also called "right judgment." It helps us to choose to do what's right.

3. What was wrong with Chris' jacket?
   A) missing a button   C) wrinkled collar
   B) torn sleeve   D) hole in elbow

Segment 2: Gifts of the Spirit (Part 2)

1. Three gifts are oriented toward the will, to help us to love God. They are fortitude, fear of the Lord, and **piety**.

2. **T** or F? The gift of fortitude is also called "courage."

3. Fear of the Lord is the beginning of all _____.
   A) understanding   B) wisdom   C) piety   D) fortitude

Segment 3: The 12 Fruits of the Holy Spirit

1. The Fruits of the Holy Spirit flow from the **Gifts** of the Holy Spirit.

2. Which of the following is NOT a fruit of the Holy Spirit?
   A) Joy   B) Kindness   C) Judgment   D) Self-control

Small-Group Discussion

Segment 1: Gifts of the Spirit (Part 1)

1. What was the most exciting gift you ever received?

2. What was the most *helpful* gift you ever received? How was it helpful to you?

Segment 2: Gifts of the Spirit (Part 2)

1. What are the seven Isaiahan Gifts of the Holy Spirit,[1] and what are some examples of how they help us in our daily lives?

2. What are some of the gifts you see play out in your life, and how can you make better use of them?

Segment 3: The 12 Fruits of the Holy Spirit

1. Name the charismatic Gifts of the Holy Spirit.[2] Which of these gifts would you most like to have, and why?

2. Name the twelve Fruits of the Holy Spirit.[3] Give some examples of how they play out in everyday life.

3. Have you selected a Confirmation saint name? How did that saint show the fruits, gifts, and charisms of the Holy Spirit in his or her life?

Step 5

Watch It!/Small-Group Discussion (50 minutes)

On the video, click on Lesson 13, Segment 1. When Segment 1 ends, have students fill in the "Watch It!" questions (2 to 3 minutes). Run through them to be sure they wrote the correct answers so they will have them to prepare for the next "Review Game."

Next, lead students in a small-group discussion for Segment 1. You may begin by asking general questions like: "What part of the video spoke to you the most?" Discussion questions for each segment are provided in the blue box above.

Follow the same steps for Segments 2 and 3. (Allow for about 10 minutes of discussion time after each segment.)

Small-Group Discussion Leader's Notes

1. See Isaiah 11:2-3.
2. See 1 Corinthians 12:4-11.
3. See Galatians 5:22-23; CCC 1832.

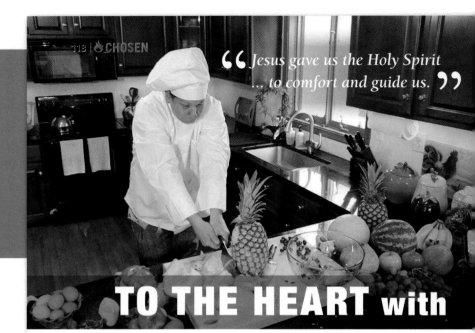

Question:

The Gifts of the Holy Spirit are a reflection of God's love for us, and we need them more than we can possibly know. What gift would you most like to focus on exercising? What gift do you think is *least* common or least used by people?

"*Jesus gave us the Holy Spirit ... to comfort and guide us.*"

TO THE HEART with

When I was a young child, my mother taught me my very first Bible verse:

The Lord is my light and my salvation; whom shall I fear? The Lord is the stronghold of my life; of whom shall I be afraid? (Psalm 27:1)

Knowing that the Lord was with me and that I needn't worry became a great consolation for me as I grew older, my parents were divorced, and I began to struggle to find my way in life. I grew up hearing songs and stories from Scripture about Jesus and God the Father. I was encouraged to value and foster a personal relationship with Jesus.

It wasn't until my mother started taking me to a charismatic Protestant church that I recall hearing about the "Holy Spirit." I have unique memories of that church: people falling down and raising their hands in prayer and praise. More than anything, I wanted the Holy Spirit to pour over me and make me speak in tongues like I'd seen so many others do. I begged the Lord to give me that gift.

But he never did. Not once. Those around me cried and called out, as though they were connected directly to heaven. But I felt ... nothing. *Why not me, Lord? Am I unworthy of the Spirit's gifts?* I didn't understand.

It wasn't until I became Catholic that I *did* begin to understand it ... or more precisely, began to understand *him*: the *person* of the Holy Spirit. As I searched the Scriptures and learned of the actions of the Holy Spirit in the early Church, I realized that, just as the Spirit is not a dove or a flame of fire, the Holy Spirit is also not a *feeling*.

Step 6 — To the Heart (10 minutes)

After the small-group discussions, read this story aloud, have a candidate read it aloud, or have the class read it silently. After the story (written by this week's video presenter), read the thought-provoking question(s) provided in the red "To the Heart" box above. Time permitting, ask follow-up questions and encourage discussion.

Lesson 13 | 119

Jesus gave us the Holy Spirit, the third Person of the Trinity, to comfort and guide us. The Spirit reminded the early apostles of all that Jesus had said and done, so that we could have a consistent picture of Christ. The Spirit enabled the early Church to endure great difficulties ... and this same Spirit is in our lives, helping us to grow in holiness.

At Baptism, the Holy Spirit gives each of us seven special gifts: wisdom, understanding, counsel, knowledge, piety, fortitude, and fear of the Lord. These gifts are strengthened at Confirmation, and, as we exercise them and grow in virtue, our lives begin to bear beautiful fruit: charity (love), joy, peace, patience, kindness, goodness, generosity, gentleness, faithfulness, modesty, self-control, and CHASTITY. In this way, we show that we are truly "children of God," shining the love of our Father into a dark and lonely world. Jesus gave us the Holy Spirit, the Comforter, so we'd truly have no reason to fear.

In time, I came to understand that I already *had* all the gifts the Holy Spirit wanted to give me. He hadn't held anything back. I had everything I needed to do the things God wanted me to do. All I had to do was ask!

Chris Padgett

Find It!

Where in the Bible do we find the outpouring of the Holy Spirit at Pentecost?

Acts 2

120 | CHOSEN

Hero of the Week

Born:
August 28, 1774

Died:
January 4, 1821

Memorial:
January 4

Patron Saint of:
• orphans
• grieving parents
• widows

St. Elizabeth Ann Seton

Elizabeth was raised in a home of wealth and privilege in New York, but it wasn't long before she experienced great losses in her life.

Her mother died when she was only three years old. Her stepmother, whom Elizabeth adored, taught her social responsibility and to tend to the needs of the poor and sick.

Elizabeth later married a prominent young businessman, William Seton. When William's father died unexpectedly, he and Elizabeth helped to raise William's younger siblings. Then William's business went bankrupt, and he contracted tuberculosis. They moved to Italy, where they hoped the climate would improve William's health—but when the ship docked in Europe, they were placed in quarantine, worsening his condition. A short time later, Elizabeth was widowed, and she and her four children became completely dependent on the kindness of strangers—her husband's business partners in Italy, Antonio and Filippo Filicchi.

In the midst of these horrific losses, Elizabeth experienced amazing grace. Five months after she returned to America, she converted to the Catholic faith—in no small part due to the kindness of her Italian friends, who reached out to her family when they needed help most. Elizabeth's conversion represented no small challenge or sacrifice. At a time when she needed the support of family and friends most, she was criticized and rejected for her newfound faith. And yet, she once again took up the task she believed God was calling her to do.

Years later, Elizabeth took up a second calling as a religious and founded the Sisters of Charity. Mother Seton established the first free Catholic school for girls in Baltimore. The order she founded has expanded to include work for the poor in hospitals, schools, and charitable institutions.

Elizabeth became the first American-born saint to be canonized. In his homily for the canonization of St. Elizabeth Ann Seton, Pope Paul VI gave a great definition of a saint: "A saint is a human creature fully conformed to the will of God." While the stories of other saints are full of drama and bloodshed, Elizabeth's story is different. There is no over-the-top drama, no "special effects." Her obedience did not make her life easier—just the opposite, in fact. And yet, in Elizabeth, we see a wonderful example of what happens when the Holy Spirit is unleashed in a heart fully open to receiving his transforming grace.

St. Elizabeth Ann Seton, pray for us. Help us to open our hearts to the Holy Spirit.

Step 7

Hero of the Week (5 minutes)

This saint story will help to highlight and reinforce this lesson's topic. You may choose to read it aloud, have a candidate read it aloud, or have the class read it silently.

Lesson 13 | 121

Challenge of the Week

 Give a gift. This week, do a favor, buy a present, create something artistic for someone, or help someone do some work. Watch for signs that your gift has strengthened, encouraged, or inspired the other person. Write what you did in the space below, and be ready to talk about it next week.

Do some weight lifting. First, measure your biceps with a measuring tape. Write the measurement below. Then, select light weights and curl them until your muscles burn. Rest for a count of fifteen and repeat. Now measure again. Did the number change? Reflect on how using your gifts makes them expand and grow stronger.

Read Isaiah 11:1-9. The Holy Spirit frequently predicted the coming of the Messiah through the prophets of the Old Testament. Read this passage slowly and carefully, and think about how it applies to Christ. As followers of Jesus, how can we put these Gifts of the Spirit to better use in our own lives?

_____

_____

_____

_____

_____

_____

_____

Closing Prayer

"And the Spirit of the Lord shall rest upon him, the spirit of wisdom and understanding, the spirit of counsel and might, the spirit of knowledge and the fear of the Lord."

—*Isaiah 11:2*

Lord, you don't just demand holiness from us; you offer us spiritual treasures that help us get there. It's a great mystery to us that you delight in such weak creatures, pouring your graces out on us whenever we approach you in humility. Your life-changing gifts are there for the asking. Give us the grace to ask, so that we may receive. Amen.

 Step 8 **Challenge of the Week** (2 minutes)

Ask your candidates to read the "challenges" above and choose one of the three to complete this week. Have them check the box next to the challenge they intend to complete. Encourage them to write about their experiences in the space provided.

Step 9 **Homework Instructions and Updates** (2 minutes)

Remind candidates to read the "Wrap-Up" and the "What's That Word?" sections in the "Taking It Home" section of the Student Workbook. They should also review the "Watch It!" questions to prepare for the next "Review Game."

Step 10 **Closing Prayer** (3 minutes)

As a way of building up community, ask if there are any prayer intentions. Write them down (or have candidates share them aloud) and after praying for those intentions, have the class read the "Closing Prayer" together (provided in the Student Workbook).

Taking It Home

For next week's "Review Game," be sure to read over the following ...

1. **Watch It!** questions (page 117)
2. **Wrap-Up**
3. **"What's That Word?"**
4. **Memory Verse**

Don't forget to do your **Challenge of the Week** (page 121)

Wrap-Up

In the last chapter, we talked about who the Holy Spirit is and how he has worked throughout salvation history—up to the present day—in the life of the Church. We explained that the Holy Spirit guides both the Church and individuals within the Body of Christ, if they are willing to live their lives according to God's revealed will.

To help us understand and follow God's plan for our lives, the Holy Spirit gives us certain gifts. These "Gifts of the Holy Spirit," outlined in the book of Isaiah, are: wisdom, understanding, knowledge, counsel, piety, fortitude (or courage), and fear of the Lord.[1] These supernatural gifts complete and perfect the natural virtues to produce the FRUITS OF THE HOLY SPIRIT: chastity, modesty, and generosity, as well as "love [charity], joy, peace, patience, kindness, goodness, faithfulness, gentleness, self-control" (Galatians 5:22-23). These fruits help us grow in personal holiness.

In addition, the Holy Spirit grants, "charismatic" gifts to be used in service of the Church. While you can't grow in holiness without the Gifts of the Holy Spirit found in Isaiah 11:2-3, you can't spread the Gospel without the charismatic gifts.[2]

Some charismatic gifts are extraordinary, such as the gift of "speaking in tongues" (the ability to speak a foreign language one has never studied), prophecy, or healing. Other, more common, gifts include the gifts of counsel, preaching, and teaching. A list of gifts is found in 1 Corinthians 12:4-11.*

---

* If God does give you a more extraordinary charismatic gift to serve the Church, it would be wise to speak to a priest about it. In 1 John 4:1, we are encouraged to "test the spirits to see whether they are of God."

[1] Is 11:2-3; CCC 1831

[2] CCC 799, 951

"What's That Word?"

CHARISMS, CHARISMATIC GIFTS

The word *charism*, from a Greek word that means "gift," is found in several places in Scripture, including 1 Corinthians 12, Romans 12:5-8, and Ephesians 4.[3] CHARISMS are specific gifts given by the Holy Spirit to certain individuals to serve the Church in a particular way. Different people receive different *charisms*, depending on their role in the Church. In addition to "charismatic" gifts, such as gifts of healing, gifts of prophecy, and gifts of tongues, God grants some people special charisms of administration, teaching, or hospitality to serve the needs of the local Church.

FRUITS OF THE HOLY SPIRIT

In his letter to the Galatians, St. Paul speaks of the *"fruit of the Spirit."* These "fruits," the defining qualities of all Christians, are charity (love), joy, peace, patience, kindness, goodness, generosity, gentleness, faithfulness, modesty, self-control, and chastity.[4] As these fruits ripen and mature, their "sweetness" can often draw others into a relationship with the Lord and into the Church— and they are an important way for us to track the progress of our own spiritual growth.[5]

GIFTS OF THE HOLY SPIRIT

The seven *Gifts of the Holy Spirit* are listed in Isaiah 11:2-3: wisdom, understanding, knowledge, counsel, piety, fortitude, and fear of the Lord.[6] This Scripture passage is a prophecy describing the Messiah that the people of God were hoping would come to deliver them. These same gifts are also given to all of us who are baptized, and they remain in us as long as we remain in a state of grace. The Gifts of the Spirit make it possible for us to live and act as the Holy Spirit leads us.

[3] CCC 2003

[4] Gal 5:22-23

[5] CCC 1829

[6] Is 11:1-3; CCC 1831

Memory Verse:

"But the fruit of the Spirit is love, joy, peace, patience, kindness, goodness, faithfulness, gentleness, self-control; against such there is no law."

– Galatians 5:22-23

124 | CHOSEN

Did You Know?

Because she was willing to die, St. Thecla is considered a martyr even though the various attempts to execute her (for her faith and for refusing to marry)—by burning, wild animals, and, finally, poisonous snakes—were thwarted by miracles.

Any questions

How can I grow in the Gifts of the Holy Spirit?

Simply following God every day makes your heart more and more open to these special strengths from the Holy Spirit. You follow God by engaging in daily prayer and Scripture reading; attending Mass and receiving the Eucharist whenever possible; making yearly retreats; getting involved with your parish; joining a good Catholic youth group; making regular confessions; and serving others.

The Sacrament of Confirmation will increase these gifts in your soul in a special way. But if there is a specific gift you need to develop to become the person you're meant to be, just ask the Holy Spirit for it!

Holy Trinity - 3 coeternal Consubstantial persons
He is the comforter and helper sent to the apostles.
7 Gifts of the Holy spirit

The Gift of Wisdom the ability to
Isaiah 11:2-3   Value spiritual things over worldly ones.

Understanding helps us grasp the
truths of the faith more easily and
                                  profoundly.

Piety is our obedience and
reverence to God. our willingness to serve him

Fear of God we dread
sin and fear offending God. We fear losing our
connection.

Knowledge is awareness of
God's Plan of God's purpose, and how we ought to respond.

Counsel
acknowledge the difference between right and
wrong and bestows proper judgement. Helps
avoid sin.

Fortitude sustains our
decision to follow the will of God in any situation.
Stand up and defend our faith.

Pentecost   beginning of the Church.

✗ Rite of Confirmation anointing by the
                          Holy Spirit
into the Soul of every baptized Christian
it is the final Sacrament of initiation into the
Catholic Church. Performed by a Bishop or priest

Lesson 14
Leader's Notes

Overview

The purpose of this lesson is to help prepare students to receive the Sacrament of Confirmation and to see it not as the "end" of their spiritual formation, but as a powerful outpouring of the Holy Spirit. The goal is that they may "share more completely in the mission of Jesus Christ and the fullness of the Holy Spirit with which he is filled, so that their lives may give off 'the aroma of Christ'" (CCC 1294).

The Rite of Confirmation is explained, and candidates are reminded to prepare seriously for the sacrament. In the words of the *Catechism,* "Preparation for Confirmation should aim at leading the Christian toward a more intimate union with Christ and a more lively familiarity with the Holy Spirit—his actions, his gifts, and his biddings—in order to be more capable of assuming the apostolic responsibilities of Christian life. To this end, catechesis for Confirmation should strive to awaken a sense of belonging to the Church of Jesus Christ, the universal Church as well as the parish community" (CCC 1309).

Objectives of this Lesson

1. *What, exactly, is the Sacrament of Confirmation, and what does God do for us through this sacrament?* Confirmation perfects the grace of Baptism, empowering us to be followers of the Lord and co-workers for the kingdom (see CCC 1316).

2. *Throughout Scripture, the anointing of the Spirit "launches" the believer into a task God appointed him or her to do.* Confirmation is not intended to be the "end" of our Catholic journey, but a new beginning. The more we use the Gifts of the Holy Spirit, the stronger we become in them (see 2 Timothy 1:6-7).

3. *Confirmation is not "optional."* It is a necessary completion of baptismal grace (see CCC 1285).

4. *Confirmation indicates that a person has reached a level of spiritual maturity* that has little to do with chronological "age" (see CCC 1308). We need to take the preparation seriously.

"Why have I been Chosen?"

(Sealed and Sent in Confirmation)

✝

Opening Prayer

"All-powerful God, Father of our Lord Jesus Christ,
by water and the Holy Spirit
you freed your sons and daughters from sin
and gave them new life.
Send your Holy Spirit upon them
to be their helper and guide.
Give them the spirit of wisdom and understanding,
the spirit of right judgment and courage,
the spirit of knowledge and reverence.
Fill them with the spirit of wonder and awe in your presence.
We ask this through Christ our Lord. Amen."[1]

Opening Prayer

Read this prayer very slowly, allowing time for each phrase to sink in.

Today we are going to talk about the Sacrament of Confirmation. To begin the class, we are going to recite one of the prayers the bishop will say when you are confirmed. As you listen to the words, pick one line that "jumps out at you" to reflect upon a bit more.

At your Confirmation, the bishop will pray …

[1] CCC 1299

Step 1 Welcome/Review Game (5 minutes)

Begin by welcoming the class and telling them that you will be starting with a review of the previous lesson's material. On the DVD menu, click on Lesson 14; then on the sub-menu, click on "Review Game."

Have students answer the questions based on the previous lesson. For more information about how to adapt this game to meet the needs of your group, see the "Review Game" section in the Introduction to this Leader's Guide (page xvi).

Step 2 Challenge of the Week Review (5 minutes)

Ask if anyone would like to share a "challenge experience" from the previous week. Try to draw students out by prompting them with basic questions regarding the challenges from last week (e.g., "Did anyone choose the first challenge?").

Step 3 Opening Prayer (3 minutes)

Lead the class in the "Opening Prayer," which is included in the Student Workbook. Leader's Guide notes are provided above: Red text provides direction and guidance, and white text is for you to read aloud to the class.

126 | CHOSEN

Dive In:
Arise!

When I was in high school, I remember attending a retreat with a "troubled teen" from the Bronx (I grew up a thirty-minute drive from there) who had been forced to go along. He goofed off and caused problems all weekend. Even Eucharistic Adoration on Saturday night was a huge joke to him.

He knelt down with his head buried on the floor, talking to the kid next to him the whole time. Out of all the teens there, he seemed the least likely to be impacted by the retreat experience. But when the priest passed by him in procession, holding the monstrance, he suddenly broke down in tears and decided at that moment to turn his life around.

Late that night, a chaperone noticed that the young man's bed was empty. After searching the building, the chaperone finally found him in the last place anyone would have expected—with his arms outstretched and deep in prayer before the tabernacle.

For all the physical miracles we read about in Scripture and Church history, the greatest of miracles occurs when a soul changes! Jesus said as much when he asked, "Which is easier, to say to the paralytic, 'Your sins are forgiven,' or to say, 'Rise, pick up your mat and walk'?" (Mark 2:9, NAB).

As impossible as it would be for people to raise themselves from the dead or to heal themselves from disease, it's even less possible for people to forgive their own sins or to give themselves new spiritual life. That's the miracle God works in us through the sacraments. It's the miracle God wants to continue working in your life through the Sacrament of Confirmation. He isn't calling you to an ordinary life, but to life "to the full."[2] And he's ready to give it to you.

2 Jn 10:10, NIV

"Breathe in me, O Holy Spirit, that my thoughts may all be holy.

Act in me, O Holy Spirit, that my work, too, may be holy.

Draw my heart, O Holy Spirit, that I love but what is holy.

Strengthen me, O Holy Spirit, to defend all that is holy.

Guard me, then, O Holy Spirit, that I always may be holy. Amen."

—St. Augustine

 Step 4 **Dive In** (5 minutes)

Read this story aloud, have a candidate read it aloud, or have the class read it silently before watching the video segments. This thought-provoking story ties in to the lesson's topic and serves to set up the video presentation.

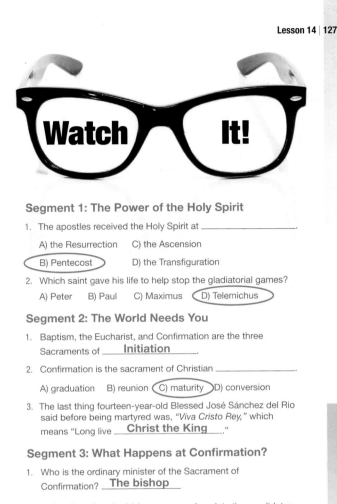

Lesson 14 | 127

Segment 1: The Power of the Holy Spirit

1. The apostles received the Holy Spirit at _____.

    A) the Resurrection   C) the Ascension

    B) Pentecost   D) the Transfiguration

2. Which saint gave his life to help stop the gladiatorial games?

    A) Peter   B) Paul   C) Maximus   D) Telemichus

Segment 2: The World Needs You

1. Baptism, the Eucharist, and Confirmation are the three Sacraments of **Initiation**.

2. Confirmation is the sacrament of Christian _____.

    A) graduation   B) reunion   C) maturity   D) conversion

3. The last thing fourteen-year-old Blessed José Sánchez del Rio said before being martyred was, *"Viva Cristo Rey,"* which means "Long live **Christ the King**."

Segment 3: What Happens at Confirmation?

1. Who is the ordinary minister of the Sacrament of Confirmation? **The bishop**

2. At Confirmation, the bishop prays and anoints the candidates with **oil or sacred chrism***

3. At Confirmation, the bishop will pray: "Be _____ with the Gift of the Holy Spirit."

    A) worthy   B) blessed   C) anointed   D) sealed

***The same oil used at Baptism**

Small-Group Discussion

Segment 1: The Power of the Holy Spirit

1. Confirmation "gives us a special strength of the Holy Spirit to spread and defend the faith by word and action" (CCC 1303) and has traditionally been associated with becoming a soldier for Christ.[1] What does it mean to be a soldier for Christ?[2]

2. Where do you see a spiritual battle going on in the world, and what is your role in it?

Segment 2: The World Needs You

1. What does the Sacrament of Confirmation do for you?[3]

2. Confirmation is "the sacrament of Christian maturity."[4] What does it mean to be spiritually mature?

Segment 3: What Happens at Confirmation?

1. What are the symbols used in the Sacrament of Confirmation, and what do they mean?[5]

2. Why do you want to be confirmed? Why do you think you are ready?

Step 5

Watch It!/Small-Group Discussion (50 minutes)

On the video, click on Lesson 14, Segment 1. When Segment 1 ends, have students fill in the "Watch It!" questions (2 to 3 minutes). Run through them to be sure they wrote the correct answers so they will have them to prepare for the next "Review Game."

Next, lead students in a small-group discussion for Segment 1. You may begin by asking general questions like: "What part of the video spoke to you the most?" Discussion questions for each segment are provided in the blue box above.

Follow the same steps for Segments 2 and 3. (Allow for about 10 minutes of discussion time after each segment.)

Small-Group Discussion Leader's Notes

1. This language is used in the Catechism of Pope St. Pius X and is also reflected in the *Baltimore Catechism*, both of which are likely making reference to 2 Timothy 2:3.

2. To be willing to resist evil, defend what is true and good, and to even endure hardship out of love for God.

3. See the "Objectives."

4. CCC 1308.

5. Holy oil, for cleansing and strengthening; the laying on of hands, conferring new status and preparing for battle; the prayer of the bishop, the sign of blessing and gift of the Holy Spirit (see CCC 1294–1299).

128 | CHOSEN

Question:

Have you ever thought God was asking you to do something requiring a level of courage that was just a bit outside your "comfort zone"? Have you ever hesitated to do the "right" thing because people around you might not understand? Share about it.

TO THE HEART with

Eleven years ago my wife and I sat at the edge of the baptismal font with our hands on Ryan's back, along with the priest's. Three dunks later, he was a child of God.

It had been no small journey. Ryan, like St. Augustine, was a philosopher. He was also an agnostic—he felt it wasn't possible to know whether God exists. Yet, despite his uncertainty and skepticism, he accepted our invitations to join us for Mass. Patiently, we answered his questions (which flowed like an endless stream), knowing all along that our dear friend might never become a brother in Christ.

One Holy Thursday, Ryan was listening to the Nicene Creed at Mass, and in that one brief moment, he allowed grace a small opening. "Do I believe that?" he asked himself. "And if not, what do I believe in?" His walls of resistance fell, one after another, as the Creed went on.

"Yes! I believe in God the Father almighty ..."

"Yes! I believe in the resurrection of the body! ..."

"Yes! I believe in the forgiveness of sin, too! Yes! I do believe!"

Soon, the holy waters rippled with his Baptism. Five years later, Ryan fell in love with a beautiful Buddhist Taiwanese woman, and she, too, converted to the faith. Recently, my wife and I became "grand-godparents" to Ryan and Elizabeth's baby, Ambrose, and I got to experience the "ripple effect" of faith. Our willingness to befriend and spend time talking about Jesus with that agnostic philosopher may end up impacting generations of people!

Step 6 — **To the Heart** (10 minutes)

After the small-group discussions, read this story aloud, have a candidate read it aloud, or have the class read it silently. After the story (written by this week's video presenter), read the thought-provoking question(s) provided in the red "To the Heart" box above. Time permitting, ask follow-up questions and encourage discussion.

The grace and gifts God gives each of us through Baptism and Confirmation are not intended only for our own benefit, but are given to help others, too. Some are called to help in extraordinary ways—but all of us are called to serve, often in ways that do not seem very important at the time.

The very first Christians had no slick websites, cool apps, or beautiful churches. They tried their best to follow Jesus, love the poor, and share the faith with a world that did not know Jesus. They lived every day by the grace of the Holy Spirit. They never could have guessed that by building small faith communities, they would set a chain of events in motion that, in two thousand years, would produce more than two billion Christians and build a civilization of love based on human dignity.

It's easy to get distracted and distressed about the problems in the world. As Christians, we need to engage the "culture war" on every front—starting with those closest to us. So, take your friends who don't know Jesus out for dinner; listen, love, and lead them to the One you are trying your best to follow. You never know what a difference you can make in the world through such simple acts of kindness.

Chris Stefanick

Find It!

This word actually means "witness," but is often used to describe those who willingly die rather than renounce their faith.

martyr

66 *... all of us are called to serve, often in ways that do not seem very important at the time.* 99

130 | CHOSEN

Hero of the Week

Born:
circa AD 5

Died:
circa AD 67

Memorial:
January 25

Patron Saint of:
- missions
- theologians

St. Paul the Apostle

Before the Second Vatican Council, it was customary for a bishop to give a very gentle "slap" to those being confirmed after they had received the sacrament.

It was intended to be a symbolic gesture to remind the person being confirmed of the adversity they would face living an authentic Christian life. While this is no longer done, the fact remains that God gives us his grace because he expects us to shine like lights in a dark world. And he doesn't call us to do his work because we are equipped to do it. Rather, he equips us with his grace *because we are called*. For example, St. Paul claims that he was the worst[3] of sinners, yet God used him to write most of the New Testament!

Prior to his conversion, the Apostle Paul (then named Saul) followed the laws of Judaism strictly, seeking (out of a misguided zeal) to stop people from believing Jesus was the Messiah. He went so far as to hunt down Christians to have them jailed and executed! In fact, Saul witnessed the stoning of St. Stephen.[4] Then, on the road to Damascus, he encountered a blinding light that flashed around him. He fell to the ground and heard the voice of Christ ask him, "Saul, Saul, why do you persecute me?" (Acts 9:4).

It was a total game-changer. And a name-changer as well: "Saul of Tarsus" was no more. He became the Apostle Paul, one of the most important leaders of the early Church. His epistles provide a snapshot of the growth of the Church,

but also give us an indication of how active and involved he was in the region. He became a missionary to the Gentiles throughout the Mediterranean and Asia Minor, moving from community to community, not only founding churches, but acting as a spiritual father and tending to a growing flock.

St. Paul's conversion was total conversion; his ardor and commitment came from his direct encounter with Christ. And yet, St. Paul's ministry was not without some controversy. He also preached in Jewish synagogues, sharing the Good News that Jesus was the Messiah. In doing so, he became the target of the kind of persecution he had previously led against Christians.

St. Paul was imprisoned twice, beaten repeatedly, persecuted, and finally beheaded in Rome during a persecution of Christians carried out under the emperor Nero. He said to his spiritual son, Timothy, "I have fought the good fight, I have finished the race, I have kept the faith" (2 Timothy 4:7). Few have influenced the Church or the world as much as St. Paul. He was far from perfect, but he opened his heart to the grace of God and became a light to the world!

St. Paul, pray for us. Help us live our faith with conviction in every circumstance of our lives.

---

[4] Acts 7

Step 7

Hero of the Week (5 minutes)

This saint story will help to highlight and reinforce this lesson's topic. You may choose to read it aloud, have a candidate read it aloud, or have the class read it silently.

Challenge of the Week

Lesson 14 | 131

☐ **Find a prayer written to or composed by your Confirmation saint.** Write it in the space below and pray it every day this week, with the intention of preparing yourself to be sealed with the gift of the Holy Spirit.

☐ **Browse your parish's website or bulletin and check out the list of active ministries.** Contact a ministry leader and ask about the work he or she does. Write about it in the space below, and talk about it in class next week.

☐ **Start a Facebook group page with at least one other Confirmation student** (from any Catholic parish, and with your parents' permission). Write brief posts about anything you are learning in class and outside of class that is helping you to think about and prepare for Confirmation. Invite your instructor and classmates to subscribe and comment.

_____

_____

_____

_____

_____

_____

_____

_____

✝ Closing Prayer

"Let no one despise your youth, but set the believers an example in speech and conduct, in love, in faith, in purity."

—*1 Timothy 4:12*

Lord Jesus, in your great mercy and kindness, you call us to lives of great heroism, purity, and peace.

Through the Sacrament of Confirmation, you offer us everything we need to find our true path in this life and to walk it boldly.

Thank you for the gifts you offer us. Help us to open those gifts and use them, to exercise them like spiritual muscles, and to become everything you have made us to be. Amen.

 Step 8 **Challenge of the Week** (2 minutes)

Ask your candidates to read the "challenges" above and choose one of the three to complete this week. Have them check the box next to the challenge they intend to complete. Encourage them to write about their experiences in the space provided.

Step 9 **Homework Instructions and Updates** (2 minutes)

Remind candidates to read the "Wrap-Up" and the "What's That Word?" sections in the "Taking It Home" section of the Student Workbook. They should also review the "Watch It!" questions to prepare for the next "Review Game."

 Step 10 **Closing Prayer** (3 minutes)

As a way of building up community, ask if there are any prayer intentions. Write them down (or have candidates share them aloud) and after praying for those intentions, have the class read the "Closing Prayer" together (provided in the Student Workbook).

Taking It Home

132 | **CHOSEN**

For next week's "Review Game,"
be sure to read over the following ...

1. **Watch It!** questions (page 127)
2. **Wrap-Up**
3. **"What's That Word?"**
4. **Memory Verse**

Don't forget to do your
Challenge of the Week (page 131)

Wrap-Up

Every summer, thousands of high-school graduates gear up for the next great adventure of their lives: college. For many, it's their first taste of "grown-up life," managing their own time, doing their own laundry, and paying their own bills.

For high-school graduation, some parents give their future college students things they will need to live life on their own: a laptop, a laundry basket, a microwave, and other things to help them set up a dorm room. These gifts are intended to help them transition to adulthood successfully. Over the years, your parents will have given you many gifts to mark the milestones of your life; as you launch out on your own, it's up to you to make the best use of those gifts.

For the past two lessons, we've been talking about the Holy Spirit and the gifts he gives us to help us grow in holiness and in our ability to serve the Church. In this lesson, we looked specifically at the Sacrament of Confirmation as a

rite of passage, preparing young Catholic men and women to become active members of the Body of Christ. Like any good parent, the Holy Spirit gives you everything you will need to succeed in this journey—it's up to you to make the best use of the gifts you have been given.

In Confirmation, the Holy Spirit comes to us in a radical way to strengthen us (*Confirmation* means "strengthening"); to increase and deepen the grace of our Baptism; and to make us soldiers for Christ. Confirmation equips us to spread and defend the faith by word and deed, as witnesses of Jesus.[5]

Some people overlook the importance of Confirmation, but the things of God are not to be taken lightly. When we get to heaven, we will see the crucial role our Confirmation played in bringing us, as well as others, to eternal peace and happiness with God.

5 Acts 8:14-19, 19:1-6; CCC 1285, 1316

"What's That Word?"

ANOINTING

Anointing was used for many purposes in the Bible and ancient culture. People and objects that were being set apart for a special or holy purpose were *anointed* by having oil poured on them. At Confirmation, Christians are anointed, or marked, with a special kind of oil (sacred chrism) that shows they are being set apart to continue the work of Jesus by helping to bring salvation to the world. Though the fragrant oil of anointing will eventually wear off, the anointing in the Sacrament of Confirmation has a sacramental character that leaves a permanent (or "indelible") spiritual mark or SEAL.

"This anointing highlights the name 'Christian,' which means 'anointed' and derives from that of Christ himself whom God 'anointed with the Holy Spirit.' ... For this reason the Eastern Churches call this sacrament *Chrismation*, anointing with chrism" (CCC 1289).

CONFIRMATION

Confirmation is a Sacrament of Initiation, along with Baptism and the Eucharist. "In the first centuries Confirmation generally comprised one single celebration with Baptism, forming with it a 'double sacrament,' according to the expression of St. Cyprian. ... The East has kept them united, so that

Confirmation is conferred by the priest who baptizes" (CCC 1290). Today, the Roman Rite uses the "age of discretion" as the reference point for the sacrament, and it is celebrated at different ages and times of the year in various dioceses. (See CCC 1306-1308.)

Confirmation completes the Sacrament of Baptism in which the confirmed receive an outpouring of the Gifts of the Holy Spirit. As with Baptism, in Confirmation, a person's soul is given an indelible mark (or *character*) that enables him or her to spread and defend the faith.

Through Confirmation, a candidate is appointed for a position in the Church and strengthened to fill that position. Unlike the other Sacraments of Initiation, the ordinary minister of Confirmation is the bishop, a successor of the apostles. He represents the Church in the appointment and strengthening of those who will take part in the work of the apostles, being witnesses of Jesus Christ and making disciples. The strengthening of Confirmation is primarily the work of the Holy Spirit. This sacrament also deepens a candidate's union with Jesus Christ.

Those preparing to receive Confirmation must take their preparation seriously. They should study

Memory Verse:

"But you shall receive power when the Holy Spirit has come upon you; and you shall be my witnesses in Jerusalem and in all Judea and Samaria and to the end of the earth."

—Acts 1:8

and pray for an openness to the Holy Spirit. Candidates should also be encouraged to celebrate the Sacrament of Reconciliation and seek the spiritual help of their sponsor, who will offer support and guidance throughout the time of preparation. (See CCC 1309-1311.)

SEAL

Ranch owners permanently mark their cattle with a branding iron to identify them as their property. In a similar way, at Confirmation, we are marked as Christ's with the *seal* of the Holy Spirit and are committed by this seal to serve him always. Just as a tattoo can strike fear into enemies of the gang who recognize the mark as a sign that the person is protected by powerful friends, so also can the *seal* of the Holy Spirit protect the Christian in spiritual battles against God's enemies—"the spiritual hosts of wickedness in the heavenly places" (Ephesians 6:12).

God the Father "set his seal" on his Son Jesus, and he "seals us" in him. This seal indicates the anointing of the Holy Spirit in the Sacraments of Baptism, Confirmation, and Holy Orders, which imprints an "indelible character" (or "mark") on the soul (see CCC 698). Because this seal is permanent, Confirmation, like Baptism and Holy Orders, can only be received once and cannot be "undone." We must strive never to betray or bring scandal to the seal that permanently marks us as servants of Christ.

[6] CCC 1313, 1314

[7] CCC 1297–1301

[8] 2 Cor 1:21-22; CCC 1303

Did You Know?

When the "Miracle of the Sun" occurred at Fatima, Portugal, in 1917, more than 70,000 witnesses reported the same story. A number of these witnesses were scholars, scientists, and unbelievers.

Any questions?

What exactly happens at Confirmation?

The bishop usually confers the sacrament, though priests can receive permission to do so in special circumstances.[6] "In the Latin rite, 'the sacrament of Confirmation is conferred through the anointing with chrism on the forehead, which is done by the laying on of the hand, and through the words: *"Accipe signaculum doni Spiritus Sancti"* [Be sealed with the Gift of the Holy Spirit]'" (CCC 1300).[7]

One of the reasons oil is used is because it is a symbol of strength. In ancient times, athletes used oil to limber up their muscles to prepare for the contest. In spiritual terms, we are being prepared for the spiritual contest ahead of us. *Christ* means "anointed one." In union with Jesus, the Sacrament of Confirmation makes us anointed ones as well!

And what are we anointed for? In this sacrament, we are given the grace of the Holy Spirit to live and profess our faith more boldly. Confirmation also strengthens the graces and gifts we received at Baptism, allowing us to fulfill our responsibility for stewardship and become the people God calls us to be.[8] The grace in Confirmation is "tailor made" for this next stage in our life of faith.

Notes

**Lesson 15
Leader's Notes**

Overview

The purpose of this lesson is to lead your students to understand the beauty and richness of the Mass and to see it as our "front row seat" in the most important event in human history. As Catholics, we are also morally obligated to attend Mass on Sundays and on holy days of obligation.[8]

The *Catechism* tells us that the liturgical celebration has remained substantially the same since the second century (see CCC 1345), and that together the Liturgy of the Word and Liturgy of the Eucharist form a "single act of worship"[9] that is reflected "on earth as it is in heaven" (CCC 1370). In a most special way, it is through this sacrament that Jesus fulfilled his promise: "I am with you always ..." (Matthew 28:20).

Objectives of this Lesson

1. *Mass is not about "having fun" or being entertained.* Mass is a divine appointment with the Creator of the universe, to worship and thank him for all he has done for us. We do this, not because he needs it, but because *we* need to acknowledge God as our Father and our place in his family (see CCC 1324–1327).

2. *Receiving Jesus in the Eucharist is our greatest gift ... and most awesome privilege.* Catholics around the world have given their lives to be at Mass. What do they see that we are missing? (see CCC 1386, 1391–1392)

3. *Learn to live the Mass all week long.* We get the most out of Mass when we prepare for it ahead of time. This allows us to draw from the power and the presence of God given to us at the altar to "go" and be that which we receive: the Body of Christ in the world (see CCC 1385–1388).

"Why do I have to go to Mass?"

(Encountering Jesus in the Eucharist)

Lesson 15

Opening Prayer

"When the hour came, Jesus and his apostles reclined at the table. And he said to them, 'I have eagerly desired to eat this Passover with you before I suffer. For I tell you, I will not eat it again until it finds fulfillment in the kingdom of God.' After taking the cup, he gave thanks and said, 'Take this and divide it among you. For I tell you I will not drink again from the fruit of the vine until the kingdom of God comes.' And he took bread, gave thanks and broke it, and gave it to them, saying, 'This is my body given for you; do this in remembrance of me.' In the same way, after the supper he took the cup, saying, 'This cup is the new covenant in my blood, which is poured out for you.'"

—Luke 22:14-20, NIV

Opening Prayer

Since the Middle Ages, Christians have practiced *lectio divina,* a slow, prayerful reading of Scripture. Every time you read the Word of God, he gives you his grace.

Today we are going to place ourselves at the Last Supper. Picture the dimly lit room. Imagine the smells of bread and wine and the feel of the old wooden table in front of you. Then imagine looking into the eyes of Jesus as he says, "This is my body." He is looking right at you—fully aware that this is his last meal and that shortly after it, he will be taken away, tortured, and killed … for you.

> *Have the teens take a deep breath and be silent for about 10 seconds before you start reading Luke 22:14-20, NIV*
>
> *(Pause for 30 seconds)*

Now, in your own words, in the silence of your heart, thank him for the gift of his life.

 Step 1 **Welcome/Review Game** (5 minutes)

Begin by welcoming the class and telling them that you will be starting with a review of the previous lesson's material. On the DVD menu, click on Lesson 15; then on the sub-menu, click on "Review Game."

Have students answer the questions based on the previous lesson. For more information about how to adapt this game to meet the needs of your group, see the "Review Game" section in the Introduction to this Leader's Guide (page xvi).

 Step 2 **Challenge of the Week Review** (5 minutes)

Ask if anyone would like to share a "challenge experience" from the previous week. Try to draw students out by prompting them with basic questions regarding the challenges from last week (e.g.,"Did anyone choose the first challenge?").

 Step 3 **Opening Prayer** (3 minutes)

Lead the class in the "Opening Prayer," which is included in the Student Workbook. Leader's Guide notes are provided above: Red text provides direction and guidance, and white text is for you to read aloud to the class.

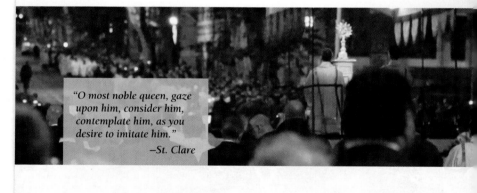

136 | CHOSEN

Dive In:
For Better, or for ... Bored?

Imagine you're sitting in math class and someone raises his or her hand to tell the teacher, "I'm bored." How would the teacher respond? "Oh, sorry, I wasn't aware that my job was to put on a *show* for you. Perhaps I should show up in a clown costume tomorrow to teach you about exponents!"

Not likely, right? There are some situations that aren't supposed to be entertaining ... and yet, the word "bored" doesn't really fit, either.

Imagine a man leaning back in his chair after dinner and saying to his wife, "Being married to you is getting boring. Entertain me."

I don't imagine that would end well.

Or think about what would happen if a man presented a woman with a ring and asked for her hand in marriage ... and she yawned in response. That would be *much* worse than a simple, "No, I won't marry you," right?

Now imagine someone being willing to die so that you might live. After the life-saving sacrifice was complete, imagine turning to your parents and saying, "I'm bored. Can we go home now?"

Crazy, huh? At every Mass, we remember Jesus' saving death for us and celebrate his Resurrection, a victory over death itself! At every Mass, he offers all of this to us. If you're thinking in terms of entertainment, you're missing the point. This week, we'll take a closer look at the miracle of the Mass.

"O most noble queen, gaze upon him, consider him, contemplate him, as you desire to imitate him."
—St. Clare

Step 4 **Dive In** (5 minutes)

Read this story aloud, have a candidate read it aloud, or have the class read it silently before watching the video segments. This thought-provoking story ties in to the lesson's topic and serves to set up the video presentation.

Lesson 15 | 137

Segment 1: What Happens at Mass?

1. When the gifts of bread and wine are consecrated, they become the ___**Body**___ and ___**Blood**___ of Christ.

2. The miracle that happens at the consecration of the bread and wine being changed into Christ's Body and Blood is called

   _____

   A) illumination   C) inauguration

   B) transubstantiation   D) *in persona Christi*

3. **T or F?** The Eucharist is the source and the summit of the Christian life.

Segment 2: Walter's Story

1. Like Walter, we are all called to remember Christ's words:

   "This is my ___**Body**___ … given up for you."

2. **T or F?** The ancient Jewish feast of Passover is a foreshadowing of the Mass.

Segment 3: Preparing for Mass

1. "Eucharist" is from a Greek word meaning _____.

   A) thanksgiving   B) sacrifice   C) bread   D) adoration

2. Anyone who commits serious (or mortal) sin must first go to ___**Confession**___ before receiving the Eucharist.

Small-Group Discussion

Segment 1: What Happens at Mass?

1. Do you think it is important to go to Mass every week? Why or why not?[1]

2. Can you describe what happens during the Eucharistic Prayers?[2]

3. Do you think that sometimes we "miss" the whole point of Mass and that is why so many people fail to make it a priority?

Segment 2: Walter's Story

1. Why would Jesus give himself to us in the Eucharist? What does he expect from us?

2. Besides the Eucharist, where else do we encounter God at the Mass?[3]

Segment 3: Preparing for Mass

1. What does it mean that we are invited to "full, conscious and active"[4] participation in the Mass? What can you do to come to Mass better prepared to pray and participate?

2. Adoration is one way to grow closer to Jesus and prepare our hearts to receive him at Mass. Have you ever been to Adoration? Describe your experience.[5]

Step 5 **Watch It!/Small-Group Discussion** (50 minutes)

On the video, click on Lesson 15, Segment 1. When Segment 1 ends, have students fill in the "Watch It!" questions (2 to 3 minutes). Run through them to be sure they wrote the correct answers so they will have them to prepare for the next "Review Game."

Next, lead students in a small-group discussion for Segment 1. You may begin by asking general questions like: "What part of the video spoke to you the most?" Discussion questions for each segment are provided in the blue box above.

Follow the same steps for Segments 2 and 3. (Allow for about 10 minutes of discussion time after each segment.)

Small-Group Discussion Leader's Notes

1. Remind them that the Third Commandment is "Keep holy the Sabbath"—and that the Church tells us we do this by going to Mass. It is the bare minimum requirement from God.

2. Look for technical answers, such as transubstantiation, but also personal answers, such as a personal encounter with Christ.

3. The people, priest, Scripture.

4. *Sacrosanctum concilium* 14.

5. If no one has ever been to Adoration, encourage them to go and consider taking your class.

Question:

What goes through your mind when you receive Jesus in the Eucharist? Why do you think Jesus chose that way to be near us?

In the Eucharist, God comes ... to raise you up to himself to make you like him.

TO THE HEART with

When I wanted to make extra money in high school, a neighbor said she would pay me to walk her dog. I remember taking that nice chocolate Lab out for a twenty-minute walk. I ran around and threw tennis balls for the dog to retrieve; we played more than walked.

When I came back to the house, the family invited me in; I was astonished to see the kitchen table covered with cash. The woman pulled a twenty-dollar bill off one of the huge bundles and handed it to me, then invited me to come back the next week. I walked home thinking, *This is the best job ever! I get to play with a dog and make a dollar a minute!*

I enjoyed "walking the dog" and getting paid like a rock star for a few more weeks. Then, early one morning, our whole family woke up to the sound of shouting. A S.W.A.T. team was swarming the neighbor's home. They were busted for running a multi-million-dollar drug ring. Suddenly, the supersized cash stash on the kitchen table made sense.

As I mourned the loss of my best job ever, I thought of what my parents so often said to me: *If it sounds too good to be true, it probably is.*

Probably ... but with one important exception: the Eucharist—which is *even greater* than you could possibly imagine! In the Eucharist, God shares with us his perfect love and power: his Body, Blood, Soul, and Divinity. When we receive the Eucharist, we receive the strength we need to follow Christ ... all the way to heaven! In the words of St. Athanasius, "For the Son of God became man so that we might become God" (CCC 460).

Step 6 **To the Heart** (10 minutes)

After the small-group discussions, read this story aloud, have a candidate read it aloud, or have the class read it silently. After the story (written by this week's video presenter), read the thought-provoking question(s) provided in the red "To the Heart" box above. Time permitting, ask follow-up questions and encourage discussion.

In the Eucharist, God comes to you, just as you are, to raise you up to himself and to make you like him. You may feel broken, unworthy, lonely, or afraid. Yet, it is precisely into the pain and sin of the world that Jesus comes to us.

Pope Benedict XVI says that in the Mass, Christ "has stridden through the Red Sea of death itself, descended into the world of shadows, and smashed open the prison door."[1] In the Eucharist, the entire reality of our Christian story comes to a brilliant climactic moment, where heaven and earth are united, with Jesus' Body and Blood becoming one with *your* body and blood. And all of this happens daily in churches throughout the world. Jesus gives us himself over and over again in order to love us, purify us, strengthen us, and remain with us.[2] And that's something that's definitely *not* too good to be true!

[2] cf Jn 14:3

Brian Butler

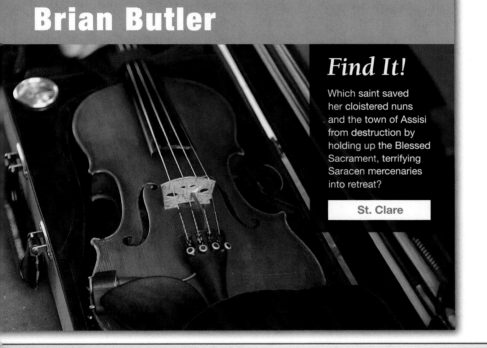

Find It!

Which saint saved her cloistered nuns and the town of Assisi from destruction by holding up the Blessed Sacrament, terrifying Saracen mercenaries into retreat?

St. Clare

140 | CHOSEN

Hero of the Week

Born:
January 13, 1891

Died:
November 23, 1927

Memorial:
November 23

Blessed Miguel Pro,
Martyr

Fr. Pro on the day of his execution.

Getting your face plastered on a "wanted" poster is not the typical route to sainthood ... but it was for Fr. Miguel Pro.

Wrongly accused of bombing a federal building in Mexico, he courageously declared the reign of God before a firing squad, leading to one of the most dramatic martyrdoms of the last 100 years.

Miguel Agustin Pro Juarez, known as Miguel Pro, was born in Guadalupe, Mexico, in 1891. Following the example of his two sisters who had entered religious life, Miguel gave up his work in his family's business and entered the Jesuit novitiate in 1911.

It was a turbulent time for Catholics in Mexico. By 1914, anti-Catholic laws made life for the young seminarian extremely difficult. He fled Mexico, went to California and then to Spain, where he finished his studies and was ordained a priest in Belgium in 1925.

His superiors allowed him to return to Mexico in 1926 at the height of violent persecution against Catholics. The Catholic Church had gone underground, and priests were being imprisoned or shot for celebrating Mass. Fr. Pro's good-natured sense of humor and fervent prayer life served him well in that hostile time.

In spite of the danger, Fr. Pro fearlessly and repeatedly risked his life to serve the spiritual needs of his flock. He often disguised himself as a beggar or street cleaner to get past watchful government informants so he could administer the sacraments to the faithful. Once, in an audacious insult to the local authorities, he disguised himself as a police officer to get into the jail and minister to the prisoners!

Ultimately, his activities were discovered, and he was arrested. The Mexican government, eager to make an example of him, charged him and his brother with trumped-up charges of an assassination attempt against ex-President Obregon in November of 1927.

He had no trial. Instead, Fr. Pro faced the firing squad ten days after his arrest. He went to his death declaring his innocence and forgiving his executioners. Arms outstretched like a cross, he held a crucifix in one hand and a rosary in the other. His last words continue to inspire us today: *Viva Cristo Rey! – Long Live Christ the King!*

Blessed Miguel Pro, pray for us. Inspire in us a love of the Holy Mass and a yearning for the Eucharist.

Step 7

Hero of the Week (5 minutes)

This saint story will help to highlight and reinforce this lesson's topic. You may choose to read it aloud, have a candidate read it aloud, or have the class read it silently.

Challenge of the Week

 Spend some time at Adoration or in front of the tabernacle. The red sanctuary lamp is lit to let you know that Jesus is truly present. Bring a spiritual book to read or just sit quietly. Any time spent in the presence of the Blessed Sacrament is good for your soul. Write about your visit in the space below.

Memorize the "Anima Christi" (Soul of Christ), a wonderful prayer for after Communion. Search online for it, and write it down to help you memorize it. Write it in the space below (or take a copy with you) to pray after you receive Jesus in the Eucharist at Mass this week.

Search online for "Eucharistic miracles," and write about what you find in the space below. Tell about it in class next week.

_____

_____

_____

_____

_____

_____

_____

_____

_____

_____

 Closing Prayer

"'I am the bread of life; he who comes to me shall not hunger, and he who believes in me shall never thirst.'"

—John 6:35

Lord Jesus, you are infinitely powerful, but it's so easy to overlook you, so easy to forget the great mystery of your presence in the Holy Eucharist. You call to us in your quiet way, waiting for us to seek you. You hunger to transform our lives. You thirst to save our souls. Give us the grace to recognize our own hunger for you and to seek you at Mass with a holy reverence. Amen.

Step 8 **Challenge of the Week** (2 minutes)

Ask your candidates to read the "challenges" above and choose one of the three to complete this week. Have them check the box next to the challenge they intend to complete. Encourage them to write about their experiences in the space provided.

Step 9 **Homework Instructions and Updates** (2 minutes)

Remind candidates to read the "Wrap-Up" and the "What's That Word?" sections in the "Taking It Home" section of the Student Workbook. They should also review the "Watch It!" questions to prepare for the next "Review Game."

Step 10 **Closing Prayer** (3 minutes)

As a way of building up community, ask if there are any prayer intentions. Write them down (or have candidates share them aloud) and after praying for those intentions, have the class read the "Closing Prayer" together (provided in the Student Workbook).

142 | CHOSEN

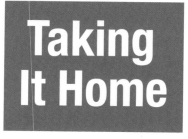

Taking It Home

For next week's "Review Game," be sure to read over the following …

1. **Watch It!** questions (page 137)
2. **Wrap-Up**
3. **"What's That Word?"**
4. **Memory Verse**

Don't forget to do your
Challenge of the Week (page 141)

Wrap-Up

Jesus gave his disciples the Eucharist for the very first time at the Last Supper, just before he died. Blessing the bread and wine, he passed them around to his disciples, saying, "Take this, all of you, and eat of it: for this is my body which will be given up for you. Take this, all of you, and drink from it: For this is the chalice of my blood, the blood of the new and eternal covenant, which will be poured out for you and for many for the forgiveness of sins. Do this in memory of me" (see Matthew 26:26-28).

From the very beginning, the Church has obeyed Jesus' command by celebrating the Liturgy of the Eucharist at Mass.[3] In the Mass, Jesus' sacrifice on the cross is "re-presented," or made present for us.[4] Jesus didn't want his followers to simply hear about his saving Death, Resurrection, and Ascension. He wanted every generation to "take and eat" and have a direct encounter with him in the Eucharist.

Some people resist doing this, of course. They can think of a million ways they would rather spend their Sundays. "I feel close to God when I'm outside in nature!" they might argue. "Why do I need to go to church?"

But in the Ten Commandments, we read that God commanded his people to "remember to keep holy the Sabbath day" (Exodus 20:8, NAB). At minimum, this means going to Mass (and actively participating!) every Sunday and on holy days of obligation.[5] You can't fulfill that command by just walking through the woods; nor can you encounter God as profoundly there.

In the Mass, God is present in four specific ways:

In his people. God dwells in our hearts through Baptism. We image God through our ability to know (intellect) and love (free will).

In his priest. Jesus Christ is present to us in a sacramental way through the priest who, by virtue of the Sacrament of Holy Orders, stands IN PERSONA CHRISTI CAPITIS ("in the person of Christ the Head").

[3] CCC 1342

[4] CCC 1366

[5] CCC 2177–2178

In the Scriptures. Every time Sacred Scripture is proclaimed, God pours out his life-changing grace upon his people so that they can put this word into action. "For in the sacred books, the Father who is in heaven meets his children with great love and speaks with them" (CCC 104; see *Dei Verbum* 21).

In the Eucharist. This is where we most fully and intensely encounter Jesus, who is truly present under the appearance of bread and wine—Body, Blood, Soul, and Divinity.

It's still a good idea to go for a walk on Sunday afternoons—God is *spiritually* present to us in the woods and everywhere. So, if nature nourishes you spiritually, then by all means, spend some time praying there. Many of the saints did! But if you want to experience God in the deepest way possible in this life—if you want to encounter him both spiritually and *physically*—go to Mass. Your soul will thank you!

"What's That Word?"

EUCHARIST

In the Sacrament of the Eucharist (Greek for "thanksgiving"), we receive the Body, Blood, Soul, and Divinity of Jesus under the appearance of bread and wine. The Eucharist is not merely a symbol; it is truly Jesus, given so we can share in the life of God.[6] Through the Eucharist, we are united to the sacrifice of Christ and offer praise in thanksgiving for all of creation.

The Eucharist is our greatest treasure, and it unites us more fully to Christ and his Church. For this reason, though people from other faiths are welcome at Mass, only baptized Catholics who share the Church's belief in the Real Presence can receive Communion.

To be prepared to receive this great gift, we must fast for one hour prior to receiving Communion and have confessed any serious sins in the Sacrament of Reconciliation. The words of St. Paul should encourage us to examine our consciences before communion: "Whoever, therefore, eats the bread or drinks the cup of the Lord in an unworthy manner will be guilty of profaning the body and blood of the Lord" (1 Corinthians 11:27; see CCC 1385). While reception of the Eucharist does not forgive mortal sins, it does help strengthen us against sinning in the future by filling us with God's sanctifying grace.

[6] CCC 1357

Memory Verse:

"'Lord, to whom shall we go? You have the words of eternal life; and we have believed, and have come to know, that you are the Holy One of God.'"

– John 6:68-69

144 | CHOSEN

LITURGY

The LITURGY is the public prayer of the Church. It includes the Mass, celebrations of the other sacraments, and celebrations of the seasons and feasts of the LITURGICAL YEAR, such as Advent, Lent, and Pentecost.

The biblical word *liturgy* comes from the Greek word meaning "work."[7] In the liturgy, God invites us to participate in his work of saving us from sin and blessing us so that we can share his life. Participating in the *liturgy* is the most important thing we can do on earth. In the liturgy, God makes it possible for us to have a taste of eternity and experience the "work" we will do one day with all the angels and saints in heaven.

MASS

The English word "Mass" (*missa* in Latin) comes from the same root as the word "mission." God empowers and sends us out from the Mass into the world on a mission: to love others as Christ has loved us.[8]

The two main parts of the Mass are: 1) the *Liturgy of the Word*, in which we hear readings from the Scriptures proclaimed and taught; and 2) the *Liturgy of the Eucharist*, in which the consecrated bread and wine become the very Body and Blood of Christ, whom we receive in Holy Communion.[9]

According to the *Catechism*, the Eucharist is the "source and summit of the Christian life" (CCC 1324). "Before the greatness of this mystery St. Augustine exclaims, '*O sacrament of devotion! O sign of unity! O bond of charity!*'" (CCC 1398). For this reason, the Church never ceases to pray for the unity of all Christians. At Mass the entire Church on earth joins the Church in heaven to feast on the gift of redemption.[10] This is an awesome mystery. (*See also* TRANSUBSTANTIATION.)

[7] CCC 1069

[8] Jn 13:1-15

[9] CCC 1346

[10] CCC 1382–1383

Did You Know?

When French forces invaded the city of Turin, Italy, in 1640, soldiers sacked the Church of St. Maria del Monte in order to loot the church and murder the civilians who had taken refuge there. But when a French soldier forced open the tabernacle full of consecrated hosts, a miraculous fire erupted from inside the tabernacle, singeing his face and clothing. As he fell to the ground, repentant, the violence ceased. An imprint of the soldier's hand is still visible on the tabernacle door to this day.

Notes

**Lesson 16
Leader's Notes**

Overview

The purpose of this lesson is to communicate the holiness and beauty of the Sacrament of Matrimony (marriage) and to help students understand the importance of preparing for this sacrament, not as the world does, but according to God's design.

The prevalence of social media and the tendency to "hang out" has produced a generation that to a great extent has been deprived of authentic friendships with those of the opposite sex. And yet, these friendships are an important part of discerning whether one has been called to marriage (and to whom)—always with an emphasis on self-respect and refusing to "use" others for physical or emotional gratification.

Objectives of this Lesson

1. *Marriage is a sacrament.* Many young people have suffered through the divorce of their parents and are unclear about why God thinks marriage is important (see CCC 1603).

2. *There are four "characteristics" of the Sacrament of Matrimony.* We will examine the four characteristics of Catholic marriage (free, total, faithful, and fruitful) to understand why God defines marriage as the union of one man and one woman ... for life.

3. *Marriage is a lifelong commitment: A sacramental union cannot be broken, even if the couple is divorced* (see CCC 1644). This lesson touches upon the subject of annulments and dispels some misconceptions about what the Church teaches. For example, an annulment is not a "Catholic divorce," but a ruling by the Church that a sacramental bond never happened (see CCC 1629).

4. *Learn how to discern a vocation to marriage.* We will examine the importance of forming healthy relationships in terms of discerning future vocations. We must always be careful to show self-respect and refuse to "use" others physically or emotionally (see CCC 2333, 2338).

"What does it mean to say, 'I do'?"

(Marriage, a Sign of God's Love)

✝

Opening Prayer

"He who has the bride is the bridegroom; the friend of the bridegroom, who stands and hears him, rejoices greatly at the bridegroom's voice; therefore this joy of mine is now full."
—*John 3:29*

"On the third day there was a marriage at Cana in Galilee, and the mother of Jesus was there; Jesus also was invited to the marriage, with his disciples."
—*John 2:1-2*

"Then I heard what seemed to be the voice of a great multitude, like the sound of many waters and like the sound of mighty thunderpeals, crying, 'Hallelujah! For the Lord our God the Almighty reigns. Let us rejoice and exult and give him the glory, for the marriage of the Lamb has come, and his Bride has made herself ready ...'"
—*Revelation 19:6-7*

Opening Prayer

One powerful image we have for how God loves us is the love shared between a husband and wife. That is how much he loves us. Let's prayerfully listen to just a few of the verses from Scripture that drive this point home.

> *Ask for volunteers or assign a teen to read each passage, pausing between each to allow students to reflect on the words.*

Let's pray. In the name of the Father ...

 Step 1 ## Welcome/Review Game (5 minutes)

Begin by welcoming the class and telling them that you will be starting with a review of the previous lesson's material. On the DVD menu, click on Lesson 16; then on the sub-menu, click on "Review Game."

Have students answer the questions based on the previous lesson. For more information about how to adapt this game to meet the needs of your group, see the "Review Game" section in the Introduction to this Leader's Guide (page xvi).

 Step 2 ## Challenge of the Week Review (5 minutes)

Ask if anyone would like to share a "challenge experience" from the previous week. Try to draw students out by prompting them with basic questions regarding the challenges from last week (e.g.,"Did anyone choose the first challenge?").

Step 3 ## Opening Prayer (3 minutes)

Lead the class in the "Opening Prayer," which is included in the Student Workbook. Leader's Guide notes are provided above: Red text provides direction and guidance, and white text is for you to read aloud to the class.

146 | 🔥 CHOSEN

Dive In:
Wedding Bell Blues

Imagine you are at your best friend's wedding, standing there, decked out in your tuxedo (or bridesmaid's dress). What would you do if you heard the bride and groom make the following vows to one another? Would you object?

Bride: "I take you, *(name),* to be my husband. I promise to be true to you for as long as you are romantic and give me everything I want, like taking me out to dinner every week plus birthdays and month-a-versaries. I promise to honor you ... when you deserve it. You WON'T deserve it if you: leave the toilet seat up; snore or chew with your mouth open; say another woman is cute; or watch football every weekend.

"I promise to love you, except when I'm tired or stressed out. I will always tell you exactly what I think ... unless I'm too mad to talk to you. Then you'd better read my mind!"

Groom: "I take you, *(name),* to be my wife. I promise to be true to you and love you as long as you don't nag me too much. But not if I have to work a lot of overtime and not when you are cranky and tired. When that happens, I will love you from a safe distance. If that.

"I promise to honor you, except when you fail to keep the house clean or forget to make snacks when I watch football with the guys. I will be faithful to you all the days of my life ... so long as we both shall feel like it."

Obviously, most people don't go into marriage thinking this way. Most couples believe they will beat the odds—that *their* marriage will last forever. And yet, we live in a broken world, full of broken people. Sadly, far too many marriages end in DIVORCE. Families are destroyed, hurting everyone involved. Maybe that's happened in your own family.

Despite all these things, God's high call (and our high hopes) for a love that is authentic and true remains. Today we're going to take a deeper look at that beautiful vocation (calling) that most of us have and at God's plan for man and woman.

"If a marriage is to preserve its initial charm and beauty, both husband and wife should try to renew their love day after day, and that is done through sacrifice, with smiles and also with ingenuity."

— St. Josemaría Escrivá

Step 4 — **Dive In** (5 minutes)

Read this story aloud, have a candidate read it aloud, or have the class read it silently before watching the video segments. This thought-provoking story ties in to the lesson's topic and serves to set up the video presentation.

Lesson 16 | 147

Segment 1: What Is Marriage?

1. The commitment of each spouse in a marriage must be: free, total, faithful, and __fruitful (life-giving)__.

2. Which of these is a "purpose" of marriage?

   A) The procreation of children   C) The education of children

   B) The mutual sanctification   (D) A, B, and C
   of the spouses

Segment 2: Tough Questions

1. Those who cohabit before marriage have higher rates of

   _____

   A) divorce   B) infidelity   C) abuse   (D) A, B, and C

2. **T** or **F?** An annulment is a decree that states that the relationship in question was not a valid marriage.

Segment 3: Free. Total. Faithful. Fruitful.

1. Jason says that fidelity is something we do with our

   A) heart   B) eyes   C) imagination   (D) A, B, and C

2. You shouldn't enter into a relationship looking for the kind of love only _____ can give you.

   A) your parents   B) your puppy   (C) God   D) chocolate

Small-Group Discussion

Segment 1: What Is Marriage?

1. Do you know of a married couple with the kind of marriage you would like to have some day? What is it about their relationship that stands out to you?

2. What did you think about the idea of a groom wearing black to represent "dying to self"? What does "sacrificial love" in marriage mean to you?

Segment 2: Tough Questions

1. Why do you think it is so important that marriage is permanent, that it binds a husband and wife together for life?

2. Do you know anyone who has received an annulment? What is the difference between an annulment and a divorce?[1]

Segment 3: Free. Total. Faithful. Fruitful.

1. In light of love being free, total, faithful, and fruitful, what are some ways you can start to love your future spouse now?[2]

2. What qualities would you look for in a potential spouse?

3. Why is it important to make God part of any dating relationship? How can you do this?

 Step 5 **Watch It!/Small-Group Discussion** (50 minutes)

On the video, click on Lesson 16, Segment 1. When Segment 1 ends, have students fill in the "Watch It!" questions (2 to 3 minutes). Run through them to be sure they wrote the correct answers so they will have them to prepare for the next "Review Game."

Next, lead students in a small-group discussion for Segment 1. You may begin by asking general questions like: "What part of the video spoke to you the most?" Discussion questions for each segment are provided in the blue box above.

Follow the same steps for Segments 2 and 3. (Allow for about 10 minutes of discussion time after each segment.)

Small-Group Discussion Leader's Notes

1. See the "Objectives" and the Glossary.

2. Hints: practicing chastity now, avoiding pornography.

148 CHOSEN

TO THE HEART with

Question:

What do you think "true love" looks like when a couple has been married a long time? In what ways is it different from what it was like at the beginning? What qualities are most important to cultivate to make sure your future marriage will last "for life"?

In her book, *Girls Gone Mild*, Wendy Shalit recounts:

I once traveled by car with some elderly friends going to a family event, and it was a humbling experience. The wife was suffering from Alzheimer's, and every twenty seconds she would ask somewhat fearfully, "Where are we going?" … Her husband would always respond gently and cheerfully, as if for the first time, "We're going to a party!"

Years later, I heard from my grandparents about this couple, and how the husband gallantly continued to care for his wife during her mental degeneration. By the time she died, she no longer recognized her husband of fifty years. But she did tell him, offhand, something very beautiful: "You know, I don't know who you are, but you're the best."[1]

What woman does not want to be loved like this? What man does not wish to lose himself so fully in his beloved? We are drawn to such love for a reason: Our hearts are made for it. Because we are made in the image and likeness of God—and God is love—we are made in the image and likeness of love.

Some people are unable to give and receive this kind of love because of wounds from the past. Some people think they don't deserve to be loved this way; their ability to receive love needs healing. Others are trapped in vices that have impaired their ability to give authentic love. Still others wonder if real love even exists. Perhaps they have never known a marriage like the one Wendy Shalit describes in her book.

We all struggle to overcome obstacles to love, but if we want to experience love that truly satisfies, we can't just wait and hope this love will simply "happen" to us when the time is right. We need to prepare ourselves for it, receive healing for our

Step 6 **To the Heart** (10 minutes)

After the small-group discussions, read this story aloud, have a candidate read it aloud, or have the class read it silently. After the story (written by this week's video presenter), read the thought-provoking question(s) provided in the red "To the Heart" box above. Time permitting, ask follow-up questions and encourage discussion.

Lesson 16 | 149

wounds, and battle our imperfections. This might be a frightening or daunting task, but St. John Paul II has reassured us: **"Do not be afraid, then, when love makes demands. Do not be afraid when love requires sacrifice."**[2] He also said, "Real love is demanding. I would fail in my mission if I did not clearly tell you so."[3]

People spend countless hours preparing for their wedding day. But how many hours are these couples spending preparing for *marriage?* While marriage may not be on your immediate radar, the choices you make today about your relationships and God's place in them can help you prepare for the love that should last a lifetime.

Jason Evert

We all struggle to overcome obstacles to love ...

Find It!

Are wedding rings necessary for a sacramental marriage to take place?

No, they are a cultural symbol. However, they can become sacramentals and dispose us to receive graces.

150 | CHOSEN

Hero of the Week

Born:
July 7, 1207

Died:
November 17, 1231

Memorial:
November 17

Patron Saint of:
- nurses
- bakers
- brides

St. Elizabeth of Hungary

Imagine you wanted to impress a certain girl in your English class (if you're a guy) or get a certain football player to notice you (if you're a girl).

How would you go about it? Would you come up with a clever text, slip a note or rose or bag of homemade cookies in that person's locker, or do something really crazy to get that person to notice you?

Chocolate chips and love poems are great, of course. And if you really love someone, you look forward to spending time with that person—taking long walks on a beach or even just around the block. But real love—married love—is much more than a few tender moments captured in a photograph. It involves a lifetime of loving and serving one's spouse, as a pathway to holiness. We see this in the life of St. Elizabeth of Hungary and her husband, Louis IV of Thuringia.

Both Elizabeth and Louis were raised to rule. The creature comforts of courtly life could have insulated them from the suffering of the poor. Elizabeth, however, had a soft spot for the poor ... and Louis had a soft spot for *her*. He not only accepted but encouraged her loving, charitable works, sharing his wealth as a way to grow in love.

Sometimes that love worked in miraculous ways. St. Elizabeth was in the habit of taking food from the royal coffers to feed needy families, even though the royal household disapproved. One day, she came across her husband, who happened to be out in the woods. When he gently asked her to reveal what was hidden in her cloak, she opened it to show him the bread and cheese she'd hidden there—and out came a bouquet of roses!

On October 20, 2011, in his weekly audience, Pope Benedict XVI said, "Elizabeth's marriage was profoundly happy: she helped her husband to raise his human qualities to a supernatural level and he, in exchange, stood up for his wife's generosity to the poor ... A clear witness to how faith and love of God and neighbor strengthen family life and deepen ever more the matrimonial union."

Sadly, Louis died young. St. Elizabeth made arrangements for the care of their three children and devoted the next few years of her life to charitable works, including building a hospital for the poor. She, too, died very young. And yet her legacy of married love continues to this day.

St. Elizabeth, pray for us. By your example, show us the fruits of a loving, authentic marriage.

Step 7 **Hero of the Week** (5 minutes)

This saint story will help to highlight and reinforce this lesson's topic. You may choose to read it aloud, have a candidate read it aloud, or have the class read it silently.

Challenge of the Week

☐ **What makes a happy marriage?** What does it mean to love someone "heroically"? Poll some of the adults in your life to get their thoughts; add a few of your own ideas; and write about it in the space below.

☐ **Prayerfully inventory your wardrobe.** Is there anything that doesn't reflect the dignity of a child of God? Think of one way you exercise the virtue of modesty this week, and write it in the space below.

☐ **Ask your parents or grandparents about their wedding day.** Discuss what their plans were at the time, and how they feel "God's plan" has worked out in their marriage. Write about it in the space below.

_____

_____

_____

_____

_____

_____

_____

_____

_____

✝ Closing Prayer

"The body is not meant for immorality, but for the Lord, and the Lord for the body."

—*1 Corinthians 6:13*

Heavenly Father, you have made us in your image and likeness. Thank you for the dignity and beauty of our sexuality. The world tells us that promiscuity is freedom and then enslaves us to the emptiness of sin, loneliness, and despair. Help us to repent of any impurity that has taken hold of our lives and to make a gift of ourselves to you, knowing that when we trust you, our lives will become abundant and beautiful. Amen.

 Step 8 **Challenge of the Week** (2 minutes)

Ask your candidates to read the "challenges" above and choose one of the three to complete this week. Have them check the box next to the challenge they intend to complete. Encourage them to write about their experiences in the space provided.

 Step 9 **Homework Instructions and Updates** (2 minutes)

Remind candidates to read the "Wrap-Up" and the "What's That Word?" sections in the "Taking It Home" section of the Student Workbook. They should also review the "Watch It!" questions to prepare for the next "Review Game."

 Step 10 **Closing Prayer** (3 minutes)

As a way of building up community, ask if there are any prayer intentions. Write them down (or have candidates share them aloud) and after praying for those intentions, have the class read the "Closing Prayer" together (provided in the Student Workbook).

152 CHOSEN

Taking It Home

For next week's "Review Game," be sure to read over the following …

1. **Watch It!** questions (page 147)
2. **Wrap-Up**
3. **"What's That Word?"**
4. **Memory Verse**

Don't forget to do your **Challenge of the Week** (page 151)

Wrap-Up

When God created the first man and woman, he intended marriage to be a sign to the world of the love of the Trinity–a perfect communion of love. "For this reason a man shall leave his father and mother [and be joined to his wife], and the two shall become one flesh" (Mark 10:7, NAB).

God designed married love to be like his love for us–free, total, faithful, and fruitful.[4] In authentic marriage, the bride and groom love each other completely and faithfully, for the rest of their lives. First in their words and then in their actions, they reflect the self-giving love of the Trinity. Spouses become a source of SACRAMENTAL GRACE for each other and a sign and source of God's love for their children and others.

Given how much confusion some people have today about marriage, it is good to keep in mind that the Church's teaching on marriage and family life is not at all based on discrimination. It is based on both NATURAL LAW and DIVINE LAW and, therefore, cannot be changed, since both come from the Creator.

It is important to understand that God made male and female bodies to have a "complementarity" that makes it possible for them to biologically produce children together (the fourth quality of authentic love … fruitfulness). Even if they are infertile, this "language" of life-giving love still exists.*

So, while some people do struggle with same-sex attraction, it is not biologically possible for two men or two women to "marry" because they do not have the capacity to consummate a marriage through a physical act that is meant to be life-giving.

Complementarity is not just a "skin deep" physical reality; it affects how men and women think and interact as well–and it's all a part of God's plan for the human family, which reflects the divine love of the Blessed Trinity.

The Church's teaching on sexual ethics and marriage is applied to everyone regardless of marital status or personal sexual struggle. The Church teaches that people who experience same-sex attraction are to be treated with dignity and love.[5] The Church is clear that no one should ever

4 CCC 1643

5 CCC 2358

---

* While some married couples are physically unable to conceive children, this "complementarity" (imprinted on their bodies) enables them to fulfill God's plan in other ways, such as through adoption or through other forms of spiritual parenthood.

be looked down on or treated with disrespect, regardless of his or her personal struggles.

However, the Church is equally clear that it does not have the authority to redefine marriage. This is because marriage is not a "right," but a calling—a vocation—that is about far more than the personal, emotional fulfillment of the couple.

Marriage empowers us to love like God loves—for better, for worse, and for life.

"What's That Word?"

DISCERNMENT

DISCERNMENT is a process by which someone, through personal reflection and with guidance from others who are spiritually mature, makes an important decision. VOCATIONAL DISCERNMENT is the process by which we make ourselves ready and able to hear and answer God's call for our lives—for example, the call to marriage or religious life—and to distinguish his voice from all the other voices in our lives. In his will we find our peace and joy. (*See also* CELIBATE.)

DIVORCE

Divorce marks the end of the legal, civil contract of marriage. However, because of the permanent, indissoluble bond of sacramental marriage, those who divorce are not free to remarry. Jesus affirmed this permanence of marriage: "What God has joined together, no human being must separate" (Mark 10:9, NAB). It is this bond that enables husbands and wives to give of themselves totally, faithfully, freely, and fruitfully—according to God's plan for married life. Sometimes divorce is a necessary tragedy—for instance, if it is no longer safe for a woman to remain with a man who has become abusive. But the divorce does not "dissolve" the marriage.

Catholics who wish to enter into marriage while their first spouse is still living must seek a decree of nullity (an *annulment*) from the Church, which is a ruling that because of some impediment to marriage, God did not "bond" the couple in the Sacrament of Matrimony. In cases where the Church is unable to identify impediments to marriage, an ANNULMENT would not be possible. (*See also* TRIBUNAL *and* CONSENT.)

Memory Verse:

"You are not your own; you were bought with a price. So glorify God in your body."

—*1 Corinthians 6:19-20*

MARRIAGE

Marriage is an exclusive, indissoluble, and lifelong covenant between a man and a woman, which has as its purpose the good of the spouses and the procreation and raising of children. Because the human family reflects the love of God in the world, and because spouses encounter Jesus Christ sacramentally through one another, the marriage of baptized Christians is called the Sacrament of Matrimony. In marriage, human love is taken up into divine love, and the couple becomes a witness to the truth that we were created to live in loving communion with others and, ultimately, in eternal communion with God who is love. A sacramental union has four defining characteristics: It is *free, total, faithful,* and *fruitful.* (See also COVENANT.)

Did You Know?

St. Catherine of Siena was able to see guardian angels from the age of six. She had many visions of Jesus, Mary, and the saints throughout her life. Once she had a vision of the baby Jesus presenting her with a wedding band, making her a "bride of Christ."

Any questions?

How do people who don't marry fit into God's "family plan"?

Everyone is called to live out God-like love—singles included! While the sexual expression of love is reserved to married couples, God calls *all* people to experience self-giving love. Those who are single because of life circumstances, because they're still looking for a spouse, because they are called to the single life (which includes a commitment to celibacy), or because they have an impediment to marriage (such as a prior marriage for which they have not received an annulment), are called to live like Jesus, who never got married, but modeled perfect love, making a gift of himself to the world. Most of the saints were celibate and lived in this way–finding fulfillment through self-giving love, service, deep friendships, and community.

Like all vocations, the single state can be difficult. Single people can look to the Church, in both its teachings and sacraments, as a source of encouragement, strength, and healing. Even in our brokenness, God does not abandon us. Instead, he urges us to "take up our cross and follow."

Loneliness and pain are sometimes part of life (for married and single people!)–it certainly was for Christ. But God gives us the strength to persevere if we ask him for it. The Church gives us many saintly examples of individuals who courageously and joyfully lived out the single life, such as St. Zita and Blessed Pier Giorgio Frassati.

Notes

Lesson 17
Leader's Notes

Overview

The purpose of this lesson is to instill an understanding of the Sacrament of Holy Orders. In addition, students will be offered an opportunity to learn a bit more about the process of discerning a vocation to the priesthood, religious life, married life, or single life (which includes a commitment to celibacy).

Oftentimes teens have a "knee jerk" reaction to considering whether God might be calling them to serve him in the Church. They simply cannot imagine a satisfying, fulfilling life without the benefits of marriage, and they do not stop to consider that all vocations have both a crown and a cross, both benefits and sacrifices. This lesson will encourage them to consider this.

Objectives of this Lesson

1. *All of us share the fundamental vocation of love.* Most people live out that call through the vocation of marriage. Others are called to the priesthood or religious life, where—like married couples—they witness to God's love. Those with religious vocations make a gift of themselves to the Church and to the whole world with "undivided heart" (CCC 1579, 2392; 1 Corinthians 7:32).

2. *Christ established the priesthood to share in his ministry for the Church.* The ordained priest has received an indelible mark on his soul and becomes a living icon of Christ, living *in persona Christi* and bringing the light of Christ to the world (see CCC 1563–1566).

3. *Through their celibacy, priests and religious sacrifice one good for an even greater good:* to reflect *in their bodies* our destiny in heaven, where we will be "neither married nor given in marriage" (Matthew 22:30; CCC 1579–1580).

4. *God calls us all to various vocations.* Both men and women must learn to listen to God and to ask him for the desire to follow his plan for their lives. In *vocational discernment*, we prayerfully consider our own gifts and what we sense God is asking of us—with the help of those who have made similar choices—to determine the state of life to which God is calling us.

Lesson 17

"Who's calling?"

(Holy Orders and Vocational Discernment)

✝

Opening Prayer

"Dearest Jesus,
teach me to be generous,
teach me to love and serve you as you deserve,
to give and not to count the cost,
to fight and not to heed the wounds,
to toil and not to seek for rest,
to labor and to look for no reward,
except that of knowing that
I do your Holy Will. Amen."

—*St. Ignatius of Loyola*

Opening Prayer

Today we will begin with a short, powerful prayer from St. Ignatius of Loyola, who is renowned for his writing on discernment, which is figuring out what God wants you to do. I encourage you to write out this prayer and pray it every day. Let's pray. In the name of the Father ...

 Step 1 **Welcome/Review Game** (5 minutes)

Begin by welcoming the class and telling them that you will be starting with a review of the previous lesson's material. On the DVD menu, click on Lesson 17; then on the sub-menu, click on "Review Game."

Have students answer the questions based on the previous lesson. For more information about how to adapt this game to meet the needs of your group, see the "Review Game" section in the Introduction to this Leader's Guide (page xvi).

 Step 2 **Challenge of the Week Review** (5 minutes)

Ask if anyone would like to share a "challenge experience" from the previous week. Try to draw students out by prompting them with basic questions regarding the challenges from last week (e.g.,"Did anyone choose the first challenge?").

Step 3 **Opening Prayer** (3 minutes)

Lead the class in the "Opening Prayer," which is included in the Student Workbook. Leader's Guide notes are provided above: Red text provides direction and guidance, and white text is for you to read aloud to the class.

156 | CHOSEN

Dive In:
A Soldier's Story

September 29, 2006

On a hot, sweltering day on the streets of Ramadi, Iraq, four SEALs of Delta Platoon stood alongside eight Iraqi soldiers to provide rooftop cover for joint American-Iraqi operations against insurgent forces. Twenty-five-year-old Michael Monsoor of southern California provided extra security with his heavy machine gun for the two SEAL snipers on either side of him.

After hours of sporadic and at times intense engagement with insurgents, a hand grenade was thrown toward Michael. It bounced off his chest and landed on the rooftop in front of him.

Instantly, Monsoor reacted. "Grenade!" he shouted, alerting the others to the danger at hand. He then threw his body upon the device, absorbing the blow into his own chest in order to save the lives of his two brothers-in-arms. They were wounded, but survived.

In critical condition, Monsoor was medevaced to a field hospital. This Catholic sailor who always attended Mass "with devotion" before missions, fought for life for a full half-hour before succumbing to his injuries—just long enough to receive last rites from his chaplain, Fr. Paul Halladay.

It was the feast day of Saint Michael the Archangel.[1]

2 1 Jn 4:8

3 Mk 12:30-31

The fundamental call of every person is summed up in one word: love. Love is our participation in the very life of God, who *is* love.[2] Love is how we become holy.[3]

This kind of love is neither a vague sentimentality nor a warm, fuzzy feeling people get while holding hands on Valentine's Day. Rather, it's the kind of love Jesus showed us perfectly on the cross. "Greater love has no man than ... [to] lay down his life for his friends" (John 15:13). We're called to live the way Jesus died ... for others.

The vocation to give ourselves to others in love is written on our very bodies. We may never have the opportunity to jump on a grenade to save our friends, but we are called to live in a way that radically puts others before ourselves; that is, to be gifts to one another. Some live out this self-gift through marriage, others as single people, and others as priests or religious. Those who accept the call to the consecrated life lay down their lives not just for one person, but for us all. Today we're going to talk about how to figure out how God is calling us to love, and especially about the heroic gift of love as we see it lived out in the Sacrament of Holy Orders.

Step 4

Dive In (5 minutes)

Read this story aloud, have a candidate read it aloud, or have the class read it silently before watching the video segments. This thought-provoking story ties in to the lesson's topic and serves to set up the video presentation.

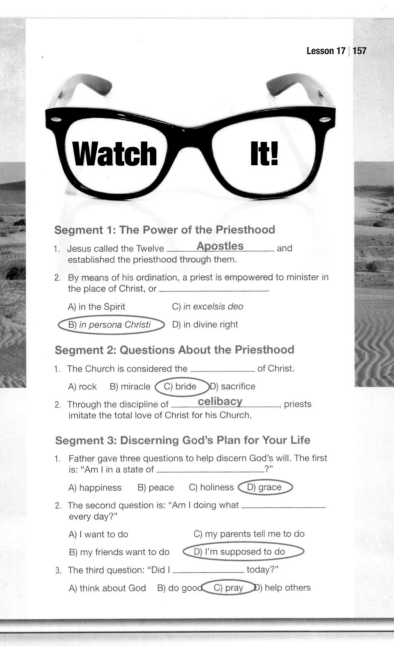

Watch It!

Segment 1: The Power of the Priesthood

1. Jesus called the Twelve _____**Apostles**_____ and established the priesthood through them.

2. By means of his ordination, a priest is empowered to minister in the place of Christ, or _____.

   A) in the Spirit   C) *in excelsis deo*

   B) *in persona Christi*   D) in divine right

Segment 2: Questions About the Priesthood

1. The Church is considered the _____ of Christ.

   A) rock   B) miracle   C) bride   D) sacrifice

2. Through the discipline of _____**celibacy**_____, priests imitate the total love of Christ for his Church.

Segment 3: Discerning God's Plan for Your Life

1. Father gave three questions to help discern God's will. The first is: "Am I in a state of _____?"

   A) happiness   B) peace   C) holiness   D) grace

2. The second question is: "Am I doing what _____ every day?"

   A) I want to do   C) my parents tell me to do

   B) my friends want to do   D) I'm supposed to do

3. The third question: "Did I _____ today?"

   A) think about God   B) do good   C) pray   D) help others

Small-Group Discussion

Segment 1: The Power of the Priesthood

1. Do you know any priests, deacons, or religious personally? What are some ways they have helped you or others you know?

2. How are priests different from other Catholics? In what ways are they the same?

3. What could you do for the world as a priest or religious sister that you could not do as a married person?

Segment 2: Questions About the Priesthood

1. How can you offer your support to our priests and religious?

2. How is a priest like a "spiritual father" and a religious sister like a "spiritual mother."

3. What do you think your parents and friends would say if you told them you were considering becoming a priest or religious sister?

Segment 3: Discerning God's Plan for Your Life

1. Have you ever asked God to reveal to you his plans for your life? What is one way to find out if God wants you to serve him in a particular way?

2. What are some things you can do to help discern your vocation to marriage, Holy Orders, or religious life?[1]

Step 5

Watch It!/Small-Group Discussion (50 minutes)

On the video, click on Lesson 17, Segment 1. When Segment 1 ends, have students fill in the "Watch It!" questions (2 to 3 minutes). Run through them to be sure they wrote the correct answers so they will have them to prepare for the next "Review Game."

Next, lead students in a small-group discussion for Segment 1. You may begin by asking general questions like: "What part of the video spoke to you the most?" Discussion questions for each segment are provided in the blue box above.

Follow the same steps for Segments 2 and 3. (Allow for about 10 minutes of discussion time after each segment.)

Small-Group Discussion Leader's Notes

1. Hints: Encourage them to draw closer to God by confessing their sins, praying, reading Scripture, and attending daily Mass. Also suggest going on a vocation retreat and talking to someone who is already living one of these vocations.

Question:

Dedicating your life completely to God, either as a priest or in the religious life, takes great courage. Because these vocations represent God and the Church in a special way, priests and religious have unique opportunities to bless the lives of others. Have you ever considered the priesthood or religious life or talked to someone who chose that state of life? If you had a friend who was thinking about it, how would you suggest they begin making this decision?

God, if that was the only soul you ever let me bring back to you, I want to thank you for asking me to be your priest.

TO THE HEART with

In 1913, Sir Ernest Shackleton was trying to recruit men for his third attempt to reach the South Pole. He ran an ad in the *London Times* that read: "Men wanted for hazardous journey. Small wages, bitter cold, long months of complete darkness, constant danger, safe return doubtful, honor and recognition in case of success."

The response was so great that the line of applicants wrapped around the block! *The Endurance* set sail for Antarctica with twenty-eight men willing to give up everything for the chance to be part of something great.

Jesus' "recruitment plan" was similar. He said, "If any man would come after me, let him deny himself and take up his cross and follow me" (Matthew 16:24). He also warned his disciples that people would hate them because of his name. In spite of this, there have always been men and women willing to give up everything for the chance to be a part of God's rescue mission on earth.

As a priest, I've had many opportunities to take part in someone's "rescue." When I was a newly ordained priest in a parish in Northern Minnesota, I was awakened one morning around 3 AM by a call from a hospital official asking me if I could come to the hospital to visit with a patient and his daughter.

When I walked through the sliding-glass doors, a nurse said, "I don't know, Father. I think the family needs you in there, but I don't think they will be happy you are here."

She was right. When I walked into the waiting room, two women looked up. The first smiled at me, and I recognized her as one of my parishioners. The other woman's face contorted with hatred and disgust when she saw me. Clearly, she had not known her friend had asked the hospital to call me. I had no idea what to say.

Step 6 **To the Heart** (10 minutes)

After the small-group discussions, read this story aloud, have a candidate read it aloud, or have the class read it silently. After the story (written by this week's video presenter), read the thought-provoking question(s) provided in the red "To the Heart" box above. Time permitting, ask follow-up questions and encourage discussion.

The first woman stood up and shook my hand. "Father, I'll give you two a chance to talk," she said and then left.

I breathed a quick prayer and inquired about the woman's father, the patient. As we talked, I found out why she wasn't happy to see me. "I've been living a very bad life, Father," she began. "When I saw you walk in here, all I could think about was how I've wasted my whole life running from God and the Church. My friend said I should pray, but God doesn't want to hear from someone like me."

I reminded her that God loved her and hadn't forgotten her. Then I asked her if she wanted to go to Confession.

"What? Here?"

"Yes."

I guided her through her first Confession in more than twenty years. As I pronounced Christ's absolution of her sins, her tears of sorrow and desperation were transformed. The look of hatred was replaced by a look of joy.

As I walked to my car afterward, I thought, "God, if that was the only soul you ever let me bring back to you, I want to thank you for asking me to be your priest."

This kind of experience happens every day in the life of a priest. The South Pole would be an adventure, but the priesthood is *the* adventure of a lifetime.

Father Mike Schmitz

Find It!

What Albanian nun started life with the name Agnes Gonxha Bojaxhiu and became known as "the saint of the gutters"?

Blessed Teresa of Calcutta, also known as Mother Teresa

160 | CHOSEN

Hero of the Week

Born:
May 8, 1786

Died:
August 4, 1859

Memorial:
August 4

Patron Saint of:
- priests
- confessors

St. John Vianney

The young deserter grew more and more exhausted as he ran through the woods in the dead of night to evade Napoleon's soldiers.

As he passed a local farm, he threw himself in a pile of fermenting hay in desperation. It was an unpleasant—but effective—hiding spot.

He had never wanted to be a soldier or a farmer. What he wanted more than anything in the world was to become ... a priest. As a young child, he and his family had often traveled many miles to attend Mass in secret, because the French Revolution had sent priests into hiding. To an impressionable child, the priests who undertook these heroic efforts represented an ideal.

Called to the priesthood as a young man, St. John Vianney initially flunked out of his studies. A priest who knew of John's fervent devotion intervened on his behalf, suggesting that John's zeal would more than make up for his poor academic background.

This, combined with a severe shortage of priests, led to him being assigned to the tiny, remote parish of Ars, where he became one of the hardest working priests of his time. He understood the people's great need for the sacraments— it is said he regularly heard confessions for sixteen hours a day, eating nothing more than a few boiled potatoes.

He lived a simple life of sacrifice and charitable works, with a special place in his heart for orphans. But it was his zeal for his priestly duties that distinguished him with his bishop. St. John served so many faithful in the sacraments, that the bishop gave him a special dispensation from attending his annual spiritual retreat because so many souls were lined up to have their confessions heard by him. The bishop understood St. John's special gift to the hundreds of faithful waiting for him.

St. John did all this for love of Christ and his neighbors. He understood that his call to holiness was his vocation to love. He was a champion of the poor. He was a miracle worker, reportedly curing the sick, especially children. He converted souls with a mere word.

And he did this humbly, because all he wanted was to be a good priest.

St. John Vianney, pray for us. Teach us to love Jesus as you did, with every breath you took and each beat of your heart.

 Step 7

Hero of the Week (5 minutes)

This saint story will help to highlight and reinforce this lesson's topic. You may choose to read it aloud, have a candidate read it aloud, or have the class read it silently.

Lesson 17 | 161

Challenge of the Week

 If you want to hear from God, make sure the line is "clear." Go to Confession. A clear conscience makes it easier to listen to the voice of God. Then go to Adoration and spend a few minutes with Jesus. Write a prayer asking him for guidance in the space provided.

☐ **Explore a vocation.** One of the best ways to discern is to "investigate" what a specific vocation is like. Ask your priest or a religious what life is like for him or her. Ask a married couple (your parents, perhaps?) about the joys and sacrifices of their vocation. Write about something you found out that surprised you below.

☐ **Make a sacrifice this week.** You might get up extra early to go to daily Mass or refrain from desserts, TV, or gossip. Ask the Holy Spirit to help you conform your will to Christ's and to make your vocation clearer to you. Write what you did below.

_____

_____

_____

_____

_____

_____

_____

✝ Closing Prayer

"You did not choose me, but I chose you and appointed you that you should go and bear fruit and that your fruit should abide; so that whatever you ask the Father in my name, he may give it to you."

—John 15:16

Lord, you want to shower us with graces and bring our lives into focus. If we could see how perfectly our vocations match our deepest desires, we would be overcome with joy. Thank you for giving each of us the talents and abilities that will best serve your heavenly kingdom and lead to our greatest joy. Amen.

 Challenge of the Week (2 minutes)

Ask your candidates to read the "challenges" above and choose one of the three to complete this week. Have them check the box next to the challenge they intend to complete. Encourage them to write about their experiences in the space provided.

Step 9 **Homework Instructions and Updates** (2 minutes)

Remind candidates to read the "Wrap-Up" and the "What's That Word?" sections in the "Taking It Home" section of the Student Workbook. They should also review the "Watch It!" questions to prepare for the next "Review Game."

 Closing Prayer (3 minutes)

As a way of building up community, ask if there are any prayer intentions. Write them down (or have candidates share them aloud) and after praying for those intentions, have the class read the "Closing Prayer" together (provided in the Student Workbook).

⁴ CCC 1141, 1268, 1547

⁵ CCC 1548, 1566, 1570

⁶ CCC 1120, 1552

⁷ CCC 1545

162 | 🔥 CHOSEN

Taking It Home

For next week's "Review Game," be sure to read over the following …

1. **Watch It!** questions (page 157)
2. **Wrap-Up**
3. **"What's That Word?"**
4. **Memory Verse**

Don't forget to do your **Challenge of the Week** (page 161)

Wrap-Up

Did you know that, at Baptism, every new believer is anointed "priest, prophet, and king"? It's true— listen for it the next time you attend a Baptism. Though our priesthood is "essentially different" than that of the ordained, all the baptized share in Christ's priesthood and are called to be intercessors for the world and to offer God the sacrifice of their daily lives.⁴

Throughout our lives, we encounter God in powerful ways through other people. Christ came into the world through a humble, teenage girl. Mary said, "He who is mighty has done great things for me, and holy is his name" (Luke 1:49). God loves to use lowly creatures as a way to pour out blessings upon his people. This is a fundamental rule in our sacramental life as Catholics; the priesthood is a striking example of it.

When a priest receives Holy Orders, he no longer ministers in his own name or by his own particular gifts and charisms; rather, he ministers "in the person of Christ the Head" (*in persona Christi Capitis*). Jesus acts through bishops, priests, and deacons whenever they administer the sacraments, preach, or lead the Church.⁵

The priest does not say, "This is *Jesus'* body," but, "This is *my* body." And when hearing confessions, he does not say, "Jesus absolves you from your sins," but, "*I* absolve you."⁶ In a real way, each priest shares in the one priesthood of Jesus Christ, who works in and through him to minister to his people.⁷

As St. John Vianney, the patron saint of parish priests, puts it, "The priest continues the work of redemption on earth … If we really understood the priest on earth, we would die not of fright but of love. … The Priesthood is the love of the heart of Jesus" (CCC 1589).

"What's That Word?"

CELIBATE

When the disciples asked Jesus about marriage, he responded that some people choose not to get married "for the sake of the kingdom of heaven" (Matthew 19:12). CELIBATE describes those who choose not to get married so that they can better serve God.

Because Jesus affirmed *celibacy*, and because he himself was celibate, the Church finds it to be an appropriate discipline for priests who stand *in persona Christi Capitis* for us. However, because some of the apostles Jesus chose were married, married men can be ordained as permanent deacons in the Roman rite and to the priesthood in certain Eastern rites of the Church. (With a special permission granted by the Holy See, certain Protestant ministers who enter the Catholic Church can also be ordained to the priesthood even though they are married.)

HOLY ORDERS

Holy Orders is the sacrament by which the mission entrusted by Christ to the apostles continues to be exercised within the Church. This apostolic ministry of bishops, priests, and deacons is received at ordination through the laying on of hands and the calling down of the Holy Spirit.[8]

By virtue of ordination, priests and bishops have the power to re-present the sacrifice of the Mass. All ordained men are called, like Christ, to serve and teach God's people and to lay down their lives, often in public and heroic ways. This self-sacrifice recalls St. Paul's challenge to husbands to love their wives by "handing [themselves] over for her" (Ephesians 5:25, NAB). The Church sees the ordained man filling the role of Christ as Bridegroom of the Church.

Because Christ chose twelve men as apostles, and because the Church celebrates the sacraments as the Lord gave them to us, only men are ordained to the priesthood in the Catholic Church. Obviously, men are not "better" or "holier" than women. Mary had a "singular" role in the saving work of Christ,[9] yet she was not ordained. Whether we are married, single, or religious men or women, we are all called to serve God in different, yet equally important, ways that are consistent with our vocations. (*See also* CONSECRATION.)

VOCATIONAL DISCERNMENT

Vocation refers to the calling God has for each person's life. In the Bible, St. Paul explains the difference in vocations by describing the body: "If the whole body were an eye, where would be the hearing?" (1 Corinthians 12:17). God calls all people to serve in different ways: some in ordained ministry as deacons, priests, or bishops; others in the religious life; still others as lay persons, who may also receive a calling to marriage. (*See also* DISCERNMENT.)

[8] CCC 1536–1538

[9] CCC 968

Memory Verse:

"We know that in everything God works for good with those who love him, who are called according to his purpose."

—Romans 8:28

Any questions ?

How will I know if God is calling me to the priesthood or religious life?

St. Augustine once said, "Love God and do what you want." Obviously, he was presuming that if we love God, we will want things that are good. If you are right with God, and the idea of a vocation attracts you, it may be because God made you for it. This week, we learned three questions we can ask ourselves to help us discern:

1. Am I in a state of grace (or do I need to go to Confession)?

2. Am I doing my daily duties (studying, family time)?

3. Did I pray today?

Being able to answer "yes" to these questions will help you to be open to hearing God's voice more clearly. Since the Church began, men and women around the world have been inspired to dedicate themselves entirely to the service of God and the Church. Single men may discern the diocesan priesthood or a religious order. Single women may discern a life in one of hundreds of religious communities. The priesthood and religious life are powerful signs of God's love in the world. They are also signs of our ultimate destiny as the bride of Christ.

How does someone begin the discernment process?

Whether you are considering becoming a priest or an engineer, you can't really discern your options fully until you've talked to people who actually do what you are considering doing. Talk to a few priests or religious and ask them about their vocation. Consider going on a vocation discernment weekend sponsored by a nearby seminary or religious order.

Remember, every state of life has distinctive benefits and requires some kind of personal sacrifice. That's what love is—a willingness to give yourself to someone else. Each vocation has its unique challenges and joys, if we embrace our calling completely.

Pray and ask God what he has in mind for you! God doesn't want to take anything from you. He's never outdone in generosity. Ask him for a heart that's open to his will.

Did You Know?

In the fifth century, Pope St. Leo the Great met the ferocious pagan general, Attila the Hun, at the gates of Rome and talked him out of sacking the city. Attila and his army soon retreated and left the Romans in peace.

Notes

**Lesson 18
Leader's Notes**

Overview

The purpose of this lesson is to instill a hunger in the hearts of students to get to know God (and not simply *about* God) through prayer. As St. Thérèse of Lisieux observed in her *Autobiography*, "For me, prayer is a surge of the heart; it is a simple look turned toward heaven, it is a cry of recognition and of love, embracing both trial and joy"[10] (CCC 2558).

Our Catholic tradition has many different ways to approach God in prayer, including verbal prayer (both spontaneous and drawn from the treasury of the saints), meditation, and contemplation (see CCC 2700–2719). Through prayers of blessing and adoration, petition (also called *supplication),* intercession, thanksgiving, and praise, we experience God both through personal prayer and as a people of God, especially in the liturgy (see CCC 2626–2643).

Objectives of this Lesson

1. *Learning about God is not the same as getting to know God personally.* Prayer is essential to our relationship with God because it is the means by which we can experience his presence: "You will call upon me and come and pray to me and I will hear you" (Jeremiah 29:12; CCC 2559–2560).

2. *God calls man first:* "He tirelessly calls each of us to the mysterious encounter known as prayer" (CCC 2567). Because he is always there, calling to us, any step we make toward God is always a response (see CCC 2561, 2567).

3. *As Catholics, we have a treasure trove of both formal and personal prayer traditions* (see CCC 2625). Formal prayers include the Liturgy of the Hours, the Rosary, and the Divine Mercy Chaplet. One very powerful personal prayer tradition is *lectio divina* (Latin for "divine reading"), which has helped people pray with Scripture for 2,000 years (see CCC 2708).

4. *A commitment to prayer can change your life.* Prayer is not always easy, but God honors every attempt. It takes effort, dedication, and patience—but we are rewarded abundantly as we develop a deep friendship with God, allowing ourselves to be "taken over by the light of Christ" (John Paul II).[11]

This week you will need ...

A candle, crucifix, or other devotional for the "Opening Prayer."

"Are you talking to me?"

(Getting to Know God Through Prayer)

✝

Opening Prayer

"Our Father, who art in heaven,
hallowed be thy name;
thy kingdom come,
thy will be done, on earth as it is in heaven.
Give us this day our daily bread,
and forgive us our trespasses
as we forgive those who trespass against us;
and lead us not into temptation,
but deliver us from evil. Amen."

Lesson 18

Opening Prayer

Since prayer is a simple conversation with God, being able to pray informally, from the heart, is very important. We are going to do that right now.

We will go around the room, and each person will thank Jesus for one or two things and ask him for one or two things that he or she or a loved one needs.

Rather than saying, "I'd like to ask for_____" or, "I'm thankful for_____," instead say, "Jesus, I ask you for_____" and, "Jesus, thank you for_____." Talk *to* him.

Pass a sacramental or other devotional object (like a candle or a small crucifix) around the room for each student to hold as he or she prays.

Let's begin with the prayer that Jesus taught us. In the name of the Father …

 Step 1 **Welcome/Review Game** (5 minutes)

Begin by welcoming the class and telling them that you will be starting with a review of the previous lesson's material. On the DVD menu, click on Lesson 18; then on the sub-menu, click on "Review Game."

Have students answer the questions based on the previous lesson. For more information about how to adapt this game to meet the needs of your group, see the "Review Game" section in the Introduction to this Leader's Guide (page xvi).

 Step 2 **Challenge of the Week Review** (5 minutes)

Ask if anyone would like to share a "challenge experience" from the previous week. Try to draw students out by prompting them with basic questions regarding the challenges from last week (e.g.,"Did anyone choose the first challenge?").

Step 3 **Opening Prayer** (3 minutes)

Lead the class in the "Opening Prayer," which is included in the Student Workbook. Leader's Guide notes are provided above: Red text provides direction and guidance, and white text is for you to read aloud to the class.

166 | CHOSEN

Dive In:
Blessed Chiara Badano
"For You, Jesus"

A popular Italian teenager from a loving family, Chiara "Luce" Badano had a rock-solid faith that was nurtured by retreats and youth ministry programs. Chiara loved to hang out in coffee shops, and she was great at tennis, swimming, and mountain climbing. Her outgoing personality and adventurous spirit inspired her to dream of becoming a flight attendant. Chiara had a bright future ahead of her.

Then, one day, while playing tennis, Chiara experienced excruciating pain in her shoulder. Shortly afterward, she was diagnosed with a rare form of bone cancer. It's here that the real story of her life begins—the story of heroic virtue.

Chiara's explosive joy only increased with suffering. Cardinal Saldarini heard of this amazing teen and visited her in the hospital. Awestruck, he said, "The light in your eyes is splendid. Where does it come from?" Chiara's reply was simple. "I try to love Jesus as much as I can."

She often repeated the phrase, "If this is what you want, Jesus, so do I." When locks of her hair fell out, she would pray, "For you, Jesus." She endured great pain with even greater patience, always saying, "I want to share as much as possible in his suffering on the cross."

She would walk around the hospital counseling depressed patients. When she was encouraged to stop and rest, she said, "I'll have time to rest later." Ever thinking of others, she said, "*I have nothing left, but I still have my heart, and with that I can always love.*"

Chiara asked to be buried in a wedding gown. As the end of her short life drew near, she told her mother, "When you're getting me ready, Mum, you have to keep saying to yourself, 'Chiara Luce is now seeing Jesus.'"

She died on October 7, 1990 at age eighteen. Her parents and friends were with her. Her last words were, "Goodbye. Be happy because I'm happy."

Several years later, a young boy in Italy was dying from meningitis. His organs were shutting down, and there was no way to save his life. His parents learned of Chiara's story and sought her intercession. Their son was fully healed. A panel of doctors ruled that there was no medical explanation for this turn of events. Chiara was beatified on September 25, 2010.

Sometimes prayer changes the course of events in history. Sometimes prayer just changes us. Prayer didn't heal Chiara, but it gave her the grace to suffer with love and joy. Prayer, united with the communion of saints, worked a miracle in the life of the young boy with meningitis.

Prayer is one of the mightiest things we can do. Today we're going to learn how.

Step 4

Dive In (5 minutes)

Read this story aloud, have a candidate read it aloud, or have the class read it silently before watching the video segments. This thought-provoking story ties in to the lesson's topic and serves to set up the video presentation.

Watch It!

Segment 1: What Is Prayer?

1. In speaking about prayer, Father Toups calls the Book of
_____ the "masterpiece of the Old Testament."

   A) Proverbs (B) Psalms C) Wisdom D) Genesis

2. In the story of Martha and Mary, who feels overwhelmed with
chores and goes to the Lord with her burden? __Martha__

Segment 2: How to Pray (Lectio Divina)

1. *Lectio divina* is Latin for "divine _____."

   (A) reading B) prayer C) meditation D) mercy

2. There are four steps to praying *lectio divina*:

   Read, Reflect, __Relate__, and __Rest__

Segment 3: What Happens When I Pray?

1. **T** or **F?** Father Toups said that if prayer becomes dry or
difficult, stop and try again when it feels easier.

2. Although God is always waiting for us, prayer still takes
_____ on our part.

   A) discipline B) effort C) patience (D) A, B, and C

Small-Group Discussion

Segment 1: What Is Prayer?

1. When and where do you like to pray?

2. Share a time you experienced God while praying.

3. If a friend asked you how to pray, what would you say?

Segment 2: How to Pray (Lectio Divina)

1. What are some different kinds of prayer?[1]

2. Father Toups says, "Prayer is responding to and relating to God." What does this mean to you?

3. We often forget to listen to God when we pray. One way to listen is to read and reflect on Scripture. How is praying with Scripture different from studying it as we would do in a theology class?

Segment 3: What Happens When I Pray?

1. Was there ever a time when you found it difficult to pray? What, if anything, did you do about it?

2. Are you willing to make a commitment to deepening your prayer life? If so, be specific. When will you pray? For how long will you pray? What will you pray? Challenge yourself, but set realistic goals.[2]

Step 5 **Watch It!/Small-Group Discussion** (50 minutes)

On the video, click on Lesson 18, Segment 1. When Segment 1 ends, have students fill in the "Watch It!" questions (2 to 3 minutes). Run through them to be sure they wrote the correct answers so they will have them to prepare for the next "Review Game."

Next, lead students in a small-group discussion for Segment 1. You may begin by asking general questions like: "What part of the video spoke to you the most?" Discussion questions for each segment are provided in the blue box above.

Follow the same steps for Segments 2 and 3. (Allow for about 10 minutes of discussion time after each segment.)

Small-Group Discussion Leader's Notes

1. Formal prayers include the Rosary and the Liturgy of the Hours. *Lectio divina* is another form of personal prayer with Scripture in which we (1) Read, (2) Reflect, (3) Relate, and (4) Rest.

2. If students are hesitant to share, make it more general, and ask them what they think would be realistic for everyone (e.g., how many minutes we should pray per day or how often we should read the Bible).

Question:
How is talking to God like staying in touch with a friend you do not see every day? How is it different?

... God doesn't just want to tell you how to get there—he wants to go with you.

TO THE HEART with

I drive a lot: to the church, to the gym, to the homes of parishioners. As a busy priest on the highways in Cajun country, my life would look very different if I didn't have *her* ... you know, *Siri*. My world changed when Apple introduced Siri on the iPhone. She types my texts. She sends my emails. She even wakes me up in the morning.

My favorite feature of the iPhone is that Siri can tell me how to get to my destination. Siri tells me where to go and how to get there, and she lets me know if I'm heading in the wrong direction. Driving is much easier, especially when I don't know where to go, all because of Siri's voice. Gotta love that GPS!

Now, imagine this: Wouldn't the iPhone be even better if it had a *God* app? Think what life would be like if, at any moment, we could plug into God and know what to do in any given situation. Need

to know why life is so tough sometimes? Need to know where God is in this crazy world? Grab your phone and simply ask the app and *voila:* God's voice.

The good news is that God already has the app for us to hear his voice. It's called *prayer.* And, unlike Siri (who really doesn't know or care about me ... I know ... hard to believe), God is tirelessly pursuing every one of us![1]

Now, many of us want to pray. Many of us would love to hear God clearly. However, prayer can sometimes feel dry. Oftentimes, we get distracted. Moreover, many of us don't know what to do or how to start.

You're not the first person to want to go deeper with God. The good news is that for the past 2,000 years, people of every generation have wanted God just like you do. The Church in its wisdom

[1] CCC 2567

Step 6 **To the Heart** (10 minutes)

After the small-group discussions, read this story aloud, have a candidate read it aloud, or have the class read it silently. After the story (written by this week's video presenter), read the thought-provoking question(s) provided in the red "To the Heart" box above. Time permitting, ask follow-up questions and encourage discussion.

can teach us about prayer. And, if we persevere in learning how to pray, it's like having our own GPS in life. God can tell you how to get to your ultimate destination. God can tell you where to go, how to get there, and if you're heading in the wrong direction. Furthermore, God doesn't just want to tell you how to get there—he wants to go *with* you. God wants a relationship with you.

All you need is an open mind and a hungry heart. You can go deeper in your relationship with God. Set aside your phone, along with Siri and the other apps. God is ready to teach you. The Church is ready to teach you. Your personal GPS for life is called *prayer*.

Father Mark Toups

Find It!

What are the four types of mysteries prayed in the complete Rosary?

1. Joyful
2. Sorrowful
3. Glorious
4. Luminous

170 | CHOSEN

Hero of the Week

Born:
March 25, 1347

Died:
April 29, 1380

Memorial:
April 29

Patron Saint of:

- Europe
- against bodily ills
- against miscarriage
- against sexual temptation
- firefighters
- nurses

St. Catherine of Siena

Have you ever seen your guardian angel?

St. Catherine of Siena did. In fact, when she was a little girl, she could see other people's guardian angels, too. She also saw Jesus, Mary, and many saints. Sometimes her mystical experiences were witnessed by others—she would amaze her mother by literally flying upstairs, her feet never quite touching the steps!

Catherine wanted nothing more than to be with Jesus in prayer. One day, he came to her when she was in prayer and slipped a ring with four pearls and a diamond on her hand—a ring no one else could see. From that moment, she considered herself married to the Lord. Her heart beat so loudly for love of God, it would disturb others at Mass; she lived for years sustained by nothing but the Eucharist at Mass.

This amazing intimacy produced a strong faith that led her to do amazing things. At sixteen, she joined the Dominican Order as a tertiary—a lay member who would live in the world instead of in a convent. Her family had other plans for her that included marriage, but she put up a strong defense, and eventually she was allowed to follow her heart.

When the Plague swept her city in 1374, killing more than 80,000 people, she tended to the sick and cured many of them miraculously through her prayers. Many were converted on the spot. Soon, she had many followers.

Catherine began to travel extensively and to wield some influence through the power of her letters, not just to the people with whom she came into contact, but with political and influential figures. She suffered greatly over the Western Schism, a time when two papal courts existed, one in Rome and one in Avignon, France. Catherine worked diligently to establish peace, and because of her challenge to Pope Gregory XI, the pope and his administration returned to Rome. Catherine even served as an Ambassador from Florence in order to make peace in the Papal States.

She died of a stroke at age thirty-three, leaving behind a powerful legacy in her writings, which are considered some of the most profoundly brilliant writings in the Church, leading to the honor of her being proclaimed a doctor of the Church, a distinction she shares with just three other women (Teresa of Avila, Thérèse of Lisieux, and Hildegard of Bingen).

St. Catherine, pray for us. Show us, through your example, the power of prayer for consolation as well as change.

Step 7

Hero of the Week (5 minutes)

This saint story will help to highlight and reinforce this lesson's topic. You may choose to read it aloud, have a candidate read it aloud, or have the class read it silently.

Challenge of the Week

 Start a prayer journal. For each entry, note the date and what you prayed for. As you accumulate entries, go back and see which of your prayers have been answered. Be sure to thank God, even if you didn't get the answer you wanted. Write a question or comment from your journal in the space below.

 Try LECTIO DIVINA **at home.** Choose a passage from Scripture, and read it in a quiet place. Ask the Holy Spirit to show you connections between the Scripture reading and your own life. Stop to reflect, and talk to God about what you read. Then, choose one action to help you apply that passage to your life. Finally, "rest" and give God a chance to speak to your heart. Write about it in the space below.

 Choose a relationship in your life that needs attention, and do something concrete about it. Does someone need a kind word, a little of your time, an apology, forgiveness, or a simple greeting? Without violating anyone's privacy, tell a little about it next week.

_____

✝ Closing Prayer

"Ask, and it will be given you; seek, and you will find; knock, and it will be opened to you."

—Matthew 7:7

Lord Jesus, you invite us to pray with confidence, expecting answers and an outpouring of graces. But sometimes when we pray, our hearts are in the wrong place. Show us what parts of our lives need to change in order for our prayers to become holy and our wills to be conformed to yours. Give us the grace to make time for daily prayer and to listen for your gentle voice in our lives. Amen.

Step 8 Challenge of the Week (2 minutes)

Ask your candidates to read the "challenges" above and choose one of the three to complete this week. Have them check the box next to the challenge they intend to complete. Encourage them to write about their experiences in the space provided.

Step 9 Homework Instructions and Updates (2 minutes)

Remind candidates to read the "Wrap-Up" and the "What's That Word?" sections in the "Taking It Home" section of the Student Workbook. They should also review the "Watch It!" questions to prepare for the next "Review Game."

Step 10 Closing Prayer (3 minutes)

As a way of building up community, ask if there are any prayer intentions. Write them down (or have candidates share them aloud) and after praying for those intentions, have the class read the "Closing Prayer" together (provided in the Student Workbook).

172 | CHOSEN

Taking It Home

For next week's "Review Game," be sure to read over the following ...

1. **Watch It!** questions (page 167)
2. **Wrap-Up**
3. **"What's That Word?"**
4. **Memory Verse**

Don't forget to do your
Challenge of the Week (page 171)

Wrap-Up

Imagine you had a good friend who was moving away. How would you make sure you stayed in touch? Would you just *talk about* your friend? Would you text or email a line or two, without bothering to read or respond to your friend's messages? Would you avoid picking up the phone when that person's number came up on Caller ID? Of course not.

God gives us lots of ways to stay in touch with him through personal prayer, which is a two-way conversation with God. There are many helpful devotional prayers the Church offers us to help us pray: The Rosary, litanies, novenas, and the Stations of the Cross are just a few of these. The highest and most powerful form of prayer is liturgy, specifically the Liturgy of the Eucharist (i.e., the Mass). Take advantage of that!

One of the most important ways to stay in touch with God, however, is through personal, conversational prayer. Prayer is simply a *conversation* with God, and a daily "heart-to-heart" with God needs to be the foundation of all of our prayers and the foundation of our lives.

If you're thinking about prayer, it's because God is thinking about you. If you're thirsty for prayer, it's because God is thirsty for you. As the *Catechism* reminds us: "Whether we realize it or not, prayer is the encounter of God's thirst with ours. God thirsts that we may thirst for him" (CCC 2560).

Since prayer is a conversation, like any conversation, it goes two ways. It involves *speaking* and *listening*. To listen to God, start by reading just a little from one of the Gospels each day. Search online for "USCCB Daily Mass Reading" to find the Gospel for that day's Mass. Read it prayerfully. Engage your imagination in what you read. Think of what the people in the passage looked and sounded like. Picture yourself as one of the people in the story. Then, ask yourself, "What's God saying to me today through this reading?" Next, talk to him about what you reflected on. Prayerful reading of Scripture like that is called *lectio divina,* which means "divine reading."

Lesson 18 | 173

"What's That Word?"

CONTEMPLATION

CONTEMPLATION is a type of prayer that is marked by simple silence in the presence of God. It is often considered the highest stage of prayer because it includes a special closeness to God that is a taste of what our relationship with him will be like in heaven. Some of the Church's greatest saints and mystics practiced contemplation and wrote about it to encourage others to pursue it. A good way to prepare for this kind of deep prayer is to reduce the amount of noise in your life and to take time to be silent, and, if possible, to pray in a Church where Jesus is present in the tabernacle. As you become more comfortable with silence, you will be better able to hear God speaking and be aware of his presence.

LECTIO DIVINA

Lectio divina, or divine reading, is a form of meditative prayer based on reading Scripture. The four steps of *lectio divina* are: read (*lectio*), reflect (*meditatio* or meditate), relate (*oratio* or pray), and rest (*contemplatio* or contemplate.)

MEDITATION

MEDITATION is a type of prayer in which we think about God and try to understand what he has said and is saying to us. Whereas VOCAL PRAYER is generally associated with speaking to God, either using our own words or common prayers like the Our Father, *meditation* is often associated with listening to God and making resolutions to live according to what we hear. Both *lectio divina* and the Rosary are traditional forms of Catholic meditative prayer.

Memory Verse:

"Rejoice always, pray constantly, give thanks in all circumstances; for this is the will of God in Christ Jesus for you."

—*1 Thessalonians 5:16-18*

174 | **CHOSEN**

PRAYER

God has made us for a relationship with him and longs to share his life with each one of us. *Prayer* is the communication with him that sustains and deepens that relationship. Traditionally, there are three types, or expressions, of prayer: vocal prayer, meditation, and contemplation.[2]

Jesus spent a great deal of time in prayer with his Father and taught his followers to pray, too.[3] The Our Father contains the five most common kinds of prayer: adoration, petition, intercession, thanksgiving, and praise.

Prayer is a two-way communication that includes speaking, listening, and simply being silent in God's presence. One of the best ways to hear from God is to read his Word, the Bible. The *Catechism* reminds us that "in the sacred books, the Father who is in heaven comes lovingly to meet his children, and talks with them" (CCC 104; see *Dei Verbum* 21).

[2] CCC 2721

[3] Mt 6:9-13

Did You Know?

Pope Paul VI was the first pope to do two things: visit the United States and address the United Nations General Assembly.

Any questions?

What should I say to God? I'm not sure how to start my end of the conversation ...

Just talk to him from your heart. A good way to talk to God is to remember the acronym "ACTS."

A is for "Adoration." That is simply telling God how amazing he is. Think of your favorite church song or the "Gloria" from Mass, and sing it to God in your heart.

C is for "Contrition." Contrition involves examining your conscience and asking God for forgiveness and strength. You can't grow as a person if you're not doing that every day.

T is for THANKSGIVING. Gratitude is a very powerful attitude. Count your blessings every day—especially on the days you're tempted to think your life stinks!

S is for SUPPLICATION. This means asking God for things you need or *interceding* for things other people need.

If you get up ten minutes early every morning, prayerfully read God's Word (perhaps the Gospel of the day), and then talk to God in the quiet before you go to school, it will change your life! (Set that alarm just a little earlier if you need to.)

Notes

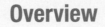

Overview

The purpose of this lesson is to inspire a deeper appreciation of Mary as Jesus' mother as well as the Queen of Heaven ... and of our hearts. We will also take a closer look at the "communion of saints" in order to understand why Catholics are so devoted to our heavenly brothers and sisters and why that is an important part of being a member of the family of God.

As Catholics, we are in constant contact with the whole Church, visible and invisible, those in heaven and those on earth—including those in Purgatory. In good times and bad, we are never truly alone in our joy or our grief, for we have an invisible "cloud of witnesses" interceding on our behalf (Hebrews 12:1). The one who is closest to Jesus, constantly praying for us, is the Blessed Mother, Mary.

Objectives of this Lesson

1. *Catholics love Jesus' mother.* We do not *adore* her (adoration is for God alone), but we honor her more than all the saints and angels, both as the mother of Jesus and as our spiritual mother. All true Marian devotion (such as the Rosary) points to Christ (see CCC 2673–2679).

2. *The Church has defined four essential beliefs (dogmas) about Mary:* (1) She is "Mother of God," (2) the Immaculate Conception, (3) her perpetual virginity, and (4) the Assumption. The Church also confirms that Mary is "our Mother in the order of grace." All of these teachings are rooted in her relationship to Jesus, who is both God and man (see CCC 466, 491, 499, 966, 969).

3. *The saints are like stained glass.* The light and beauty of the saints comes not from themselves but from Christ shining through them. This is also true of Mary, the "Queen Mother" of all the saints. The saints are alive in Christ, praying for us and cheering us on (see Matthew 17:3, 22:31-32; CCC 956–958).

This week you will need ...

A set of rosary beads and a Bible (for the opening prayer)

"What's That Word?"

APPARITIONS

An *apparition* takes place when a heavenly being appears on earth. The angel Gabriel appeared to Mary to announce that she would be the mother of Jesus, and there are many accounts of Mary and other saints appearing to people on earth. Some of the well-known appearances of Mary were to St. Juan Diego at Guadalupe (1531), to a crowd of poor people at Knock Ireland (1879), to St. Bernadette Soubirous at Lourdes (1858), and to three children at Fatima (1917).

APPARITIONS are considered "private revelations." The Church does not require anyone to believe in apparitions, but learning about Church-approved apparitions, visiting apparition sites, and following Mary's word of encouragement can certainly be a source of personal spiritual blessing. Because some claims of apparitions have turned out to be false, the Church is careful about verifying such accounts and does not encourage or approve such apparitions until after they have ended.

COMMUNION OF SAINTS

The *communion of saints* is found in the Apostles' Creed. This communion refers to the lasting connection in the Body of Christ, through Christ our Head, between all those who love God and who partake in his divine life—on earth, in Purgatory, and in heaven.[6]

MARY

Mary is the woman God chose to be the mother of Jesus. She is called the Mother of God because her son is God the Son. God prepared Mary in a special way to be free from Original Sin and its effects. Jesus was conceived in Mary's womb by the power of the Holy Spirit, although her husband, St. Joseph, was Jesus' legal father,[7] she remained a virgin after the birth of Christ. At the end of her life, Mary was taken into heaven, body and soul (the ASSUMPTION).

While he was dying, Jesus placed Mary under the care of St. John the Apostle and in so doing, offered her to all of his "beloved disciples" as their SPIRITUAL MOTHER. She served as mother to the apostles, and she continues to watch over all her son's disciples with motherly care. Devotion to Mary is a way of entrusting ourselves to her

[6] CCC 962

[7] CCC 532

Memory Verse:

"And a great sign appeared in heaven, a woman clothed with the sun, with the moon under her feet, and on her head a crown of twelve stars."

—Revelation 12:1

184 | CHOSEN

8   1 Tm 2:5

9   CCC 2116–2117; Dt 18:10; Jer 29:8

10   Mt 17:1-6

11   Dt 34:7

12   CCC 828; 1 Cor 4:16

motherly care and looking to her example in following Christ; such devotions include praying the Rosary, offering prayers and hymns that honor her, celebrating Marian feasts, and attempting to follow her example as Jesus' disciple. (*See also* IMMACULATE CONCEPTION, ASSUMPTION, *and* PERPETUAL VIRGINITY OF MARY.)

MOTHERHOOD OF MARY

God chose Mary to play an important role in his saving work by becoming the mother of Jesus. In heaven, Mary continues to be our mother, praying for her son's disciples and building up the Church. The way in which Mary continues to care for her son's spiritual children is by serving as our MOTHER IN THE ORDER OF GRACE, primarily through her prayer and powerful intercession. Though Jesus is the only true Mediator between God and humanity,[8] Mary participates in the work of salvation better than any other human being. Because of her close and one-of-a-kind (i.e., "singular") relationship with Jesus, no human being cooperates in his work for the salvation of the world better, or more deeply, than his mother. Yet we, too, mediate grace when we pray for and help others to encounter her son. (*See also* CONSECRATION TO MARY.)

Did You Know?

When St. John Paul II was a cardinal in Krakow, his motto was "Totus Tuus" ("totally yours") meaning that, like St. Louis de Montfort, he considered himself completely entrusted to Mary as his mother. In 1982, as pope, he prayerfully entrusted the whole world to her.

Any questions?

Why do Catholics pray to Mary and the saints? Isn't talking to the dead forbidden in Scripture?

The Catholic Church has always taught that it is wrong to conjure spirits or dabble in witchcraft.[9] So why does the Church *also* teach us that the saints intercede for us and that we should *ask* for their intercession?

Let's tackle the "don't talk to dead people" first. In the Gospel of Matthew, Jesus talked with Moses and Elijah.[10] Although Scripture is clear that Moses had gone through physical death,[11] he was alive and well in God. In other words, Moses and Elijah were *saints*—and saints are alive in God, even if they have experienced physical death.

When the Church canonizes saints, this means:

- These men and women lived holy lives and died in a state of grace.

- Their souls were so purified in life (through penance and the practice of heroic virtue) that they went directly to heaven, without the need for Purgatory.

- They now live with God in heaven and can intercede for us.

- We should look to them as examples of how to follow Jesus.[12]

It helps to remember that the saints of God are united to him in a special—and more complete—way now that they are in heaven. In that sense, they are more alive than when they were on earth! Just as we can ask the living on this earth to pray to God for us, we can ask those in heaven to do the same.

Notes

Overview

The purpose of this lesson is to challenge teens to live a life of radical discipleship.* Following Jesus—in the footsteps of the saints and through the guidance of the Church—is the surest path to happiness. It is the sure way to become the people God created them to be.

It will not be easy, of course. To be Christian is to be *like Christ,* who promised that we would endure persecution, just as he did. "Blessed are those who are persecuted for righteousness' sake. ... Rejoice and be glad, for your reward is great in heaven, for so men persecuted the prophets who were before you" (Matthew 5:10-12).

Objectives of this Lesson

1. *We were created with a desire to be happy. Another word for "happiness" is "blessed."* When Jesus begins each beatitude by saying "Blessed are those who ..." we can think of him saying "*Happy* are those who ..." Our deepest longings will be perfectly satisfied only in heaven. Like a hungry stomach growls for food, the soul hungers for God (see CCC 1718).

2. *In the Beatitudes, Jesus pointed the way to experiencing true success and happiness, here and now.* Jesus is not speaking of an earthly, passing happiness, but an eternal, lasting peace and joy (see CCC 1723). The Beatitudes can be found in the first twelve verses of Matthew 5.

3. *The stories of the saints are like signposts, pointing us toward heaven.* In the diversity of their callings, gifts, and personalities, we see the universal call to holiness (see CCC 828).

4. *The moral life is not something we "have" to do, but something we were created to do.* The life of virtue is motivated by a desire for greatness—and a desire for holiness (see CCC 2013).

---

* To clarify, the title of this lesson means, "What would Jesus do if he were here today?"

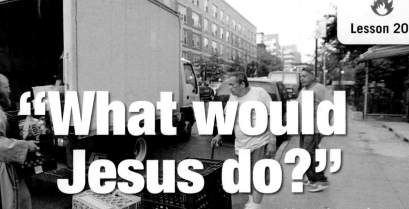

"What would Jesus do?"

(The Beatitudes as a Path to True Happiness)

✟

Opening Prayer

When he saw the crowds, he went up the mountain, and after he had sat down, his disciples came to him. He began to teach them, saying:

"Blessed are the poor in spirit,
for theirs is the kingdom of heaven.

Blessed are they who mourn,
for they will be comforted.

Blessed are the meek, for they will inherit the land.

Blessed are they who hunger and thirst
for righteousness, for they will be satisfied.

Blessed are the merciful,
for they will be shown mercy.

Blessed are the clean of heart,
for they will see God.

Blessed are the peacemakers,
for they will be called children of God.

Blessed are they who are persecuted
for the sake of righteousness, for theirs is the
kingdom of heaven.

Blessed are you when they insult you and persecute
you and utter every kind of evil against you [falsely]
because of me.

Rejoice and be glad, for your reward will be great
in heaven. Thus they persecuted the prophets who
were before you."

—*Matthew 5:1-12, NAB*

Opening Prayer

This week, we are going to take a look at the Beatitudes as taught by Jesus in the "Sermon on the Mount." For our opening prayer today, we are going to read the words of Christ as they appear in the Gospel of Matthew. Let's read them together slowly, attempting to take in all that Jesus is saying, as we begin to consider how this important passage applies to our lives here and now.

Let's pray. In the name of the Father …

 Step 1 **Welcome/Review Game** (5 minutes)

Begin by welcoming the class and telling them that you will be starting with a review of the previous lesson's material. On the DVD menu, click on Lesson 20; then on the sub-menu, click on "Review Game."

Have students answer the questions based on the previous lesson. For more information about how to adapt this game to meet the needs of your group, see the "Review Game" section in the Introduction to this Leader's Guide (page xvi).

 Step 2 **Challenge of the Week Review** (5 minutes)

Ask if anyone would like to share a "challenge experience" from the previous week. Try to draw students out by prompting them with basic questions regarding the challenges from last week (e.g., "Did anyone choose the first challenge?").

Step 3 **Opening Prayer** (3 minutes)

Lead the class in the "Opening Prayer," which is included in the Student Workbook. Leader's Guide notes are provided above: Red text provides direction and guidance, and white text is for you to read aloud to the class.

186 | CHOSEN

Dive In:
The "Eight Steps to Happiness"

Imagine you are at your graduation. The podium is set. The spotlight is on. A hush falls over the room as the commencement speaker approaches the microphone.

"I'm going to give you something very special today. They're called the 'Eight Steps to Happiness,' and I guarantee they will change your life!" she says. "Are you ready?"

A hush falls over the room—she has everyone's attention as she begins to speak.

1. "Don't obsess about money and achievement.

2. "Don't be afraid to let your heart feel sad, and to share in the hurts of others.

3. "Don't be too quick to take credit for the things you do well, or let it bother you when others don't recognize your contributions.

4. "Stay focused on God, until it feels like an unquenchable hunger.

5. "Keep your heart clean, even if it means not going to popular movies or parties.

6. "When people offend you or hurt you, forgive them right away. Don't hold on to grudges.

7. "Go out of your way to help others know God, even when it feels awkward and inconvenient.

8. "Finally: If people make fun of you for doing all of these things ... well, smile and be happy, because that's a sure sign that things are going well!"

Some people might laugh and walk out of the room if they heard this list. Pop culture gives us a totally different message, making it seem like many of these "steps to happiness" will lead to ... total failure. And yet, there is no surer path to *true* success.

> *"He is truly happy who has all that he wishes to have, and wishes to have nothing that he ought not to wish."*
> —St. Augustine

Dive In (5 minutes)

Read this story aloud, have a candidate read it aloud, or have the class read it silently before watching the video segments. This thought-provoking story ties in to the lesson's topic and serves to set up the video presentation.

Watch It!

Segment 1: The Beatitudes

1. Which of these is **not** one of the Beatitudes? Blessed are the _____.

   A) poor in spirit   B) merciful   (C) weak)   D) clean of heart

2. The beatitude "Blessed are those who are persecuted" reminds us of the need to have _____.

   A) invisibility   B) revenge   C) restitution   (D) courage)

Segment 2: The Beatitudes in Action

1. The word "beatitude" means a true and lasting _____.

   (A) happiness)   B) judgment   C) life of grace   D) covenant

2. The Franciscan Friars live out the Beatitudes by _____.

   A) feeding the poor   C) sheltering the homeless
   B) preaching the Gospel   (D) A, B, and C)

Segment 3: Living the Beatitudes

1. The happiness we experience in heaven is called the "_____ vision," when we see God face to face.

   A) blessed   B) Trinitarian   (C) beatific)   D) angelic

2. Which of these is not one of the seven Gifts of the Holy Spirit listed in Isaiah?

   A) knowledge   B) understanding   (C) intelligence)   D) counsel

---

Small-Group Discussion

Segment 1: The Beatitudes

1. Which Beatitude resonates most with you? Which one do you need to work on the most? What can you do to work on it?

2. What does being holy have to do with being happy? How can living the Beatitudes make us happier and more peaceful?

Segment 2: The Beatitudes in Action

1. What are some ways you can help the poor in your community?

2. Name some things that are important in life that people do not pay enough attention to.

3. What distracts or keeps us from paying attention to the important things in life?

Segment 3: Living the Beatitudes

1. What is the difference between being a "big deal" in the world and being truly "great"?

2. What can you do to focus more on the things that will matter forever?

Step 5 **Watch It!/Small-Group Discussion** (50 minutes)

On the video, click on Lesson 20, Segment 1. When Segment 1 ends, have students fill in the "Watch It!" questions (2 to 3 minutes). Run through them to be sure they wrote the correct answers so they will have them to prepare for the next "Review Game."

Next, lead students in a small-group discussion for Segment 1. You may begin by asking general questions like: "What part of the video spoke to you the most?" Discussion questions for each segment are provided in the blue box above.

Follow the same steps for Segments 2 and 3. (Allow for about 10 minutes of discussion time after each segment.)

188 | 🔥 CHOSEN

Question:

Have you ever asked God to provide something you needed? What happened?

" It was the first time I understood what it meant to live the Beatitudes. "

TO THE HEART with

A year after graduating from Stanford, I decided to quit my job and spend the summer as a missionary: living in a college dorm, running summer camps for children, and doing other kinds of Catholic outreach. There were forty of us from all over the world who had given up their summer to serve.

I learned so much from that experience! In particular, I learned what it means to surrender not only my "wants," but my needs as well. My wardrobe consisted of six outfits that I rotated. We ate food that was donated by people who wanted to support our work. We had no spending money for McDonalds or for coffee.

We were on the way back from World Youth Day in Toronto when the bus stopped and one of our group leaders got down and went into a restaurant. We had been on the bus for several days, and the peanut butter and jelly sandwiches we'd made for the trip had by that time grown quite stale.

I looked out the window and wondered what was going on. The minutes ticked by, and there was no movement. So I sat back and thought about the new world I was living in. I had liked my job as a coordinator for a rural health care program. I especially enjoyed working with health workers from rural Central America and the Caribbean. They had amazing stories of canoeing to work and saving people from venomous snakes in the jungle. Even so, I felt God was calling me to something deeper.

Suddenly, our leader broke my chain of thought and motioned us to come inside the restaurant. I was confused, but jumped off the bus and walked with my companions into the small Italian

---

Step 6 **To the Heart** (10 minutes)

After the small-group discussions, read this story aloud, have a candidate read it aloud, or have the class read it silently. After the story (written by this week's video presenter), read the thought-provoking question(s) provided in the red "To the Heart" box above. Time permitting, ask follow-up questions and encourage discussion.

restaurant. Someone told me that the owner of the store had donated a lunch—for all forty of us.

I was floored! Who does that? We waited happily for what I was sure would be a big pot of spaghetti. I was not expecting the beautiful shrimp linguini that came out, with iced tea and dessert, too!

I just could not understand the generosity of this stranger. What had moved him to accept the request of my group leader, who simply told him that we were Catholic missionaries returning from World Youth Day? We had no way of repaying him, but after the meal was over, we all went outside

and sang some hymns for him and his wife. I saw tears wetting their faces, and I knew that God would repay them in ways I would never know. It was the first time I understood what it meant to live the Beatitudes.

Blessed are the poor in spirit, for theirs is the kingdom of heaven. The poor in spirit: In the Old Testament, the poor (Hebrew, *anawim*) are those without material possessions, whose confidence is in God.

We had given up so much to follow him, but every day he blessed us beyond our wildest expectations.

Mary Ann Wiesinger

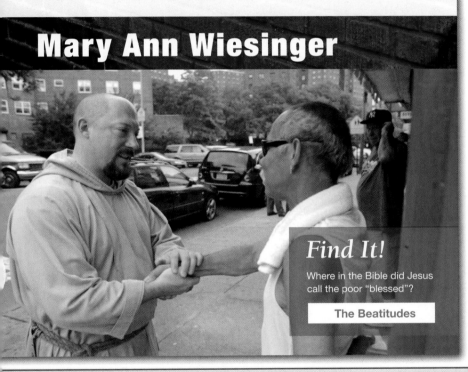

Find It!

Where in the Bible did Jesus call the poor "blessed"?

The Beatitudes

190 | CHOSEN

Hero of the Week

St. Francis of Assisi

Who is St. Francis?

Catholics around the world have statues depicting him holding birds in their gardens—especially since the election of Pope Francis. But who was this pope's namesake—St. Francis?

Francis' dad, a successful cloth merchant, had plenty of money, and Francis knew how to spend it! Francis loved to sing, wear the best clothes, and eat the best foods money could buy. Still, he wanted more. He wanted glory! That longing drove him to become a knight—a career he failed at miserably. In a battle between Assisi and Perugia, he was taken prisoner for more than a year and stripped of everything he'd *thought* was important: reputation, wealth, pleasure ... all gone, gone, gone.

A year later, ransomed with his father's gold, he set out again, but his dreams of glory were cut short, this time by illness. During this time, he had a dream telling him to go home to Assisi. And so he did—a changed man. Once the life of the party, Francis now retreated into a life of silent prayer.

Everywhere he went, Francis relinquished the trappings of wealth, for he had eyes only for "Lady Poverty." On one pilgrimage to Rome, Francis emptied his purse as a donation at St. Peter's Basilica. Upon returning home, Francis was praying before a crucifix and heard the voice of Jesus speak: "Francis, go and rebuild my Church, which as you can see is falling into ruin." He thought Jesus wanted him to renovate the little chapel where he was praying.

He rebuilt that little chapel where he'd first heard the voice of Christ, by strolling through Assisi and begging for stone and mortar. In time, it became clear that it wasn't the chapel that Jesus meant when he said to "rebuild my Church." Instead, Christ was referring to the need for renewal and healing in the universal Church.

Francis started a ministry serving the poor. He took on the poorest robes he could find (on which the Franciscan habit of today is based) and began to preach to the people of Assisi. In time, each of his followers was initiated by going to the town square and giving everything he owned to the poor. They lived in little huts around the church he had rebuilt and went out from there to preach and serve the needy. Soon, they numbered in the thousands, and Francis' preaching ministry spread throughout Italy and beyond.

Toward the end of his life, sick and going blind, he wrote his famous hymn of joy, the "Canticle of the Sun." Worn out by penance and labor, his body was brought back to the beloved chapel where his vocation began and where the huts of many of his friars had been assembled. He was overjoyed that he was able to remain faithful to Christ until the end. It hadn't been easy for him. He told his closest followers, "I have done my part. May Christ teach you to do yours."

St. Francis, pray for us. Inspire us by your humble example to always seek to do God's will.

Born:
Sometime in 1181 or 1182

Died:
October 3, 1226

Memorial:
October 4

Patron Saint of:
- animals
- merchants
- ecology

 Step 7 **Hero of the Week** (5 minutes)

This saint story will help to highlight and reinforce this lesson's topic. You may choose to read it aloud, have a candidate read it aloud, or have the class read it silently.

Challenge of the Week

 Get out of your comfort zone. Think about what makes your favorite hero great, and pick one small step you can take this week to become more like him or her. Write about it in the space below, and find a way to take that step this week!

 Meditate on the Beatitudes in Matthew 5 using the *lectio divina* techniques we learned in class. (Remember to read, reflect, relate, and rest.) Comment on the beatitude that you related to most in the space below.

 Think about your favorite saint or your Confirmation saint, and write about how that person lived the Beatitudes in his or her life.

_____

_____

_____

_____

_____

_____

_____

_____

_____

_____

✝ Closing Prayer

"You are the light of the world. A city set on a hill cannot be hid. Nor do men light a lamp and put it under a bushel, but on a stand, and it gives light to all in the house."

—*Matthew 5:14-15*

Lord Jesus, when we humble ourselves and follow you, your light shines through us and out to a dark world. Help us to be poor in spirit and meek; to mourn, to hunger and thirst for justice; to be merciful, pure of heart, and peacemakers; and to be willing to suffer for what is right. Make us heroes, Lord, by blessing us with a radical faith and willing hearts. Amen.

Step 8 — Challenge of the Week (2 minutes)

Ask your candidates to read the "challenges" above and choose one of the three to complete this week. Have them check the box next to the challenge they intend to complete. Encourage them to write about their experiences in the space provided.

Step 9 — Homework Instructions and Updates (2 minutes)

Remind candidates to read the "Wrap-Up" and the "What's That Word?" sections in the "Taking It Home" section of the Student Workbook. They should also review the "Watch It!" questions to prepare for the next "Review Game."

Step 10 — Closing Prayer (3 minutes)

As a way of building up community, ask if there are any prayer intentions. Write them down (or have candidates share them aloud) and after praying for those intentions, have the class read the "Closing Prayer" together (provided in the Student Workbook).

192 | CHOSEN

Taking It Home

For next week's "Review Game,"
be sure to read over the following …

1. **Watch It!** questions (page 187)
2. **Wrap-Up**
3. **"What's That Word?"**
4. **Memory Verse**

Don't forget to do your
Challenge of the Week (page 191)

Wrap-Up

Speaking at World Youth Day 2002, St. John Paul II noted, "I have felt the deep longing that beats within your hearts: *You want to be happy*! Dear young people, many and enticing are the voices that call out to you from all sides: many of these voices speak to you of a joy that can be had with money, with success, with power. Mostly they propose a joy that comes with the superficial and fleeting pleasure of the senses."

Yes, everyone wants to be happy. Before we even know what happiness is, we want it![1] Thousands of years ago, the Greek philosopher Aristotle wrote, "Happiness is the meaning and the purpose of life, the whole aim and end of human existence." The world would say we are "blessed" if we're rich, powerful, liked by all, and able to live for pleasure. The problem is, true and lasting happiness cannot be found in any of these things.

At World Youth Day 2002, St. John Paul II pointed out that Jesus gave us the true path to happiness—the Beatitudes—almost two millennia ago. "Christ has the answer to this desire of yours. But he asks you to trust him. True joy is a victory, something which cannot be obtained without a long and difficult struggle. Christ holds the secret of this victory … The 'Sermon on the Mount' marks out the map of this journey (to true happiness). The eight Beatitudes are the road signs that show the way. It is an uphill path, but he has walked it before us."

By "uphill path," St. John Paul II acknowledged that the kind of happiness Jesus offers can be difficult to achieve. It is the result of living by the grace of God and with our hearts set on his kingdom, rather than the passing things of this world. While it's not always easy to care about justice and peace, to mourn the pain and sin in the world, to be pure enough to see a person rather than an object in a member of the opposite sex, or to be hated for doing what's right, those are the types of things that bring us the happiness we were made for. It's a blessedness that lasts even through the hard times in life, because even in the midst of great pain, we can still know what life's all about and where we're ultimately headed. It's a happiness that nothing can take from us, both now and for eternity!

[1] CCC 1718

"What's That Word?"

BEATITUDE

BEATITUDE means ultimate happiness. Throughout history, people have pursued happiness in different ways, with varying degrees of success. We often find that the things we thought would make us happy, really don't, or that the happiness we experience does not last. God made us to find and experience beatitude, ultimate and never-ending happiness, with him. He put the desire for happiness in us and made it so strong that we would never give up the pursuit. Those who have most consistently found lasting happiness in life have found it in a life lived for and with him. Don't worry, be happy ... find God. He's waiting for you.

THE BEATITUDES

The *Beatitudes* are among Jesus' most fundamental teachings, describing the attitudes and rewards of the blessed. "Blessed are the poor in spirit, for theirs is the kingdom of heaven ..." (Matthew 5:3). The Beatitudes can seem to contradict our experience (how many people really consider it a blessing to be persecuted?), but they cause us to consider life from God's perspective. Those who try to find happiness in the pursuit of pleasure, power, wealth, or social standing are often disappointed, but those who practice the Beatitudes find that they lead to *beatitude,* that is, ultimate and lasting happiness.

Memory Verse:

"Whoever wishes to save his life will lose it, but whoever loses his life for my sake will find it."

– Matthew 16:25, NAB

HOLINESS

Holiness is a state of perfection or completeness. The Bible tells us that God is holy, but Jesus also tells us that we are to "be perfect, just as [our] heavenly Father is perfect" (Matthew 5:48, NAB). We are complete, or perfect, when we become what God made us to be. Though our own failings seem to make it impossible for God to expect perfection from us, he is not an overly demanding Father whose expectations for his children are unrealistic. He made us to be holy, and so he makes it possible, though not always easy, for us to be holy.

Holiness in one word is "love." The daily attempt to imitate the love of Jesus Christ as "people of the Beatitudes" is how we pursue holiness. By doing so, we not only become holy, but also help others become what God made them to be.

Did You Know?

The steps of St. Peter's Basilica are made from stone blocks that fell out of the walls of the Coliseum during an earthquake, placing these artifacts of Christian martyrdom under the feet of all who enter one of Rome's most holy places.

Notes

Lesson 21
Leader's Notes

Overview

In the last lesson, we examined the Beatitudes as God's path to help us discover goodness, beauty, truth, and freedom. In this lesson, we will focus on the spiritual "muscles" we need to exercise in order to have the strength we need for this journey. This exercise is called "growing in virtue."

The purpose of this lesson is to recognize that virtue is not just a high ideal, but a lifelong pursuit of holiness and *good* habits. Just as we gradually build up our physical strength and endurance through exercise, so the exercise of spiritual virtues makes us strong enough to withstand temptation and avoid the development of sinful habits (also called "vices"). Every vice has a corresponding virtue. It is not enough simply to "weed out" the bad habits—we must replace them with spiritually healthy ones.

Objectives of this Lesson

1. *If you want to be happy, practice virtue.* Each day, we take tiny steps toward virtue (good habits) or vice (sinful habits). With every choice, those habits become more and more ingrained in us, until we do them with ease (see CCC 1804).

2. *The virtuous life is not about "feelings," but actions.* Choosing to do good is hard work at first. But no pain, no gain. Not pursuing virtue means choosing vice (see CCC 1731, 1810).

3. *There are four cardinal virtues on which all other virtues "hinge":* prudence, justice, temperance, and fortitude (see CCC 1805).

4. *There are three theological virtues oriented toward God:* faith, hope, and charity (love). All the Gifts of the Holy Spirit are connected to these virtues (see CCC 1812–1813).

"Do I have what it takes?"

(Building Virtue – Your Spiritual Workout)

✝ Opening Prayer

Lord Jesus, through Mary you gave yourself to us.
So, through her Immaculate Heart, I give myself to you.
I offer you my prayers, works, joys, and sufferings of this day
in union with your sacrifice on the cross
which is offered at every Mass throughout the world.
I offer them for my family and friends, praying that you would bless them,
for the peace and salvation of the world,
and above all for the intentions of your Sacred Heart—
trusting that you know what is best for us all.
Fill me with the joy, strength, and Gifts of the Holy Spirit that I need
to live this day as your disciple
and to spread your kingdom on earth, just as your Mother did so perfectly.
Jesus, you have given your life for me; I give my life and my day for you.
Mary, pray for me. Amen.

Opening Prayer

The Christian life is not easy. Even cooperating with God's grace, it takes work and sacrifice to become the people God calls us to be. We can offer up our efforts as a type of prayer for a special intention or simply to call down God's blessing on the whole world.

It is a long-standing Catholic tradition to start every day by offering God a simple prayer, entrusting your joys, works, and sufferings to him as you strive to live a good Christian life. We are going to start today's lesson with a prayer of offering, and I encourage you to say this prayer every day when you wake up. Let's pray. In the name of the Father ...

 Step 1 **Welcome/Review Game** (5 minutes)

Begin by welcoming the class and telling them that you will be starting with a review of the previous lesson's material. On the DVD menu, click on Lesson 21; then on the sub-menu, click on "Review Game."

Have students answer the questions based on the previous lesson. For more information about how to adapt this game to meet the needs of your group, see the "Review Game" section in the Introduction to this Leader's Guide (page xvi).

 Step 2 **Challenge of the Week Review** (5 minutes)

Ask if anyone would like to share a "challenge experience" from the previous week. Try to draw students out by prompting them with basic questions regarding the challenges from last week (e.g.,"Did anyone choose the first challenge?").

Step 3 **Opening Prayer** (3 minutes)

Lead the class in the "Opening Prayer," which is included in the Student Workbook. Leader's Guide notes are provided above: Red text provides direction and guidance, and white text is for you to read aloud to the class.

196 | 🔥 CHOSEN

Dive In:
Finding Freedom – The Early Life of
Saint John Paul II

Growing up in twentieth-century Poland wasn't easy. Karol Wojtyla (St. John Paul II) was all too familiar with dictators and oppressive governments. When he was in high school, the Nazis took over his homeland. When he was in seminary, communists took over his homeland. He knew what it meant to have freedom taken away.

But he also knew that freedom doesn't consist in doing whatever you want to do, whenever you want to do it. He fought communism in Eastern Europe throughout most of his life, particularly through his work with the Solidarity Movement. Yet he knew that a false sense of unbridled freedom brings its own kind of self-centered slavery.

When he landed in the United States, John Paul II was greeted by then-president Ronald Reagan, who embraced him and said, "Welcome to the land of the free!"

"Free!" John Paul II replied, "Yes! But free for what? Free for what?"

Freedom is more than the ability to do what you want. *It's the power to do what is good.* Real freedom isn't achieved through wealth, fame, or power; it's achieved by growing in virtue.

Today we're going to find out how.

"Let us say 'yes' to love and not selfishness ... to life and not death ... to freedom and not enslavement."
—Pope Francis

Step 4 — Dive In (5 minutes)

Read this story aloud, have a candidate read it aloud, or have the class read it silently before watching the video segments. This thought-provoking story ties in to the lesson's topic and serves to set up the video presentation.

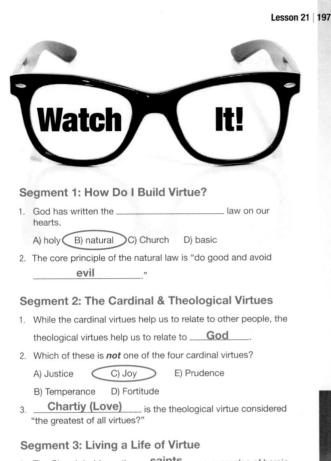

Lesson 21 | 197

Watch It!

Segment 1: How Do I Build Virtue?

1. God has written the _____ law on our hearts.

   A) holy   B) natural   C) Church   D) basic

2. The core principle of the natural law is "do good and avoid _____ **evil** _____."

Segment 2: The Cardinal & Theological Virtues

1. While the cardinal virtues help us to relate to other people, the theological virtues help us to relate to _____ **God** _____.

2. Which of these is **not** one of the four cardinal virtues?

   A) Justice   C) Joy   E) Prudence

   B) Temperance   D) Fortitude

3. _____ **Chartiy (Love)** _____ is the theological virtue considered "the greatest of all virtues?"

Segment 3: Living a Life of Virtue

1. The Church holds up the _____ **saints** _____ as examples of heroic virtue.

2. The Latin word _____ means manliness, excellence, and courage.

   A) *virtus*   B) *veritas*   C) *verbatim*   D) *vocatus*

Small-Group Discussion

Segment 1: How Do I Build Virtue?

1. How does the world define "freedom," and how does that wrong definition actually enslave people?[1]

2. What are some things you can do to "strengthen your spiritual muscles"?

Segment 2: The Cardinal & Theological Virtues

1. What are the cardinal virtues, and which one do you think you need most in your life right now?[2]

2. Why do you think love is considered "the greatest of all the virtues?"

3. What is the difference between the human virtues and the theological virtues?[3]

Segment 3: Living a Life of Virtue

1. How can the practice of virtue make someone more attractive to others and more successful in life?

2. Vices can seem like "fun," temporarily. However, in the long run, such behaviors make people very unattractive and unpleasant to be around. Why is that?

3. How do we grow in a virtue? Why is it important to develop virtuous habits, instead of just avoiding vice?

4. What are some ways we can help each other to grow in virtue?

 Step 5 ## Watch It!/Small-Group Discussion (50 minutes)

On the video, click on Lesson 21, Segment 1. When Segment 1 ends, have students fill in the "Watch It!" questions (2 to 3 minutes). Run through them to be sure they wrote the correct answers so they will have them to prepare for the next "Review Game."

Next, lead students in a small-group discussion for Segment 1. You may begin by asking general questions like: "What part of the video spoke to you the most?" Discussion questions for each segment are provided in the blue box above.

Follow the same steps for Segments 2 and 3. (Allow for about 10 minutes of discussion time after each segment.)

Small-Group Discussion Leader's Notes

1. Freedom for service vs. freedom from responsibility.

2. Prudence, justice, fortitude, and temperance (see CCC 1805).

3. The human virtues can be acquired through human effort and allow us to relate to other people in a more effective and balanced way. The theological virtues are gifts from God—received at Baptism—and make it possible to relate to him now and to live with him forever in heaven.

Question:

Why does Deacon Harold encourage the young woman to choose friends who want what she wants—to finish school and meet and marry a good man? What does choosing friends wisely have to do with living a virtuous life?

"That is a love worth waiting for."

TO THE HEART with

One Sunday, while I was greeting people after Mass, a teenager from the parish youth group approached me. She was visibly upset, so we sat down, and she shared her story.

She had been at her boyfriend's house the day before. They were sitting on the couch talking when he started making advances toward her. This made her uncomfortable, so she asked him to stop. She said, "I really like him, and I want to make him happy, but I'm not sure I'm ready for that kind of relationship."

I said, "I'm glad you're really thinking about this, instead of just doing what makes this boy happy. That's maturity! Remember, virtue is about making *positive* choices—not just avoiding bad ones. Next time, don't just go to his house and hope for the best. Go to a public place with other friends, or only go to his house when an adult is around.

"But let's say that for some reason you find yourself in that situation again: him asking you to do what you know is wrong. Stop and ask him, 'When are we getting married?' See what he says."

She gave me a funny look, so I added, "When you say that, one of two things will happen. He may get angry at you, and you'll know right away that all he cared about was what he could get from you, that he didn't really care about you as a person. Or he'll play Mr. Smooth: 'Oh, Baby, you know. Once I get my stuff together, then we can talk about all that.' If he says *that,* agree that it's important for him to 'get his stuff together' before having a family. And that's why a guy has to get himself together enough to *marry* you before he can be with you that way."

The next week I was once again greeting people after Mass, and there she was, standing in front of me, waiting to talk again. "I did what you said," she

Step 6

To the Heart (10 minutes)

After the small-group discussions, read this story aloud, have a candidate read it aloud, or have the class read it silently. After the story (written by this week's video presenter), read the thought-provoking question(s) provided in the red "To the Heart" box above. Time permitting, ask follow-up questions and encourage discussion.

told me. At her boyfriend's house the day before, they had been sitting on the couch watching television with his mom in the next room. "He still wouldn't leave me alone! So I stopped him and said, 'When are we getting married?' And guess what happened?"

"What?"

"He got real mad and stormed out of the room. So I went home." She had tears in her eyes. "I really thought he cared about me," she said.

I was proud of her. Even though her heart was bruised, this young woman had stayed strong and done the right thing. I reminded her of the good things in store for those who stay on the path of virtue: "The boy who did that to you does not deserve you. I will pray that one day, you will meet a young man who does. A man who will give his heart, his mind, his soul, and his body to you and to only you—and to the children you will have together—for the rest of your lives. That is a love worth waiting for. Trust me."

I encouraged her to find friends who, like her, wanted a bright future for themselves—to finish school, to spend time giving generously to their families and their community, and not to fall for players and "users."

Deacon Harold Burke-Sivers

Find It!

What does the Latin word *cardinal* mean?

To "hinge" or "pivot." The cardinal virtues are the four "hinges" on which the other human virtues rest.

200 | CHOSEN

Hero of the Week

Born:
April 6, 1901

Died:
July 4, 1925

Memorial:
July 4

Blessed Pier Giorgio Frassati

"Turn the other cheek, but go down swinging."

Blessed Pier Giorgio Frassati, the son of a wealthy newspaperman in Turin, Italy, was never looking for a fight, but he was not afraid to defend himself and his friends in the face of violence. During Church-organized demonstrations in Rome, he wielded a banner high and used the pole to fend off the blows of the opposition. Another time, when a group of angry fascists attacked his home, Pier Giorgio fought them off single-handedly—possibly saving his own life as well as his father's.

Pier Giorgio was what we might call a regular guy with extraordinary holiness and passion for life ... an engineering student at the Royal Polytechnic University of Turin. A lover of music, art, and literature, he was also an avid mountain climber. He loved life, had great devotion to the Blessed Mother, and loved to share his faith with his friends, whom he frequently invited to attend Mass with him. He went to daily Mass and often stayed up all night in Adoration when other young men his age would have been out at parties.

His parents never quite understood the depth of his devotion to Christ. In fact, a lot of people misunderstood him. He often gave some or all of his bus or train fare to the poor ... sometimes forcing him to run home or to ride in a third-class train car. One of his friends asked him why he rode in third class when he clearly could have afforded better. "Because there's no fourth class," he said. He lived very simply, although he came from a position of wealth and privilege. Pier Giorgio was the friend everyone wanted around because of his love of life and of his fellow man. And yet, he was also known among his friends as a man of prayer and devotion.

Pier Giorgio served the poor through various organizations such as the Society of St. Vincent de Paul. He said, "Christ comes to me daily to visit me in the Holy Eucharist. I return the visit by going to visit him in the poor."

His love of the poor and the impact of his personal connection with them became evident when he contracted polio and died at age twenty-four. The streets of Turin were lined with thousands of people who wanted to pay him homage at his funeral—most of them were the poor and needy that Pier had served! It was only then that much of his family learned of his life of extraordinary service. The cause for his canonization was brought forth by the poor of the city of Turin. At his beatification, St. John Paul II called him "the man of the eight beatitudes."

Blessed Pier Giorgio, pray for us. Invest us with a selfless love of life and of our neighbor.

 Step 7

Hero of the Week (5 minutes)

This saint story will help to highlight and reinforce this lesson's topic. You may choose to read it aloud, have a candidate read it aloud, or have the class read it silently.

Challenge of the Week

As part of your challenge, call or write your sponsor this week and invite him or her to attend the final class session and Confirmation rehearsal with you. (Your catechist will send the information home with you with the details). If your sponsor is unable to attend, invite a parent or other adult to "stand in" for your sponsor. Be sure to let your catechist know who will be coming.

☐ **What is your vision of human greatness?** Dr. Martin Luther King Jr. said, "Everybody can be great, because anyone can serve." Do you agree? Write a paragraph on the relationship between greatness and humility.

☐ **Get a spiritual workout.** Spend some time prayerfully reflecting on which vice underlies many of your bad choices or tendencies. Ask the Holy Spirit to guide you, and don't beat yourself up while doing it! Then think of the virtue that opposes that vice and two specific things you can do to grow stronger in that virtue. Do it! (If you choose to share about the experience next week, you don't have to share information about your vice, of course.)

☐ **Push-up Challenge!** Can your friends or family members name the theological or CARDINAL VIRTUES?[1] Offer to do five push-ups or sit-ups for each one they can name. (If they can't name at least one, *they* do the five push-ups or sit-ups!)

[1] CCC 1805–1809, 1813–1829

_____
_____
_____
_____
_____

✝ Closing Prayer

"Do not be conformed to this world but be transformed by the renewal of your mind, that you may prove what is the will of God, what is good and acceptable and perfect."

—*Romans 12:2*

Lord Jesus, make us hungry for holiness. You are so pleased when we take even a small step forward on the path of sanctity, and you bless our efforts a hundredfold. Help us to acquire the virtues most practiced by our Confirmation saints and to remember to ask for their help and protection every day. Amen.

 Step 8 **Challenge of the Week** (2 minutes)

Ask your candidates to read the "challenges" above and choose one of the three to complete this week. Have them check the box next to the challenge they intend to complete. Encourage them to write about their experiences in the space provided.

Step 9 **Homework Instructions and Updates** (2 minutes)

Remind candidates to read the "Wrap-Up" and the "What's That Word?" sections in the "Taking It Home" section of the Student Workbook. They should also review the "Watch It!" questions to prepare for the next "Review Game."

Step 10 **Closing Prayer** (3 minutes)

As a way of building up community, ask if there are any prayer intentions. Write them down (or have candidates share them aloud) and after praying for those intentions, have the class read the "Closing Prayer" together (provided in the Student Workbook).

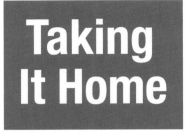

Taking It Home

For next week's "Review Game," be sure to read over the following …

1. **Watch It!** questions (page 197)
2. **Wrap-Up**
3. **"What's That Word?"**
4. **Memory Verse**

Don't forget to do your **Challenge of the Week** (page 201)

Wrap-Up

The Passover is when God freed his people from their slavery to Pharaoh, King of Egypt. In his Easter homily on March 31, 2013, Pope Francis observed that the "Passover" from the bondage of sin to the freedom of goodness must take place in all of us. "How many deserts, even today, do human beings need to cross—above all, the desert within, when we have no love for God or neighbor, when we fail to realize that we are guardians of all that the Creator has given us and continues to give us. God's mercy can make even the driest land become a garden, can restore life to dry bones."

Like Pharaoh, sin wants to make us its slave.[2] It doesn't "play nice" with us. The more we give in to our temptations, the more difficult it becomes to resist them—and the more we become enslaved. A habit, or tendency, to do what's wrong is called a "vice." Once you're caught in the grip of a vice, it takes some serious work to get out of it!

To the contrary, a virtue is the power to do what's right and good, even if it's difficult. A virtue isn't a restriction; it's an interior freedom that comes from the habit of choosing the good, until it comes naturally. We can achieve this freedom with the help of the Holy Spirit, who is prefigured as the "pillar of fire" that led God's people out of slavery in Egypt.

2   Gn 4:7

"What's That Word?"

VIRTUE

A VIRTUE is a good habit that makes it possible to act in a way that is pleasing to God. It is developed through practice and repeated good actions.[3] God created us to be virtuous, to possess habits that make us brave, fair, humble, and calm during trials. Due to the effects of Original Sin, however, we struggle to act as we should, and we have a tendency to do what we should not do. When we fight this tendency and try to act as we should in every situation, good habits develop, and we do what we should more easily. Just as working out is necessary for the athlete, so too is the pursuit of virtue necessary for the disciple.

CARDINAL VIRTUES

The cardinal virtues are prudence, justice, fortitude, and temperance. All other human (or moral) virtues "hinge" upon these four.[4]

Cardinal virtues are considered human virtues because they influence our conduct with others and are developed through practice (like good habits). Prudence makes it possible to recognize the right thing to do in a particular situation. Justice enables us to give others what is due to them. Fortitude gives us the strength to do the right thing when it is difficult, and temperance helps us keep our natural appetites in order.

THEOLOGICAL VIRTUES

The THEOLOGICAL VIRTUES are faith, hope, and charity. They are infused into our souls at Baptism along with sanctifying grace (see CCC 1266). While human virtues allow us to relate to other people, theological virtues make it possible for us to relate to God now and to live with him forever in heaven. Although these virtues are not acquired by effort, like the human virtues, we can grow in them or gradually lose them through the choices we make.

St. Paul taught that charity (from the Latin *caritas*) is the highest and greatest of the theological virtues.[5] Although this word is sometimes translated "love," we use the word "charity" to distinguish this kind of love from all others: It is the kind of love Christ showed us when he died on the cross. As we seek to perfect ourselves in charity, the other virtues will follow.

[3] CCC 1804

[4] CCC 1806–1809; Wis 8:7

[5] 1 Cor 13:13

Memory Verse:

"Resist the devil and he will flee from you. Draw near to God and he will draw near to you."

– James 4:7-8

Any questions?

How do I gain a virtue and escape a vice?

Change takes work—especially spiritual change. The good news is that it isn't too complicated. Here are a few tips to help you overcome "problem areas" in your life:

1. *Take it to Confession.* It's called "the sacrament of conversion" because it gives you the grace to change!

2. *Find a coach.* It's hard for us to critique ourselves objectively. That's why even the best pro-baseball players have multiple coaches and high-tech computer programs to critique their swing. A parent, solid friend, your Confirmation sponsor, or anyone who isn't afraid to challenge you will do. If there is a vice (sinful habit) that you find difficult to beat, your priest can be your coach! Just go face to face to Confession each time with the same priest, so he can give you the sacramental graces *and* practical advice (coaching) you need. It takes humility to do Confession like that, but it's worth it!

3. If you're really stuck in a vice, you should also think about when you are most tempted to sin, and *commit to staying out of those situations.* Also pray for the strength and resolve to persevere and remain strong. When you are tempted, even a short prayer such as, *"Lord, help me!"* can make you strong.

4. *Remember: Virtues and vices are both built up one decision at a time*—and every vice has a corresponding spiritual "antidote." For example, if you struggle with lust (looking upon a person as an object of gratification), practice chastity (keeping your eyes in the right places and recognizing the dignity of each person as a child of God). Work on the virtue that opposes whatever vice you have by doing things that you think a person with that virtue would do—even if it doesn't come naturally to you. Set specific goals for yourself.

5. God never gives up on you. *Don't give up on yourself!* Be patient.

Did You Know?

St. Nicholas was the Bishop of Myra (in Turkey) during the Emperor Diocletian's brutal suppression of Christianity, in the fourth century. Tortured and imprisoned for many years, he never denied the faith. The legend of Santa Claus (which comes from the Dutch for "Saint Nicholas") originated from the great charity he showed by making secret gifts to help the poor.

Notes

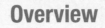

Overview

The purpose of this lesson is to present chastity as the path to authentic love and to introduce the "Theology of the Body" principles to this age group. We want to show how the personal expressions of authentic love mirror (truly, yet imperfectly) the love of the Blessed Trinity—that we are, indeed, "made in the image and likeness of God."

For teens, the virtue of chastity is best interpreted, not as a prohibition (avoid sex), but as an invitation (seek and reflect real love to others out of love for God). At the same time, we must offer practical applications in order to help them distinguish between authentic love and cultural counterfeits (e.g., lust).

Objectives of this Lesson

1. *God created us as sexual beings, and chastity is the path to authentic love.* Our sexuality is part of God's perfect plan. When he created man and woman and brought them together in marriage, God caused them to mirror, in a real way, the love of the Blessed Trinity—a creative, life-giving, sacrificial kind of love (see CCC 2331).

2. *The world often confuses lust with love.* Lust selfishly uses other people; love serves and puts the highest good of others above one's own desires (see CCC 2527–2532).

3. *The Church's teachings on sexuality are often misunderstood and misrepresented.* Teachings on subjects like contraception, pornography, and homosexuality are explained within the context of God's plan for all of us to experience true and authentic love (see CCC 2370, 2396).

4. *While sexual sin has serious consequences, God's grace is available for those who want to experience authentic love and joy.* Through the sacraments, we receive the healing and strength we need to live holy lives (see CCC 1468, 1695).

"Why wait?"
(God's Plan for Love and Sex)

Lesson 22

✝ Opening Prayer

"Only the chaste man and the chaste woman are capable of true love."
—*St. John Paul II*

"Holy Purity is granted by God when it is asked for with humility."
—*St. Josemaria Escriva*

"Lust indulged became habit, and habit unresisted became necessity."
—*St. Augustine*

"Purity is the fruit of prayer."
—*Blessed Teresa of Calcutta*

"Chastity is a difficult, long term matter; one must wait patiently for it to bear fruit. ... But at the same time, chastity is the sure way to happiness."
—*St. John Paul II*

Opening Prayer

Ask for or assign five students who will each read one of the saint quotes in the Student Workbook.

We often enter into prayer by reflecting on a passage of Scripture. For our opening prayer today, we are going to "chew" on the words of some saints about our topic: chastity. We are going to go around the room and read the saints' quotes in your workbook. We will pause for about five seconds between each quote to think about it.

Have each student read his or her saint quote.

Now, silently talk to Jesus in your own words about what was read.

Give them 60 seconds. If you have a little extra time, ask if they would like to share what impressed them.

Step 1 — Welcome/Review Game (5 minutes)

Begin by welcoming the class and telling them that you will be starting with a review of the previous lesson's material. On the DVD menu, click on Lesson 22; then on the sub-menu, click on "Review Game."

Have students answer the questions based on the previous lesson. For more information about how to adapt this game to meet the needs of your group, see the "Review Game" section in the Introduction to this Leader's Guide (page xvi).

Step 2 — Challenge of the Week Review (5 minutes)

Ask if anyone would like to share a "challenge experience" from the previous week. Try to draw students out by prompting them with basic questions regarding the challenges from last week (e.g.,"Did anyone choose the first challenge?").

Step 3 — Opening Prayer (3 minutes)

Lead the class in the "Opening Prayer," which is included in the Student Workbook. Leader's Guide notes are provided above: Red text provides direction and guidance, and white text is for you to read aloud to the class.

206 | CHOSEN

Dive In:
Finding Real Love

Bob Rice offered to share his story about finding real love.

I consciously gave my life to Jesus when I was fourteen years old. At that time, I knew only a few important things about the faith: I shouldn't steal stuff, I shouldn't lie, I should go to church every Sunday, and I should save sex for marriage. So I made a commitment to stay a virgin until I got married.

Sounds noble, right? Well, at that age, no girl was even remotely interested in me. But as time went on, I did eventually attract some girlfriends (playing guitar helped), and I entered the exciting world of male/female romance. How did I do? Not well. I understood virginity, but hadn't a clue about chastity. And so I really made a mess of things, hurting the women I dated—and myself as well.

I didn't really "get" the chastity message until I heard a conference speaker give an amazing talk about what chastity really is. It's not a restriction—it's a gift! God wants us to live in purity so we can have the greatest experience of love. I realized why sexual activity confuses and destroys beautiful relationships and why chastity protects them! I was thrilled to hear the truth.

When they passed out "chastity pledge cards," I hastily filled one out.

A little over a year later, I began dating a beautiful woman, and we were careful to keep the relationship chaste. I was amazed at how happy we were.

One day, after a few months of dating, we were praying together when I opened my Bible and the pledge card fell out. My new girlfriend picked up the card, then reached into her Bible and pulled out *her* card. "Look!" she said. They were the exact same card. From the same conference. On the same date.

While I was in one corner of the room, committing myself to purity for God and my future spouse, she was in another corner of the room, pledging the same thing.

We were married a year later.

Bob's story, like many others, shows us that chastity isn't the restraint that keeps you from experiencing life. It's the virtue that helps you experience real love. This week we're going to explore how.

> *"In dangers, in doubts, in difficulties, think of Mary, call upon Mary. Let not her name depart from your lips, never suffer it to leave your heart."*
>
> —St. Bernard

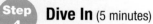

Step 4 — **Dive In** (5 minutes)

Read this story aloud, have a candidate read it aloud, or have the class read it silently before watching the video segments. This thought-provoking story ties in to the lesson's topic and serves to set up the video presentation.

Watch It!

Segment 1: Love vs. Lust

1. Chastity frees us to _____love_____.

2. In Jason's story, the girl gave him a _____ indicating she was breaking off an unhealthy relationship.

   A) ring   B) note   C) hard time   (D) necklace)

Segment 2: Tough Questions About Chastity

1. Chastity calls us to a love that is free, total, _____, and fruitful (life giving).

   (A) faithful)   B) holy   C) joyful   D) pure

2. Taking birth control ("the Pill") causes more than _____ biological changes in a woman's body.

   A) 50   B) 75   C) 100   (D) 150) *

Segment 3: Tips for Practicing Chastity

1. The first thing Jason recommends for being and staying chaste is _____prayer_____.

2. When we fail in chastity, the Sacrament of _____Confession_____ gives us the grace to continue to pursue virtue and holiness.

*Malcolm Potts and Peter Diggory, *Textbook of Contraceptive Practice,* 2nd ed. (Cambridge: Cambridge University Press, 1983), 155.

Small-Group Discussion

Segment 1: Love vs. Lust

1. How is chastity a "positive" virtue (something to do, rather than to avoid)?

2. What is the difference between love and lust?

Segment 2: Tough Questions About Chastity

1. What are some ways that sexual impurity destroys relationships and hurts people?

2. Do you think living a chaste life is possible? If there are so many benefits to living a chaste life, why do you think we seldom, if ever, hear this message?

Segment 3: Tips for Practicing Chastity

1. What practical things can you do to live out the love God is calling you to in purity?

2. In the Beatitudes, Jesus said that purity of heart was necessary to see God. What does this mean to you?

Step 5 **Watch It!/Small-Group Discussion** (50 minutes)

On the video, click on Lesson 22, Segment 1. When Segment 1 ends, have students fill in the "Watch It!" questions (2 to 3 minutes). Run through them to be sure they wrote the correct answers so they will have them to prepare for the next "Review Game."

Next, lead students in a small-group discussion for Segment 1. You may begin by asking general questions like: "What part of the video spoke to you the most?" Discussion questions for each segment are provided in the blue box above.

Follow the same steps for Segments 2 and 3. (Allow for about 10 minutes of discussion time after each segment.)

208 | CHOSEN

Question:

God created us to be in relationship with other people. How can we express what we feel—including physical attraction—in ways that are positive and "pure of heart"?

Chastity ... is about wanting heaven for the person you love.

TO THE HEART with

A few months before my wedding, I received a phone call from England, asking if my fiancée and I would be willing to be part of a BBC documentary on chastity. Apparently, news of an American couple who wasn't living or sleeping together prior to marriage had traveled all the way to Europe. It sounded like a fun opportunity.

The producer and her camera crew flew to California and followed us around the Gaslamp Quarter of downtown San Diego. They watched a few of my groomsmen and me as we surfed, and they accompanied Crystalina as she tried on her wedding dress for the first time. And, of course, they asked us all kinds of awkward questions about why we weren't sleeping together.

A few months after Crystalina and I returned from our honeymoon, we received a package from England containing the footage that had been aired. Excitedly, she and I turned on the TV. The show, *Anna in Wonderland,* featured our interviewer, Anna, who travels the world ... experiencing bizarre cultures. As the closing credits rolled, we heard: "Join us next week, when Anna visits a colony of vampires!"

A little (belated) research on my part uncovered that Anna had also done shows on female professional wrestlers, psychics, prostitutes, people who believe they have animals living inside of them ... and, now, my wife and me. Yep, a chaste young couple is *bizarre*—right up there with vampires.

Granted, it's not easy to follow the Church's teachings on sexuality when the rest of the world is bent on instant gratification (and is suffering the consequences). St. John Paul II declared,

Step 6

To the Heart (10 minutes)

After the small-group discussions, read this story aloud, have a candidate read it aloud, or have the class read it silently. After the story (written by this week's video presenter), read the thought-provoking question(s) provided in the red "To the Heart" box above. Time permitting, ask follow-up questions and encourage discussion.

Lesson 22 | 209

"... chastity is a difficult, long-term matter; one must wait patiently for it to bear fruit, for the happiness of loving kindness which it must bring. But at the same time, chastity is the sure way to happiness."[1]

If you're reading this, maybe you're thinking, "How could following a bunch of religious rules bring happiness?" *Chastity isn't about following a litany of regulations so you don't go to hell. It's about wanting heaven for the person you love.* The point of purity is not to deny our desires, but to acknowledge their presence and their power and to ask God for the strength to love other people as God loves them. If we do this, our sexuality won't be something we hide from God. Rather, he will empower us to put our sexuality at the service of authentic love—a love that never reduces someone to an object for pleasure and that always puts what's good for another first.

Jason Evert

Find It!

What Ugandan martyr willingly lay down on a pyre to be burned, rather than allow young men at court (pages) to be sexually exploited by an evil king (Mwanga II)?

St. Charles Lwanga

210 | CHOSEN

Hero of the Week

St. Kateri Tekakwitha

Born:
1656

Died:
April 17, 1680

Memorial:
July 14

Patron Saint of:
- ecologists
- people in exile
- Native Americans

Television, movies, billboards, and magazines create misleading images of beauty, which try to persuade us that real beauty is on the outside—photo shopped, cropped, and enhanced.

When we buy into this false construct, we lose sight of the truth that a person's true value, dignity, and—yes—beauty is based on more than externals. By getting caught up in external trappings, we risk objectifying those around us, thereby forgetting their dignity—and our own as well.

St. Kateri Tekakwitha, an Iroquois convert to Catholicism, lived a brief life of suffering. Orphaned when her parents died in a smallpox outbreak, Kateri's face was scarred and her vision damaged by the same disease. In spite of this, she cultivated an inner beauty born from her understanding that the path to authentic love came from Jesus Christ alone.

Her remaining family tried to get her to marry, but her conviction and love of Christ was so profound that she professed, "I have consecrated myself entirely to Jesus, son of Mary. I have chosen him as my husband. He alone will take me as wife."

Kateri was ostracized and bullied for her Christian faith and for her vow to perpetual virginity, yet she held fast to both. She traveled over two hundred miles through rough woods, swamps, and dangerous rivers to settle in relative safety in the Jesuit mission of St. Francis Xavier near Montreal. There she spent time in the woods deep in prayer or with the Blessed Sacrament. It is said that people loved to listen to her and be near her because of her radiant inner beauty.

St. Kateri lived a life of service and penance, working with other young women in the tribal community. However, she suffered from poor health from her bout with smallpox, and she finally died at age twenty-four. Just after her death, the scars from Kateri's smallpox miraculously disappeared, leaving her skin perfect—a sign of God's recognition of her inner beauty. St. Kateri is the first Native American to be canonized a saint and is known as the Lily of the Mohawks because of her purity and virtue.

St. Kateri, pray for us. Your fidelity inspires us to live our lives chastely within our vocation, whether called to marriage, Holy Orders, the religious life, or the single life.

Step 7 — Hero of the Week (5 minutes)

This saint story will help to highlight and reinforce this lesson's topic. You may choose to read it aloud, have a candidate read it aloud, or have the class read it silently.

Challenge of the Week

 Think of some of your favorite songs. Choose one that has lyrics dealing with a relationship. Look at the lyrics and consider the tone and the message. Does the song reflect a Christian understanding of sexuality? Why or why not? Write about it in the space below.

 Try a new habit. Our culture bombards us with sinful images and words. Every time an impure thought or temptation comes to your mind, silently turn to the Blessed Mother in your heart by calling her name: "Mary, help me ..." Take note of any positive changes in your thoughts this week.

 Chastity is about more than not having sex. It's about loving rightly. How can you put this into practice this week? How can you, as a young man or young woman, do something to honor the opposite sex? Write about it here, and tell about it next week.

_____

✝ Closing Prayer

"For this is the will of God, your sanctification: that you abstain from immorality; that each one of you know how to control his own body in holiness and honor ..."

—*1 Thessalonians 4:3-4*

Loving Father, you created our bodies to be holy. Help us to recognize and resist the lie that sexual promiscuity is freedom. Help us hold to the truth: Purity is true freedom, freedom to love, while vice and sin only make us slaves! Inspire us, Lord, to trust in you, as we patiently wait for love. Amen.

Step 8 Challenge of the Week (2 minutes)

Ask your candidates to read the "challenges" above and choose one of the three to complete this week. Have them check the box next to the challenge they intend to complete. Encourage them to write about their experiences in the space provided.

Step 9 Homework Instructions and Updates (2 minutes)

Remind candidates to read the "Wrap-Up" and the "What's That Word?" sections in the "Taking It Home" section of the Student Workbook. They should also review the "Watch It!" questions to prepare for the next "Review Game."

Step 10 Closing Prayer (3 minutes)

As a way of building up community, ask if there are any prayer intentions. Write them down (or have candidates share them aloud) and after praying for those intentions, have the class read the "Closing Prayer" together (provided in the Student Workbook).

212 | CHOSEN

Taking It Home

For next week's "Review Game,"
be sure to read over the following ...

1. **Watch It!** questions (page 207)
2. **Wrap-Up**
3. **"What's That Word?"**
4. **Memory Verse**

Don't forget to do your
Challenge of the Week (page 211)

Wrap-Up

CHRISTIAN SEXUALITY embraces what St. John Paul II called the "Theology of the Body," which teaches that, when he made men and women, God was revealing to the world a glimpse of the love shared within the Blessed Trinity. In our bodies, we reflect that love to the extent that we give of ourselves for the good of others and use our gifts and abilities to serve others out of love for God.

Exercising the virtue of chastity prepares us for our future vocations. For most of us, dating helps us figure out (a) whether God is calling us (individually) to marriage and (b) what qualities we want in a future marriage partner. Dating is not an excuse to use each other selfishly, for pleasure or emotional affirmation. The virtue of chastity (the antidote to lust) empowers us to do what's good for others—protecting and respecting them, even when feelings of attraction are strong. When we do this, we protect ourselves—and we honor God as well as the other person's future spouse (whoever that may be).

Did You Know?

The early popes mostly kept their own names, but when a Roman priest named for the pagan god, Mercury, was elected in 533, he chose to take the name John II as more appropriate for his office. Since then, most popes have chosen new names for themselves.

"What's That Word?"

CHASTITY

Chastity is the virtue that helps us live according to God's plan for our sexuality. Chastity helps us use the great gift of our sexuality for authentic love and gives us the strength to save sexual activity for marriage. Use of our sexuality for selfish reasons or engaging in sexual activity outside of marriage is an abuse of the purpose for which God gave it to us. The pain of broken relationships, depression, sexually transmitted diseases, and unwanted pregnancy are a reminder that sexual relations are intended for the exclusive and lifelong relationship of marriage. Married couples, too, are called to chastity by avoiding using their spouse in a lustful or selfish manner.

LOVE (CHARITY)

Because the word *love* is used not only to express our deepest feelings for another person, but also to express our desire for our favorite food, the word *charity* (also called "agape" in ancient Greek) is used to express the kind of love that God has for us—and the kind of love he calls us to live. Jesus demonstrated this kind of love when he willingly gave up his life for us. We keep the crucifix on our wall not so much to remind us of the ugliness of his death, but to remind us of the greatness of his love for us. Christian love is more than the feelings of affection we have for another person; it is an imitation of Jesus' sacrificial love for us, a love that seeks the good of the other above our own—even to the point of laying down our lives.

SEXUALITY

Sexuality is a word that is used to refer to the distinction between genders and the characteristics that are unique to males and females. A Christian perspective of sexuality acknowledges that God made men and women different but complementary for a reason. The physical aspects of men's and women's sexuality make it possible for them to conceive children, but sexuality is not just skin deep. Men and women think and act in accordance with their "maleness" or "femaleness" and experience emotions differently as well. These differences are part of God's plan for people to support each other and live in relationship with one another and not just as individuals.[2]

² CCC 2332

Memory Verse:

"So shun youthful passions and aim at righteousness, faith, love, and peace, along with those who call upon the Lord from a pure heart."

—2 Timothy 2:22

Any questions?

How can sex hurt someone, if you really love the other person?

It's time we stop confusing lust with love. St. John Paul II rightly remarked that the "fire of pleasure ... burns quickly like a pile of withered grass. Passing encounters are only a caricature of love."[3] And because these feelings can be so powerful, they can trick us into doing something that can change our lives in a split second—and not for the better.

Authentic love does what's good for someone else, plain and simple. Is premarital sex good for someone? Let's look at the facts: Sexually active high-school girls are three times more likely to become depressed; sexually active boys are twice as likely. There are physical risks as well, including HIV and other diseases.

Chastity is good for your future! Those who wait are about seventy percent less likely to get divorced. On average, sexually active teens go on to earn sixteen percent less money than teens that waited. Finally, chastity is the only foolproof way to avoid the life-changer of teenage pregnancy.

Premarital sex is a grave sin and has a devastating effect on future romantic relationships, destroys your spiritual health, and can seriously damage family relationships. Promiscuity risks all these things. Conversely, the sooner someone commits to chastity, the better off that person will be!

Chastity makes real love possible. It is the virtue that gives us the power to say to another person: "*I love you so much that you don't have to prove anything to me. Let me protect your emotional and physical health. Let me protect your relationship with your parents. Let me guard your relationship with God.*" Now that is love!

How far is "too far"?

Asking that question is like driving down the freeway with someone you love in the car and saying, "Let's see how close we can get to the oncoming traffic." If you love someone, you will keep that person as far away as possible from what might hurt him or her—physically, emotionally, and spiritually.

If you really want to be safe, commit to dating in public places, with other people around. Prove your love by staying in your lane!

What if we have already gone too far? Is it too late for us?

One of the great things about being Catholic is that when we sin, God is ready to forgive us and help us get back on track. That doesn't mean that he magically removes the consequences of sin (which is why we need to exercise virtue). But you are worth far more to God than the sum total of your good or bad choices. You are a beloved, irreplaceable child of God. He loves you and wants you to experience authentic love!

Go to Confession—the graces of the sacrament will strengthen you to practice virtue. Talk with an adult you can trust about your struggle. It might be wise for you to take a break from dating, at least until you grow spiritually stronger. Spend some time with God, and create a list of "do's" and "don'ts" for dating, to help you avoid temptation. And don't date someone who doesn't agree with your list in the future! Then ask God to give you the strength to follow through.

Notes

Overview

Spreading the kingdom of God—through words and actions—is a mandatory part of the Christian life, not just for priests and religious, but for all believers. In the first days of his pontificate, Pope Francis visited a juvenile prison, washed the feet of single mothers, and went into the crowds to touch the hands of those who reached for him—putting his own safety at risk. Why did he do these things? We find the answer in an interview in 2012, when, as Cardinal Bergoglio (before being named pope), he observed:

"We need to avoid the spiritual sickness of a church that is wrapped up in its own world: When a church becomes like this, it grows sick. It is true that going out on to the street implies the risk of accidents happening, as they would to any ordinary man or woman. But ... if I had to choose between a wounded church that goes out on to the streets and a sick, withdrawn church, I would definitely choose the first one."[12]

To follow Jesus is to show concern and care for all, especially the poor and marginalized who are most in need of love and care. In the book of James, we read, "Religion that is pure and undefiled before God and the Father is this: to visit orphans and widows in their affliction, and to keep oneself unstained from the world" (James 1:27). Through these tiny acts of generosity and compassion, the Church has reached to the farthest corners of the world. And through the Sacrament of Confirmation, each of us is equipped to go out and do this most important work in the name of Christ and his Church.

Objectives of this Lesson

1. *The kingdom of God is both now and yet to come.* The Church is not comprised of spectacular buildings, but of the entire people of God—spanning the world and the centuries (see CCC 769, 2818).

2. *The Church is, by its very nature, "missionary."* It is the duty of every Christian to take part in the mission of the Church: to build up and spread the kingdom of God (see CCC 768).

3. *We will be called to account for what we do—or do not do—"to the least of our brothers."* Jesus is very clear about our obligation to those in need in his parable of the sheep and goats in Matthew 25 (see CCC 1039).

"How do I build the kingdom?"

(Saying "Yes" to the Mission of Christ and His Church)

Lesson 23

✝

Opening Prayer

"Then the king will say to those on his right, 'Come, you who are blessed by my Father. Inherit the kingdom prepared for you from the foundation of the world.'

"'For I was hungry and you gave me food, I was thirsty and you gave me drink.'

"'[I was] a stranger and you welcomed me.'

"'[I was] naked and you clothed me.'

"'[I was] ill and you cared for me.'

"'[I was] in prison and you visited me.'

"Then the righteous will answer him and say, 'Lord, when did we see you hungry and feed you, or thirsty and give you drink? When did we see you a stranger and welcome you, or naked and clothe you? When did we see you ill or in prison, and visit you?'

"And the king will say to them in reply, 'Amen, I say to you, whatever you did for one of these least brothers of mine, you did for me.'"

—*Matthew 25:34-40, NAB*

Opening Prayer

Today we are going start by reading what Jesus told us about the Last Judgment.

> *Read Matthew 25:34-40, NAB.*

Now close your eyes and consider how this Gospel applies to you and the people in your life … Who in your life is hungry or thirsty for love, attention, or friendship? What can you do to feed them? Who in your school is lonely, left out, or rejected? Do you approach them at lunch or let them sit alone for fear of looking "uncool"?

Who are those who are literally hungry or who are so poor they cannot even afford clothes. What can you do to help? Who in your life is sick or elderly? Do you make the time to reach out to them? Do you know anyone in prison, or their family members? In what ways can you support or encourage them? Now, silently, talk to Jesus in your own words about the reading.

> *Give them 60 seconds. If you have a little extra time for the class, ask if they would like to share what moved them.*

Step 1 — Welcome/Review Game (5 minutes)

Begin by welcoming the class and telling them that you will be starting with a review of the previous lesson's material. On the DVD menu, click on Lesson 23; then on the sub-menu, click on "Review Game."

Have students answer the questions based on the previous lesson. For more information about how to adapt this game to meet the needs of your group, see the "Review Game" section in the Introduction to this Leader's Guide (page xvi).

Step 2 — Challenge of the Week Review (5 minutes)

Ask if anyone would like to share a "challenge experience" from the previous week. Try to draw students out by prompting them with basic questions regarding the challenges from last week (e.g., "Did anyone choose the first challenge?").

Step 3 — Opening Prayer (3 minutes)

Lead the class in the "Opening Prayer," which is included in the Student Workbook. Leader's Guide notes are provided above: Red text provides direction and guidance, and white text is for you to read aloud to the class.

216 | CHOSEN

Dive In:
At St. Peter's Basilica

Sentenced to crucifixion by Nero, this apostle didn't think himself worthy to die like the Lord, and so he requested that his cross be turned upside down. According to tradition, St. Peter was buried as close as possible to the site of his martyrdom. Today, towering over his tomb, is one of the world's most beautiful works of architecture: St. Peter's Basilica.

The basilica, one of the most sacred places on earth, has a rich history that extends back to the time of Peter's burial. After St. Peter was buried, a simple shrine was placed atop his tomb. In AD 323, the Emperor Constantine had a beautiful church built there. It was finished after the emperor's death.

Centuries later, the basilica was in disrepair. Pope Nicholas V decided to demolish the old church and build a new basilica in its place. He commissioned Bernardo Rosselino from Florence to oversee the project. When Pope Nicholas died in 1455, little had been done to restore the site. Pope Julius II picked up Pope Nicholas V's initiative and commissioned Donato Bramante as the chief architect and grand designer. However, they also died before its completion, and over the years, other great artists like Raphael and Michelangelo Buonarroti became instrumental in the final design.

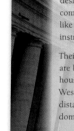

Their work paid off. Many popes and great saints are buried in this magnificent basilica, which also houses some of the most precious artwork in the Western world, including Michelangelo's *Pietà*. The distance from the marble floor to the top of the dome above the altar is 395 feet. More than two-and-a-half full-sized replicas of the Statue of Liberty, foot to torch, could be stacked inside it! Millions of pilgrims visit St. Peter's Basilica every year to lift their hearts and minds to heaven.

Was St. Peter actually buried there? Beneath the altar, archeologists unearthed a box with bones and an inscription that read, "Peter is here." Careful study determined the bones were that of a man who was between sixty-five and seventy years of age, and 5 feet 6 inches tall. All the bones were present except those of the feet—consistent with the way Peter died, feet fastened to the top of a cross. Indeed, this particular church is built upon "the rock" of Peter's faith.

But perhaps the most notable thing about the holy site is the fact that people spent their entire careers working on it with no hope of seeing the full fruit of their labor in their own lifetimes. St. Peter's Basilica wasn't finished until 1626—176 years, twenty-six popes, many architects, and countless artists and laborers after Nicholas V and Rosselino began working on it. But it wasn't about them. They knew they were part of building something bigger than themselves, and because of that, they left a great gift to humanity.

Jesus has invited his followers to do the same, not necessarily with brick and mortar, but as builders of his kingdom on earth—a kingdom we will only see completed, on earth as it is in heaven, at the end of time.

Step 4 **Dive In** (5 minutes)

Read this story aloud, have a candidate read it aloud, or have the class read it silently before watching the video segments. This thought-provoking story ties in to the lesson's topic and serves to set up the video presentation.

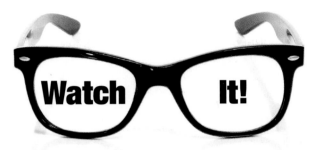

Lesson 23 | 217

Segment 1: We're on a Mission

1. Chris says that he looks like a banana but is shaped like a ___pear___.

2. To combat the evil we see in the world today, we are called to build a "culture of ___life___."

Segment 2: Building the Kingdom

1. Jesus is the Way, the ___Truth___, and the Life.

2. St. Paul tells us that we are all part of the Body of Christ. In his analogy, which part of the body is Christ?

   A) Feet   B) Hands   (C) Head)   D) Eyes

Segment 3: The Works of Mercy

1. The ___corporal___ works of mercy are oriented toward the body, that is, toward other people.

2. To comfort the sorrowful and to bear wrongs patiently are examples of the ___spiritual___ works of mercy.

3. Chris says we need to be "needy for ___Christ___."

Small-Group Discussion

Segment 1: We're on a Mission

1. How have you grown spiritually during this time of Confirmation preparation?

2. In Matthew 25, Jesus talks about "the least" and says that the way we treat them is the way we treat him. Who are some of "the least" among us today? The weak, small, vulnerable, forgotten, or unprotected?[1]

Segment 2: Building the Kingdom

1. What are some ways you can be Christ in your world?

2. Why do you think people are so hesitant to talk about their faith? Why is it easy to talk openly about other relationships, but not our relationship with God?

Segment 3: The Works of Mercy

1. Chris talked about getting out of our comfort zones. What does he mean, and how can we do that?

2. In what ways will Confirmation empower and oblige us to spread the kingdom of God in word and action?

 Step 5 **Watch It!/Small-Group Discussion** (50 minutes)

On the video, click on Lesson 23, Segment 1. When Segment 1 ends, have students fill in the "Watch It!" questions (2 to 3 minutes). Run through them to be sure they wrote the correct answers so they will have them to prepare for the next "Review Game."

Next, lead students in a small-group discussion for Segment 1. You may begin by asking general questions like: "What part of the video spoke to you the most?" Discussion questions for each segment are provided in the blue box above.

Follow the same steps for Segments 2 and 3. (Allow for about 10 minutes of discussion time after each segment.)

Small-Group Discussion Leader's Notes

1. Be sure to bring up unborn babies and the elderly as examples.

Question:

Tell of a time when you felt you were a part of something really great—in school, at church, or in your family. What made it "great"?

> *We serve a King who cares, a King who knows and loves his people.*

TO THE HEART with

In the year 2000, I went to Rome for the first time. A recent convert, I was excited beyond belief to spend ten days in the Eternal City. Every street and building told a story about my newfound faith. I vividly recall walking into St. Peter's Basilica and being struck by the grandeur of it. I looked up at the statues and felt as if they were saying to me, "Take this seriously. You're a part of something great."

Later that week, I joined a million other people in St. Peter's Square, awaiting the arrival of John Paul II. At the start of the ceremony, dozens of people emerged from the crowd carrying glowing lamps, which they placed in front of statues and icons on display. Someone explained that each lamp-bearer was honoring the original missionary who had brought the Gospel to his or her homeland. In that moment, I realized we were all the beneficiaries of a legacy thousands of years in the making.

The story of our Christian faith is a tale of epic proportion without a single insignificant plot detail or character. There are heroes and villains, battles and quests, sinister plots, and unseen adversaries. It is an adventure full of unsung heroes, majestic cities, and shepherds becoming kings. Most of all, it is the story of a group of people following in the footsteps of a Servant King, living the life and sharing the gifts entrusted to them for the good of the kingdom of God. Not only do we get to be a part of that kingdom, but we also are given the chance to find and bring others into something great—just like those original missionaries!

When all is said and done, I want my life to have been such a gift to others that, thousands of years

Step 6 **To the Heart** (10 minutes)

After the small-group discussions, read this story aloud, have a candidate read it aloud, or have the class read it silently. After the story (written by this week's video presenter), read the thought-provoking question(s) provided in the red "To the Heart" box above. Time permitting, ask follow-up questions and encourage discussion.

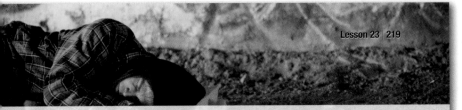

later, the effects of that gift can still be felt, even if the people touched have no idea who I am. We need to work together to build this kingdom of God, both in this world and for the one to come.

Each of us is entrusted with a different task and is given certain gifts to get the job done. While each of us must use our unique gifts to build up God's kingdom, all of us as followers of Christ are called to take a public stand against evil, to assist the poor and hurting, and to teach people about Jesus and his Church. We serve a King who cares, a King who knows and loves his people.

This is the profound reality: The kingdom we build is one that is resting upon our willingness to serve others, to follow in the steps of the One who first served us. The more we learn from the King who is a Servant, the more we will be the saints we are called to be in his kingdom. You and I truly are a part of something great!

Chris Padgett

Find It!

Which saint lived as a soldier and gambler before becoming a priest and starting the Red Cross movement, caring for the outcast poor and sick in prisons, on battlefields, and in hospitals?

St. Camillus de Lellis

Northbound

AT&T Station

220 | CHOSEN

Hero of the Week

Born:
July 22, 1515

Died:
May 27, 1595

Memorial:
May 26

Patron Saint of:
- Rome
- laughter
- joy
- humor

St. Philip Neri

"Smile, it makes people wonder what you're up to."

Is that an attitude you'd associate with holiness? It was for St. Philip Neri, a sixteenth-century Italian priest who dedicated his life to meeting the needs of ordinary people. Though he could have lived a life of comfort and privilege, he established the Oratory where he and the other "Fathers" of the community ministered to people who needed a listening ear.

Today, St. Philip Neri speaks to "ordinary" saints, those who aren't called to disappear into the desert, dressed in sackcloth and eating locusts like St. John the Baptist. He shows us that building the kingdom of God right here and now in the "real world" is a job for everyday saints! And one of the ways he spread the kingdom in his day was through the simple joy he brought to everything he did.

St. Philip Neri was joyfully Christian! In fact, he was known for having a sense of humor and even liked playful practical jokes. He often used humor as a means of evangelization, reminding others—and himself—to stay humble. He would occasionally shave off half his beard—making others laugh while reminding himself that it's the INTERIOR LIFE

that matters, not what others see on the outside.

He felt that laughter and smiles more perfectly fit the Christian than being sad and serious:

"A joyful heart is more easily made perfect than a downcast one."

That's not to say that he advocated a silly approach to living a Christian life, but rather, that our baptismal call is a joyful one, so we must live it with a joyful heart.

One of the remarkable things about St. Philip Neri is the story about his heart. When he died, doctors discovered that he had two broken ribs. They were attributed to the miraculous size of his heart, which, it is said, grew from the love he had for Christ and his brothers and sisters.

St. Philip Neri lived a life of *evangelization and* SOCIAL JUSTICE, serving not only the poor who needed to have their basic needs met, but also searching for the spiritual poor, who needed to hear the Good News. And that's something to smile about.

St. Philip Neri, pray for us. Help us spread the joy of God's boundless love to everyone we meet.

Step 7

Hero of the Week (5 minutes)

This saint story will help to highlight and reinforce this lesson's topic. You may choose to read it aloud, have a candidate read it aloud, or have the class read it silently.

Challenge of the Week

 Give a little! Start this week. Even if your earnings are minimal, put something in the collection basket on Sundays for the parish and its ministries. If you don't have any money, donate some of your time or some of the clothes collecting dust in your closet. Write about it below.

□ **Advocate for someone.** Do you know someone who needs a friend? Is there someone lonely or bullied at school? Step in, offer your friendship, and help this person to connect with friends or services he or she may need. Restoring another person's dignity is holy work and very pleasing to God. In the space below, write about your experience.

□ **Spread the word!** We're all called to evangelize. Find a way to share your faith this week, perhaps by inviting someone to church or to a youth ministry event, or even by simply posting your favorite Scripture passage on Facebook (or whatever social media you use).

_____

_____

_____

_____

_____

_____

Closing Prayer

"'Come, O blessed of my Father, inherit the kingdom prepared for you from the foundation of the world; for I was hungry and you gave me food, I was thirsty and you gave me drink, I was a stranger and you welcomed me ...'"

—*Matthew 25:34-35*

Lord, you love the poor and disadvantaged, and you're calling us to love them, too.

Help us to see *you* when we see anyone suffering, spiritually or physically, and give us the courage to reach out and help someone this week.

Every good thing comes from you, so increase our faith and make us generous, Lord, like you. Amen.

Before leading them in the closing prayer, remind candidates to bring their sponsors (or a parent or other "stand in") to the next session and to the Confirmation "rehearsal." If you have not already communicated directly with the adults, consider sending a reminder (via email, regular mail, or through the candidates) with the details.

 Step 8 **Challenge of the Week** (2 minutes)

Ask your candidates to read the "challenges" above and choose one of the three to complete this week. Have them check the box next to the challenge they intend to complete. Encourage them to write about their experiences in the space provided.

Step 9 **Homework Instructions and Updates** (2 minutes)

Remind candidates to read the "Wrap-Up" and the "What's That Word?" sections in the "Taking It Home" section of the Student Workbook. They should also review the "Watch It!" questions to prepare for the next "Review Game."

Step 10 **Closing Prayer** (3 minutes)

As a way of building up community, ask if there are any prayer intentions. Write them down (or have candidates share them aloud) and after praying for those intentions, have the class read the "Closing Prayer" together (provided in the Student Workbook).

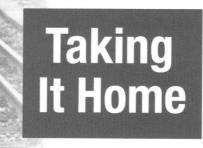

222 | CHOSEN

Taking It Home

For next week's "Review Game," be sure to read over the following …

1. **Watch It!** questions (page 217)
2. **Wrap-Up**
3. **"What's That Word?"**
4. **Memory Verse**

Don't forget to do your **Challenge of the Week** (page 221)

Wrap-Up

In his homily on March 24, 2013, Pope Francis had an encouraging word for the Catholic youth of the world:

"Dear young people! With Christ, the heart never grows old! Yet … all of you know very well that the King whom we follow and who accompanies us is very special: he is a King who loves even to the Cross and who teaches us to serve and to love. And you are not ashamed of his Cross! On the contrary, you embrace it because you have understood that it is in giving ourselves, in emerging from ourselves that we have true joy. … You carry the pilgrim Cross through all the Continents, along the highways of the world! You carry it in response to Jesus' call: Go, make disciples of all nations" (Matthew 28:19).

At the end of every Mass, God sends us out on a mission to build up the kingdom of God in our world by serving our families, our friends, and all those in our communities.

When we encounter Jesus alive in the Eucharist, we should be like the apostles, standing in awe before the empty tomb. They had encountered a love, a hope, and a power that was far too great to keep to themselves. They had to share it! Likewise, the love that Christ gives us in the Eucharist is far too great to keep to ourselves. The dismissal (*missa*) from Mass is "a starting point" for our mission to share not just a way of life, but the person of Jesus Christ, with the entire world.

For some people, the idea of evangelizing can be pretty intimidating. So let's start with a couple of simple ways to share your faith without feeling foolish.

First, some "don'ts":

1. ***Don't make it harder than it is.*** You don't need a theology degree or to travel across the globe to spread the faith (though if you get to do that, great!) The patron saint of foreign missions, St. Thérèse of Lisieux, did small things with great love, and her prayers helped strengthen those working to spread the Gospel.

2. ***Don't get discouraged or expect results according to your personal timetable.*** St. Monica prayed for fifteen years for her wayward and promiscuous son, St. Augustine, before he came around. It is easy to forget that God wants a person's conversion much more than you do. Remind yourself of how patient God has been with *you* over the years. Be that patient with others.

3. *Don't be confrontational or take pleasure in "stumping" the other person.* You may win the argument, but could end up losing a soul.

Now, some "do's"

1. *Pray before, during, and after* each opportunity you have to lead others to Jesus and the Church.[1] Prayer is ammunition for conversions. Without prayer, you'll be pulling the trigger, but shooting blanks.

2. *Be patient.* Be calm in your conversations so that you display the peace of Christ.[2] Sometimes, the most loving response is prayerful silence—to let the Holy Spirit speak.

3. *Be creative.* Look for ways to share good Catholic resources with friends, family, and neighbors. Visit the websites of the presenters from this program (see page 260) to find some

great books, booklets, and videos to help you spread the faith.

4. *Preach through your actions.* Living a virtuous life is a powerful way to share your Catholic faith.

5. *Practice humility.* When you don't know the answer to a question, say so. When others stump you, tell them that you'll get back to them (not back *at* them), and set a time to meet again. Then do some homework and bring them the answer. And relax, knowing that every question that can be asked, has been asked and answered over the 2,000-year history of the Church.

The more you live with the gentleness and courage of Christ in your life, the more you will draw others to him.

[1] 1 Thess 5:17

[2] 2 Tm 2:24-25

"What's That Word?"

THE KINGDOM

The *Catechism* glossary refers to the *kingdom* as "the reign or rule of God." Jesus announced that "the kingdom of God is at hand" (Mark 1:15), and he used this image to encourage his disciples who were suffering under the reign of worldly rulers.

He was letting them know that, despite their current struggles, God was still in charge and had not abandoned his people.

Jesus assures us that those who submit to him and follow his commands will reap the benefits

Memory Verse:

"Blessed are those who hunger and thirst for righteousness, for they shall be satisfied."

—Matthew 5:6

224 | **CHOSEN**

of his kingdom here and now in the Church. He encourages us to pray, "Thy kingdom come ... on earth as it is in heaven" (Matthew 6:10). We can help spread his kingdom by being holy so that God reigns over us, by sharing the good news of the Gospel with our family and friends through acts of service, and by working for a more just world.

SOCIAL JUSTICE

The cardinal virtue of *justice* assists us in giving God and other people what they deserve, what is fair, or what is "due" to them. *Social justice* is when we work with others to make society a more just place, one that serves the common good. Jesus helped his disciples understand what was due to their neighbor in his parable of the Good Samaritan[3] and his teaching of the "golden rule": Do to others what you would have them do to you.[4] True justice entails not only feeding the hungry, but caring for their spiritual needs as well. The grace of Confirmation helps us to live the demands of justice.

EVANGELIZATION

The word *evangelization* is based on a Greek term meaning "good news" (or "gospel"). *Evangelization* is the process of preaching the Gospel, both through words and example. God loves us, and he sent his Son, Jesus, who died so that we might have life with him now and forever in heaven.

St. John Paul II called for a "New Evangelization" in society, which can be accomplished by the witness of a life lived for Jesus, but which also includes the willingness to tell others about him. Just as the apostles were empowered by the Holy Spirit at Pentecost to bring this message of salvation to the world, the same Spirit empowers those who receive the Sacrament of Confirmation to proclaim the Good News to our world today—using all the means of communication we have available.

[3] Lk 10:25-37

[4] Mt 7:12

Did You Know?

A twelfth-century Belgian priest, Lambert le Bègue, founded a religious order that depended entirely on donations solicited from the public. It is thought that the term "beg" was derived from his name.

Notes

**Lesson 24
Leader's Notes**

Overview

The purpose of this lesson is to conclude the program by offering a final call to the life of discipleship as your students make their final preparations to receive the Sacrament of Confirmation.

As the title of the program suggests, each of us has been *Chosen* by God to follow Jesus and to spread his kingdom individually and through our participation in the Body of Christ. In the Sacrament of Confirmation, we are invited to embark on a mature phase of our relationship with Christ, in which the seeds that were planted at Confirmation and watered and pruned through the other sacraments, begin to blossom and bear fruit in the kingdom of God. In the past twenty-three lessons, we have explored how the teachings of the Church prepare us to enter into that mature life of faith. Now we will focus on the question, "What's next?"

Objectives of this Lesson

1. *Define discipleship.* To be "Christians" is to be followers of Christ, inviting the Lord to transform us from the inside out so that his light can shine brightly in the world around us (see CCC 787–789).

2. *The choice to follow Christ is made not just once, but daily.* At Confirmation, we take an important step on that lifelong journey of faith (see CCC 166, 1888–1889).

3. *God provides all we need to sustain us on our journey.* Prayer, community, the sacraments, service, Scripture reading, and faith formation are all vital components of cultivating a strong faith life (see CCC 1426–1428).

4. *We have been* **Chosen** *to become saints.* Every day, we can choose to let the light of Christ shine more brightly through us and to become the people God created us to be. There is nothing we can do to make God stop loving us—even when we sin, he provides a way back to grace (see CCC 1695–1696, 2013–2016).

This week you will need ...

A Bible for the "Opening Prayer."

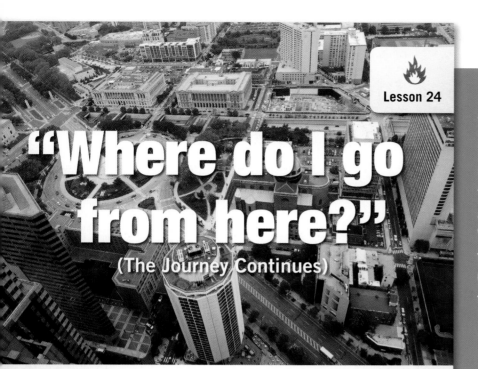

"Where do I go from here?"
(The Journey Continues)

Lesson 24

✝

Opening Prayer

Lord Jesus, you show your great love for us by inviting us to follow you. But you go further and dignify us by calling us to work with you as "fishers of men." We don't know why you love us so much, and we don't know why you believe in us so much, but we're glad you do, and we're thankful. You do not leave us without help, but give us the Holy Spirit to empower us to live as your sons and daughters. Help us, like St. Peter, to respond to you generously, knowing that you are never outdone in generosity, and that when we give you our lives, you give us eternal life and "life to the full." Amen.

Opening Prayer

We are going to start with *lectio divina*—a prayerful reading of Scripture.

Remember to engage your imagination in the reading. Put yourself in Peter's sandals as I read. What was he thinking and feeling? What did Jesus' expression say as he spoke to Peter? What changed in Peter's heart? Consider what Jesus is saying to you and me through this reading.

> *Have the teens take a deep breath and be silent for about 10 seconds; then start reading Luke 5:1-11.*
>
> *After 30 seconds of silence, say:*

Now silently talk to Jesus in your own words about the reading.

> *Give them another 60 seconds. Finish by leading the class in the "Opening Prayer."*

Let's pray. In the name of the Father …

 Step 1 **Welcome/Review Game** (5 minutes)

Begin by welcoming the class and telling them that you will be starting with a review of the previous lesson's material. On the DVD menu, click on Lesson 24; then on the sub-menu, click on "Review Game."

Have students answer the questions based on the previous lesson. For more information about how to adapt this game to meet the needs of your group, see the "Review Game" section in the Introduction to this Leader's Guide (page xvi).

 Step 2 **Challenge of the Week Review** (5 minutes)

Ask if anyone would like to share a "challenge experience" from the previous week. Try to draw students out by prompting them with basic questions regarding the challenges from last week (e.g.,"Did anyone choose the first challenge?").

Step 3 **Opening Prayer** (3 minutes)

Lead the class in the "Opening Prayer," which is included in the Student Workbook. Leader's Guide notes are provided above: Red text provides direction and guidance, and white text is for you to read aloud to the class.

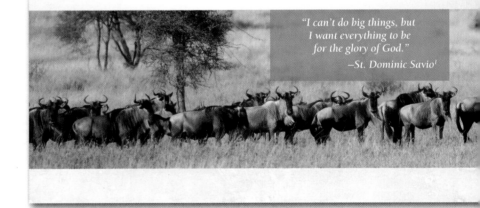

226 | CHOSEN

Dive In:
Pray... or Prey?

Poor wildebeest—it's the "Big Mac" of the Savanna. Lucky for the lion, the wildebeest has all the self-defense skills of a Happy Meal. But they travel in huge herds and can run up to forty miles per hour; each wildebeest is up to 600 pounds of pure muscle, and they have huge horns. So, despite the lack of wildebeest aggression, the lioness knows better than to run into a herd—she could get trampled. With instinctive hunting skills, a lioness watches carefully to see which wildebeest gets careless and wanders too far from the center of the herd. That's the one that gets eaten.

As you get older, you're going to leave the "herd" of family, friends, and the local church that has kept you safe for many years. Careful—there are a lot of things in this world that would devour your faith, hope, and love—temptations of the world, temptations from within, and the devil himself. St. Peter tells us that our ancient enemy prowls "like a roaring lion looking for [someone] to devour" (1 Peter 5:8, NAB).

Like the wildebeest, though, you aren't helpless! You are 600 pounds of pure spiritual muscle and can run forty miles an hour; you have huge horns, and, with your herd, you can trample anything in your way! (Okay, not exactly, but you know what I mean. You've been formed. You've been *chosen*.)

In the years ahead, you will have a chance to put all you've been given into action. You've been called and anointed at this crucial time in your life just before you get sent out into the world. Today, we're going to "dive in" to exactly how you, with the help and support of the Church, can stick to what you've learned so you won't ever become a Happy Meal!

> *"I can't do big things, but I want everything to be for the glory of God."*
> —St. Dominic Savio[1]

Dive In (5 minutes)

Read this story aloud, have a candidate read it aloud, or have the class read it silently before watching the video segments. This thought-provoking story ties in to the lesson's topic and serves to set up the video presentation.

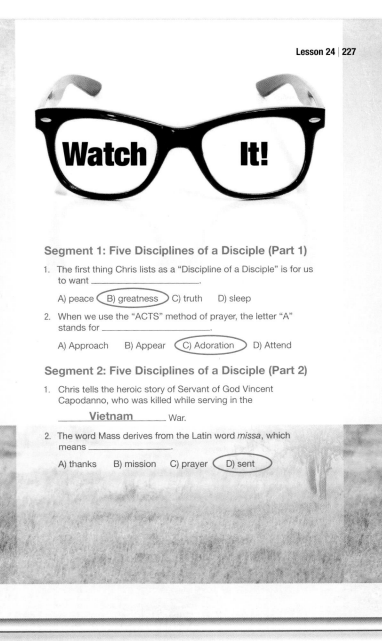

Lesson 24 | 227

Segment 1: Five Disciplines of a Disciple (Part 1)

1. The first thing Chris lists as a "Discipline of a Disciple" is for us to want _____.

    A) peace   (B) greatness   C) truth   D) sleep

2. When we use the "ACTS" method of prayer, the letter "A" stands for _____.

    A) Approach   B) Appear   (C) Adoration)   D) Attend

Segment 2: Five Disciplines of a Disciple (Part 2)

1. Chris tells the heroic story of Servant of God Vincent Capodanno, who was killed while serving in the

    _____**Vietnam**_____ War.

2. The word Mass derives from the Latin word *missa*, which means _____.

    A) thanks   B) mission   C) prayer   (D) sent)

Small-Group Discussion

Segment 1: The Five Disciplines of a Disciple (Part 1)

1. Chris says we must "desire greatness." We sometimes think of a desire as a feeling that is beyond our control, but this is not true. In what ways can we foster a healthy desire for greatness?

2. We should seek out and surround ourselves with people who will help us grow in our faith. What are some ways that we can help each other?[1]

Segment 2: The Five Disciplines of a Disciple (Part 2)

1. What does that last quote from the video mean to you?[2]

2. Ask candidates: Share a bit about your Confirmation name and why you chose this particular saint.

3. Ask sponsors: What about that saint (or perhaps another saint) do you see in your candidate?

4. Ask candidates: Why did you choose your sponsor?

5. Ask sponsors: What difference does faith in Jesus Christ make in your life?

6. Ask candidates: What do you hope to gain from your Confirmation?

7. Ask sponsors: Share one piece of advice to help your candidate live out the grace of Confirmation in his or her life.

8. Ask candidates: What will you do in the brief time ahead to prepare your heart for Confirmation?

Step 5 — Watch It!/Small-Group Discussion (50 minutes)

On the video, click on Lesson 24, Segment 1. When Segment 1 ends, have students fill in the "Watch It!" questions (2 to 3 minutes). Run through them to be sure they wrote the correct answers so they will have them to prepare for the next "Review Game."

Next, lead students in a small-group discussion for Segment 1. You may begin by asking general questions like: "What part of the video spoke to you the most?" Discussion questions for each segment are provided in the blue box above.

Follow the same steps for Segment 2. (Allow for about 10 minutes of discussion time after each segment.)

Small-Group Discussion Leader's Notes

1 Prayer, accountability, encouragement.

2. "You did not choose me, but I chose you" – John 15:16. Explain that you now have questions for both the candidates and sponsors.

Question:

Discipleship is not very complex. You just have to stick with it. How is that like any relationship?

> *God tends to widen the heart's capacity for love and joy ... through suffering.*

TO THE HEART with

For a long time, I was the kid who lived for religious retreats. I felt great! I was in my zone! I served everywhere I could. I prayed. I talked about God. I surrounded myself with Christian friends. "As the deer longs for streams of water, so my soul longs for you, O God" (Psalm 42:2, NAB). My heart learned where its fullness was, and I wanted more.

But every year, when I got home from my retreat weekend, I hit a wall. Back to sin. Back to emptiness. It took me a few years to realize that the "streams of living water" I found on that yearly retreat were also available in my daily life! I just had to work a little harder and dig a little more once I was off the "mountaintop" of the retreat experience.

Streams of living water are easy to find on a retreat. Drinking in the desert takes hard work. As St. Benedict said, "You can't even begin your ascent toward God without discipline." So I began

developing the disciplines of a disciple, and I began to drink deeply.

Daily prayer (especially the Rosary), time in silence before the tabernacle, telling my friends about the faith, reading Scripture, building solid spiritual friendships, confessing my sins to a priest—these became my new IV drip, replacing my previous "drip" of alcohol and lust. Soon, the life that had nourished the roots of my faith while on that retreat each year, was now feeding them every day.

When I first started to experience this new life in Jesus, I just assumed that I should be a priest. After all, if I wanted to go all the way for Jesus, that would be the way to do it. But God had a different calling in mind for me. Her name is Natalie. I began to see that marriage was more than a calling to marry a woman, but a calling to follow and be configured to Jesus Christ, the Bridegroom. In the Sacrament

Step 6 **To the Heart** (10 minutes)

After the small-group discussions, read this story aloud, have a candidate read it aloud, or have the class read it silently. After the story (written by this week's video presenter), read the thought-provoking question(s) provided in the red "To the Heart" box above. Time permitting, ask follow-up questions and encourage discussion.

Lesson 24 | 229

of Matrimony, I became Natalie's path to heaven, and she became mine; together, we were to become the pathway for our children to follow. All this was God's beautiful, life-giving plan for our family.

My life has its struggles. Like anyone else, I deal with disappointments and eye-opening encounters with my own human weaknesses and with the weaknesses of others. The joys of marriage and fatherhood, like the joys of DISCIPLESHIP, have far exceeded my expectations, but so has the pain. God tends to widen the heart's capacity for love and joy (in other words, for his presence) through suffering. I wish he'd pick an alternate route, but I'm learning to keep taking up my cross and following him!

Through it all, the theme of World Youth Day 1993 rings out clearly in my heart: "I have come so that they might have life, and have it to the full" (John 10:10, NIV). I found that fullness in the eighth grade, and my highest aspiration ever since has been to share it with as many people as possible. It's been an honor sharing it with you.

You are no ordinary individual. You are *chosen* by God. He is about to flood you with all the grace you need to live as one of his chosen people. I'm praying that you respond to that grace for the rest of your life. And I'm praying you respond not just for your sake, but for the sake of the whole world, which desperately needs more saints. *Be one.*

Chris Stefanick

230 | CHOSEN

Hero of the Week

St. Maximilian Kolbe, Martyr of Charity

Born:
January 7, 1894

Died:
August 14, 1941

Memorial:
August 14

Patron Saint of:
- drug addiction
- families
- journalists
- pro-life movement

The summer heat beat upon the concrete cell blocks of the Auschwitz concentration camp, and "Prisoner 16670" tried not to think about just how thirsty he was.

It all began when he had volunteered to take the place of Francis Gajowniczek, a young husband and father who had been among a group of men condemned to death when another prisoner had escaped the camp. For the previous two weeks, he had tried to keep up the spirits of the other condemned men in that basement bunker of Block Thirteen. His love of the Immaculate Virgin Mary had strengthened him during this imprisonment. He led the other prisoners in song and prayer and comforted each of his cellmates as they died of starvation, one by one, in that basement bunker. By sheer force of will, Fr. Kolbe was the last to succumb to the cruel treatment.

In his final moments, as Kolbe felt the stab of the needle that would end his suffering for good, his last act was to bless the Nazis that killed him.

On August 14, 1941, Fr. Kolbe was free at last.

As a child, he'd had a vision of the Blessed Mother, who had offered him a red crown and a white crown. The red crown signified martyrdom, and the white crown signified purity. The boy asked for both.

He had a deep devotion to the Virgin Mary and lived a life full of risks and danger. He crossed the Russian border illegally to study at his minor seminary in Lwów and opened monasteries in his native Poland as well as in Japan. During World War II, Maximilian continued to face danger, providing shelter for Polish refugees and hiding more than 2,000 Jews from Nazi persecution. This led to his arrest and subsequent imprisonment in the concentration camps. He recognized this terrible injustice against his fellow man and worked, in his own way, to help.

While St. Maximilian did not directly die a martyr's death for his faith, St. John Paul II declared that the circumstances surrounding the Holocaust constituted an assault on humanity and thus St. Maximilian died a heroic death for his fellow man in the face of such evil. He observed, "No one in the world can change Truth. What we can do and should do is to seek truth and to serve it when we have found it." Maximilian stood up for God's truth, whether it was by hiding Jews, building monasteries, or standing up to injustice. We can embrace this kind of courage in our own lives.

John Paul II canonized Maximilian in 1982. And Francis Gajowniczek was there.

St. Maximilian Kolbe, pray for us. Help us serve the truth in our daily lives with heroic conviction.

Step 7 · Hero of the Week (5 minutes)

This saint story will help to highlight and reinforce this lesson's topic. You may choose to read it aloud, have a candidate read it aloud, or have the class read it silently.

Lesson 24 | 231

Challenge of the Week

For this final week, we want to give you one more "challenge" to help get you started as a lifelong disciple of Christ. This isn't something you have to do for class. Whatever you choose, it's between you and God—the God who has Chosen you in Confirmation to be a full-fledged member of the kingdom of God! Congratulations—and God bless you!

 Find an ACCOUNTABILITY partner. Your life will just get better and better if you follow Christ every single day. Find a friend to hold you accountable for getting to Mass every week, sticking to daily prayer, going to youth group, or fulfilling any other commitment you have made to help you to follow Jesus more closely. Cheer each other on and support each other's efforts to grow in holiness. Remember, we have immortal souls, so our friendships can be eternal!

 Contemplate death. Really! Knowing that our choices matter to God makes a big difference in how we live our lives. Write down what kind of person you want to be spiritually when you breathe your last breath and three specific things you need to do to get there. Then do them.

 Commit to reading one good Catholic book a year. Visit your parish library or local Catholic bookstore, or search online for ebooks. Choose three titles you would like to read.

_____

_____

_____

_____

_____

✝ Closing Prayer

"... and let us consider how to stir up one another to love and good works, not neglecting to meet together, as is the habit of some, but encouraging one another, and all the more as you see the Day drawing near."

—Hebrews 10:24-25

Lord, we thank you for our time together. You have forged bonds of friendship and blessed our efforts. We trust that seeds of faith have been planted and will grow to maturity if we follow you.

Bless us, now and always. Give us your grace. Make us the saints you have called us to be. Amen.

Before leading candidates in the "Closing Prayer," give any last-minute instructions. Although the last "Taking It Home" section is not technically homework, encourage your students to take it home to read and to keep their workbooks handy as a reference tool as they start living as disciples of Christ.

Remind them that Confirmation is an important step on a lifelong journey of faith ... that they have been Chosen to undertake.

If time permits, take a few moments to give students a chance to share some of the highlights of the program. Then, one more time, ask if there are any prayer intentions.

Step 8 **Challenge of the Week** (2 minutes)

Ask your candidates to read the "challenges" above and choose one of the three to complete this week. Have them check the box next to the challenge they intend to complete. Encourage them to write about their experiences in the space provided.

Step 9 **Homework Instructions and Updates** (2 minutes)

Encourage candidates to read the "Wrap-Up" and the "What's That Word" sections in the "Taking It Home" section of the Student Workbook. (See above instructions in red.)

Step 10 **Closing Prayer** (3 minutes)

As a way of building up community, ask if there are any prayer intentions. Write them down (or have candidates share them aloud) and after praying for those intentions, have the class read the "Closing Prayer" together (provided in the Student Workbook).

232 | 🔥 CHOSEN

Taking It Home

Of course there is no "homework" for this final class (or "Review Game" prep). Instead, please take a moment to think about what you've learned through this program. How has it changed the way you think about God? About the Church? About yourself?

Here's one final "Wrap-Up" from Chris Stefanick ...

Wrap-Up

Now that you're finished with the *Chosen* program, you might be asking yourself, "How am I supposed to *live* it all?" Jesus is calling you to achieve true happiness, to become the best person you can possibly be (a saint!) and to live life to the full. In a word, he's calling you to *holiness*.

Thankfully, God doesn't make the path to holiness complex. By no means is it an easy path, but it's not complicated. Here are five "disciplines" that mark the life of a disciple of Jesus Christ:

1. *Desire greatness:* You're called to be more than a big deal in the eyes of the world. You're called to be truly great; that is, to succeed at the kind of person you become. Stop setting your eyes on the passing "stars" of this world. "The true stars of life are the people who have lived good lives. They are lights of hope."² Start looking up to the saints and trying to be like them.

2. *Pray:* Listen to God by reading a little of the Gospels every day and then talking to God from your heart. Remember the steps to "ACTS" (page 174) and *lectio divina* (pages 171 and 173). Commit to ten minutes of intimate, focused time with God every day (not just the last few seconds before falling asleep at night).

3. *Build community:* Watch out for people who bring you down. Focus on faith-filled people who are good for you. And go deeper with a few people you can have brutally honest conversations with, people who will hold you accountable in the ways you need to change and help you stay strong with the temptations you face.

4. *Sacraments:* Confirmation is an important step along a lifelong journey to God. But, if you want to reach the kingdom, you must live a life of faith! Go to Mass every week—it keeps you "well fed" and connected to the Body of Christ. (Plus, if you freely choose not to, it can be a mortal sin ... and we don't mess with those!) Speaking of sin, go to the Sacrament of Confession often. It's the sacrament that helps you conquer those "problem spots" that keep you from becoming the best version of yourself.

5. *Mission:* Remember that God gave you time, talent, and treasure to serve others. Be a force for good! Look for ways to love and serve and to spread the kingdom of God.

For our final "What's That Word?" section, let's take a look at two important words for you to keep in mind as you begin the next part of your journey with God.

---

² *Spe Salvi* 49

"What's That Word?"

DISCIPLESHIP

Discipleship describes the life of a follower of Jesus Christ. The word *disciple* comes from a Latin word that means "student" or "learner." To his disciples, Jesus was a teacher, but he taught them more than just information about God; he taught them how to live as children of God.

Interestingly, the word *discipline* comes from the same Latin word as discipleship. Discipline is usually understood in a negative way, as something unpleasant; but a parent disciplines a child to teach him or her how to live better. So when we live a life of discipleship by following Jesus, we learn from him and strive to imitate his life in order to become who God has made us to be.

ACCOUNTABILITY

Accountability describes a disciple's willingness to allow another person to assist him or her in taking responsibility for his or her actions. Jesus sent his disciples out in groups of two, not only to support each other, but also to help each other resist temptations. It is much easier to give in to temptation if we think no one is watching—and much easier to do what's right if we know we're not alone! If we are trying to lose weight, for instance, we might be more successful if we give a friend permission to ask us regularly whether we have been cheating on our diet. We are always accountable to God because he sees everything that we do. In addition to good friends, regular use of the Sacrament of Reconciliation helps us live out our accountability to God as well.

Memory Verse:

"You did not choose me, but I chose you and appointed you that you should go and bear fruit ..."

–John 15:16

Glossary

ACCOUNTABILITY: The process by which disciples openly share their lives—good and bad—with others who want to help them grow in virtue and avoid sin.

ACTUAL GRACE refers to a supernatural help from God that leads us to conversion and assists us in the avoidance of sin and the pursuit of holiness. Actual grace is distinct from *sanctifying grace* because it is not tied directly to the sacraments (and thus is not a share in God's divine life); we obtain it through prayer and the appropriate use of sacramentals. (See CCC 2000.) *See also* GRACE *and* SANCTIFYING GRACE.

ADORATION is a type of prayer that includes a profound expression of love, awe, and respect for God. This type of prayer is often practiced in the presence of the Eucharist. (See CCC 1378, 2628.)

ALMSGIVING is one of the three principal forms of penance emphasized in Scripture and the writings of the early Church fathers (fasting, prayer, almsgiving), in which the penitent secretly donates money or other valuables to the poor as an expression of sorrow for sin. (See CCC 1434.) *See also* PENANCE.

ANGEL: The word *angel* means "messenger." Angels are powerful, personal spiritual beings; they have no bodies, though they sometimes appear in physical form. They are powerful servants and messengers of God. "Fallen" angels, or demons, rebelled against God and were cast out of heaven with Satan. (See Revelation 12:9.) Every believer has a guardian angel. (See CCC 334–336.) *See also* DEMON.

ANNULMENT: Those who have been divorced and who wish to be married must first obtain a *decree of nullity* (commonly called an *annulment*), stating that their previous relationship was not a valid marriage. (If the Church determines the union in question was in fact valid, neither spouse is free to remarry, even after a civil divorce. See CCC 1629.) *See also* TRIBUNAL *and* DIVORCE.

ANOINTING: In the celebration of many of the sacraments, Christians are "sealed" (anointed) with one of three types of blessed, perfumed oil. Sacred chrism is associated with Baptism, Confirmation, and Holy Orders; the oil of catechumens with Baptism; and the oil of the sick with the Anointing of the Sick. Anointing claims us as members in the family of God and symbolizes the outpouring of the Holy Spirit, whose gifts we receive in the sacraments. (See CCC 695, 1293–1296.)

ANOINTING OF THE SICK imparts special graces that help the sick unite their pain with the passion of Christ; give them peace and courage; bring forgiveness of sins; and, in some cases, restore physical health. (See CCC 1523.)

APOSTOLIC: The Church is "apostolic" because Jesus founded it on the apostles; because it keeps and follows the teachings that Jesus gave to the apostles; and because it is taught, sanctified, and guided by their successors, our bishops. (See CCC 857.)

APOSTOLIC SUCCESSION: In order to safeguard the faithful proclamation of the Gospel for all time, the apostles appointed successors known as *bishops* and, by the "laying on of hands" at ordination, transferred to them the authority they had received from Christ. These successors were then equipped to represent Christ and carry on the work of shepherding the Church. (See Matthew 28:19-20; CCC 860–862.)

APPARITIONS are supernatural appearances of heavenly persons to those on earth. Apparitions usually involve spoken messages and visual signs that encourage God's people to turn from sin and grow in holiness. (See CCC 66, 67.)

ASSUMPTION: Because the Blessed Virgin Mary was preserved from Original Sin, she did not experience bodily decay after death. Rather, at the end of her life she was *assumed* (literally, "taken up") into heaven, body and soul. (See CCC 966, 2853.)

BAPTISM, the first Sacrament of Initiation, gives us a share in God's divine life through sanctifying grace, which cleanses us of Original Sin, any personal sins (if received after the age of reason), and the punishment due for sin. It unites us to the Death and Resurrection of Jesus Christ, indelibly marks our souls as belonging to God, and imparts the theological virtues and Gifts of the Holy Spirit. The baptism of infants shortly after they are born is "an immemorial tradition of the Church" (CCC 1252). Adults who wish to join the Church go through a process called the catechumenate, which prepares them to receive the three sacraments of initiation—Baptism, Confirmation, and the Eucharist. (See CCC 405, 1247-1249, 1262–1274.)

BAPTISM OF BLOOD: Unbaptized martyrs for the Christian faith are baptized by their death, a "Baptism of blood," in union with the death of Jesus on the cross. While not a sacrament, all the same effects and fruits of Baptism are received. (See CCC 1258.)

BEATITUDE: God freely offers us the chance to live forever with him in heaven, in "beatitude," or perfect happiness, and he has put the desire for happiness in each of us so that we can taste, in this life, some share of the life to come. (See Matthew 5:8; CCC 1720–1722.)

BEATITUDES, THE: Found in the Gospels (See Matthew 5:3-12; Luke 6:20-22), these provocative teachings of Jesus show us what life as a Christian is intended to be. By striving to live the Beatitudes, we will become ever more joyful and keep our eyes fixed on eternal life. (See CCC 1716.)

BISHOP: A priest who has been ordained to the episcopacy, the highest degree of Holy Orders. Bishops are successors to the apostles and can trace their ordination through an unbroken line of succession to one of the apostles. A bishop is appointed by the pope to lead a particular diocese. (See CCC 1536, 1555.)

CARDINAL VIRTUES: The four cardinal virtues are prudence, justice, fortitude, and temperance. All other human virtues "hinge" upon these four. (See CCC 1805–1809.)

CATHOLIC: The word *catholic* means "universal." The Church is universal because God wants everyone to be a member of the Church, to follow Jesus, and to be members of his family. Christ sent the apostles to bring the Gospel to the whole world, and he is present throughout the world through the Church he founded. (See CCC 830–831.)

Glossary continued ...

CELIBATE describes those who choose not to marry or have children so that they can be completely free to serve God. (See Matthew 19:12; 1 Corinthians 7:32-34.) Catholic priests of the Roman rite promise to live celibate lives, and religious order priests take vows of chastity. (See CCC 1579.)

CHARISMS are special gifts granted by the Holy Spirit to help our lives bear fruit for the good of the whole Church. Charisms include extraordinary gifts such as healing and prophecy, as well as others such as teaching, preaching, and discernment of spirits. (See 1 Corinthians 12:8-10; CCC 768, 798–801, 1508, 2003.)

CHARITY: The greatest of the theological virtues, the virtue of charity helps us to express the self-giving love of Christ to others. (See CCC 1822.)

CHASTITY: The virtue that helps us use the gift of sexuality to express authentic love, which reserves sexual expression for marriage. (See CCC 2337–2345.)

CHURCH: The Church is comprised of all those who, through faith in Jesus and through Baptism, have become part of the Body of Christ. The Church is one in governance (the bishops in union with the pope), one in dogma (teachings), and one in liturgy (worship). (See CCC 752–759, 830–831.) *See also* MARKS OF THE CHURCH.

COMMUNION OF SAINTS is another expression for the Church, as we are in communion with each other through Christ. The term refers to all the "redeemed": Christians living on earth, those suffering in Purgatory, and those already in the glory of heaven. (See CCC 960–962.)

CONFIRMATION is a Sacrament of Initiation and completes Baptism. The Gifts of the Holy Spirit are increased to provide the strength to live out God's call to serve the Church in various ways, especially through faithful witness. (See CCC 1285.)

CONSCIENCE is an action of the rational mind that discerns right from wrong in particular situations. The conscience, however, needs to be well formed. Prayerful study of the teachings of the Church throughout our lives helps to form the conscience to help us make positive decisions and lead happy lives. (See CCC 1778.)

CONSECRATION means to dedicate something or someone to a holy purpose. When deacons, priests, and bishops are ordained, they are consecrated to serve Jesus and his Church. Similarly, religious brothers and sisters consecrate their lives when they take their vows to serve God within a particular order. (For "consecration of the Eucharist," see CCC 1376; for "consecrated life," see CCC 914–916.)

CONSECRATION TO MARY: Mary, our sinless, spiritual mother, teaches us how to be more like Christ. Through special prayers, we can dedicate ourselves to Jesus through his mother's constant and powerful love, prayers, and protection. (See CCC 971.) *For more, search online "Montfort" or "Kolbe" and "consecration to Mary."*

CONSENT: To "consent" is to give in, or give permission, through an act of free will. We can consent to what is good or to what is bad. Either way, we are responsible. *Deliberate consent* is one of three conditions (along with "grave matter" and "full knowledge") for a sin to be "mortal." (See CCC 1857.)

CONTEMPLATION is a type of prayer that is marked by simple silence in the presence of God. It is often considered the highest stage of prayer because it draws us close to God in a way that gives us a taste of what our relationship with him will be like in heaven. We can contemplate Scripture, icons, the mysteries of the Rosary, or anything that opens our hearts and minds to an intimate communion with God. (See also "contemplative prayer" in CCC 2709–2719.)

CONTRITION is genuine sorrow for sin and a strong resolve to avoid sinning again. When we commit a mortal sin, we should go to Confession (the Sacrament of Reconciliation) as soon as possible. God never rejects a contrite heart. (See Psalm 51:17; CCC 1451.)

CONVERSION is a profound change of heart toward God. Religious conversion is always an experience of grace, brought about by the reasonableness of the faith, the personal witness of other Christians, or a deep contrition for sin that produces a genuine hunger for holiness and a reorientation of life toward God. (See Romans 15:13; CCC 1428.)

COVENANT is a solemn agreement between persons united in a permanent bond. God affirmed his covenant with Abraham after he proved willing to sacrifice his only son at God's command. (See Genesis 22:16-17.) The new covenant was established through the blood of God's only Son. (See Hebrews 12:24.)

CULPABILITY is the degree to which we are responsible for something we have done or failed to do. A lot depends on a person's intent, their understanding of right and wrong, and their willingness to make amends. (See CCC 1754; Luke 12:47-48.)

DEMON: Demons are angels who became evil by their own choice, rejecting God's authority completely and eternally. Demons tempt us to sin, thereby making us partners in their rebellion against God. (See CCC 391–392.) *See also* ANGEL.

DISCERNMENT is a process of evaluating something very carefully (with prudence) with the guidance of someone spiritually mature and with the help of the Holy Spirit. For example, the discernment of vocations, a career choice, the choice of a marriage partner, or in evaluating and avoiding temptations to sin. (See CCC 1806, 2847.)

DISCIPLESHIP: The discipline of living a life pleasing to God by imitating the example of Christ, often under the guidance and direction of someone more spiritually mature. (See CCC 787.)

DIVINE LAW (or eternal law) is the source, in God, of all law. It is known through natural law and revealed law. Revealed law includes the Old Law and the New Law of the Gospel. (See CCC 1952, 1960, 1965.)

DIVORCE is the legal dissolution of a civil marriage contract. A civil divorce has no effect on a true marriage bond, though, because no earthly authority can undo a valid sacramental marriage. (See Mark 10:9; CCC 1650.) *See also* ANNULMENT.

Glossary continued ...

DOCTOR OF THE CHURCH: A man or woman whose personal holiness, theological orthodoxy, and intellectual and spiritual insight have made a significant contribution to the Church's treasury of wisdom. Thirty-one men and four women have received this title; two recently declared doctors are St. Hildegard of Bingen and St. John of Avila.

EUCHARIST is the sacrament that is most central to the faith because it "re-presents" Jesus' sacrifice on the cross and allows us to receive him, present yet hidden, in the form of bread (unleavened in Roman Rite, leavened in the Eastern Churches) and wine (from grapes). This mystery takes place during the "Liturgy of the Eucharist." The Eucharist is no mere symbol, but is truly the Body, Blood, Soul, and Divinity of Jesus Christ. (See Matthew 26:26-28; CCC 1322–1419.)

EVANGELIZATION: The process of preaching the Gospel, by words and example.

EVIL is the absence of good, resulting from our exercising wrongly the freedom that God has given to us. Though we often do not understand why God allows evil, we do know that he sent his Son to join us in the battle against evil, over which he will triumph in the end. (See CCC 309, 403, 1040.)

EXAMINATION OF CONSCIENCE is an organized way to reflect sincerely on our sins and failures, especially before receiving Holy Communion. (See 1 Corinthians 11:27-29; CCC 1385.) *See also* **RECONCILIATION**.

EXISTENCE OF GOD, PROOFS FOR THE: St. Thomas Aquinas, the great scholastic theologian of the thirteenth century, devised the following five arguments (or "proofs") for the existence of God:

- *God is the "first mover."* Everything starts at rest and must be set in motion by something greater than itself. The greatest of all "motions," responsible for setting everything else in motion, is God.

- *God is the "first efficient cause."* Everything that exists came into being from something else; something cannot come out of nothing. This first "cause" is God.

- *God is the only "non-contingent" being.* Everything else in nature comes into being and ceases to exist (i.e., it is "contingent"). Therefore, the existence of everything is ultimately contingent on a being that had no beginning. This is God.

- *God is perfect goodness.* Things can be judged better or worse only in relationship to an objective standard of goodness. Therefore, there can be no talk of perfection or goodness unless it exists. This is God.

- *God is the "intelligent designer."* Natural bodies lack intelligence or knowledge—they achieve goals by being directed by something capable of reason (like an archer directing the course of an arrow.) That "cosmic intelligence" is God.

FAITH is a gift of God, which leads to "a personal adherence of the whole man to God who reveals himself. It involves an assent of the intellect and will to the self-revelation God has made through his deeds and words."(See CCC 176, 1816.)

FASTING is an important tradition in Catholic spirituality and involves eating less than usual to atone for sin (our own and those of the world). Fasting also helps us to learn self-control and gives us the opportunity to meditate on the sufferings of Christ and our need for God's grace. (See CCC 1430–1434.) Observing days of fasting and abstinence is the fourth precept of the Church. (See CCC 2043.)

FIAT is a Latin word meaning "let it be done [to me]." It is used to describe the Blessed Virgin Mary's gracious consent to be the mother of Jesus when confronted by the archangel Gabriel. (See Luke 1:38; CCC 973.)

FREE WILL is the power given to us by God to make our own choices, for good and ill. While God cannot force us to love him (since love must be freely given for it to be love), our will is perfected only when it is directed to the good, to fulfilling God's plan. (See CCC 1731.)

FRUITS OF THE HOLY SPIRIT are clear signs of the Holy Spirit's work within the soul of the faithful Christian. (See CCC 1832.) When we are docile to the Holy Spirit, we bear good fruit such as "... charity, joy, peace, patience, kindness, goodness, generosity, gentleness, faithfulness, modesty, self-control, chastity." (See Galatians 5:22-23.)

GIFTS OF THE HOLY SPIRIT are given to all those who are baptized, and they remain in us as long as we are in a state of grace. The Gifts of the Spirit make it possible for us to live and act as the Holy Spirit leads us. They are wisdom, understanding, counsel, fortitude, knowledge, piety, and fear of the Lord. (See CCC 1831.)

GRACE is a share in the divine life of God, a free gift of supernatural help given to us not because we deserve it, but because he loves us. Grace makes it possible for us to respond to God's call, to grow in holiness, and to live with God in heaven for all eternity. (See John 1:12, 14; CCC 1996–1999.) *See also* ACTUAL GRACE *and* SANCTIFYING GRACE.

HAPPINESS: The desire for happiness has been placed in our hearts by God, who is the only one who can fulfill us and make us happy. He gave us this need in order to encourage us to come closer to him, to love him, and to live with him forever in heaven. (See CCC 1718.)

HEAVEN is our true home, where the saved will live in the company of the Blessed Trinity and all the saints. We don't know exactly what it will be like, since "no eye has seen ... what God has prepared for those who love him" (1 Corinthians 2:9). But Scripture uses words such as "wedding feast," "life," and "paradise." (See CCC 1025–1027.)

HELL: Those who freely and willfully persist in a state of mortal sin until death cannot be saved. God cannot force us to love him and be with him forever in heaven. The place for those who reject God is called hell. (See CCC 1033–1037.) *See also* MORTAL SIN *and* JUDGMENT.

HOLINESS is the state of Christian perfection to which we are all called. Since we cannot achieve it on our own, we must rely on the grace and mercy of God. By prayerfully embracing the cross, we discover our unique, individual calling and the very best of ourselves. (See CCC 2012–2016.)

Glossary continued ...

HOLY ORDERS is the sacrament through which men are ordained as bishops, priests, and deacons. Anointed by a bishop, the ordained receives special Gifts of the Holy Spirit necessary for carrying on the sacramental and pastoral mission of the apostles. (See CCC 1536–1538.)

HOLY SPIRIT: The third Person of the Blessed Trinity, the Holy Spirit, is the living love between the Father and the Son. Also called the "Spirit of Truth," he dwells in us through Baptism and makes our lives, sacraments, prayers, and liturgies effective and fruitful. (See CCC 691.)

HOMOSEXUALITY: See "Same-Sex Attraction"

IMMACULATE CONCEPTION is one of the titles of Our Lady, since she was conceived in her mother's womb completely free of Original Sin. The angel, Gabriel, referred to her as "full of grace." (See Luke 1:28; CCC 490–492.) She called herself the "Immaculate Conception" at Lourdes in 1858. *For more, search online "Bernadette Soubirous."*

IN PERSONA CHRISTI CAPITIS: Latin for "in the person of Christ the Head," this term refers to the special role bishops and priests, by virtue of their ordination, have to act with the authority of Christ in celebrating the sacraments and teaching the faithful. (See CCC 875–876, 1548–1549.)

INCARNATION: This refers to the Eternal Son of God, the second Person of the Trinity, *assuming* ("taking on") a human nature at a specific moment in history. Jesus, then, is true God and true man, like us in all things except sin. (See CCC 464–464, 470.)

INFALLIBILITY refers to an inability of the Church's Magisterium (i.e., the pope and the bishops united with him) to err when defining a doctrine of faith or morality. It also refers, in an extended sense, to the entire people of God, whose *sensus fidelium* ("sense of the faithful") prevents the Church as a whole from believing an erroneous doctrine. (See CCC 889–891). *See also* MAGISTERIUM.

INSPIRATION: The books of the Bible are divinely "inspired," which means that their human authors—writing freely using their own intellect and talents under the inspiration of the Holy Spirit—wrote down only "the truth which God, for the sake of our salvation, wished to see confided to the Sacred Scriptures" (CCC 107).

INTERCESSION is a type of prayer in which we place the needs of others before God. When someone says, "I'll pray for you," they are offering to be intercessors. When we ask Our Lady, the saints, or our guardian angels to pray for us, they become our intercessors. (See CCC 2635.)

INTERIOR LIFE refers to the private relationship we have with God in our hearts, minds, and souls. Whereas we often relate to God in union with others (in families, churches, and communities), our interior life is strictly personal and unique and must be cultivated like any important relationship. (See CCC 2697–2699.)

JESUS CHRIST is the second Person of the Blessed Trinity, God's only-begotten Son, the Word made flesh (see John 1:14), who suffered and died to save us from our sins (see John 3:16). He is the Messiah, the Lord of Creation, and the Head of the Church present to us in the sacraments. (See CCC 1698, 1701.)

JUDGMENT: At the end of our lives, we will experience the judgment of God, which will determine how we spend eternity, either with God in heaven or separated from him in hell. The Church distinguishes between the *particular* judgment, which occurs immediately after death, and the *Last Judgment*, which will transpire at the Second Coming of Christ. (See CCC 1021, 1040–1041.)

KERYGMA (Greek): The Gospel, in brief: We were created by the Trinity (Father, Son, Holy Spirit) to live in heaven forever, but sin alienated us from God. God gave his Son, Jesus, to save us from our sins and sent the Holy Spirit to build up the Church and share his divine life through the sacraments.

LECTIO DIVINA (literally, "divine reading"): A traditional practice of meditation that is finding renewed popularity. It involves the prayerful reading of a passage of Scripture (read); personal reflection (reflect); application (relate); and quieting the heart to give God a chance to speak (rest). (See CCC 1177.) *For more, search online "Ignatius of Loyola" and "lectio divina."*

LITURGICAL YEAR: This refers to the calendar of the Church's liturgies, including Lent, Easter, Ordinary Time, Advent, Christmas, feast days, memorials, and holy days of obligation. Through the rhythms of the liturgical year, the faithful experience a deeper connection with the paschal mysteries they recall. (See CCC 1168–1171.)

LITURGY is "the participation of the People of God in 'the work of God.' Through the liturgy Christ, our redeemer and high priest, continues the work of our redemption in, with, and through his Church" (CCC 1069). Through divine worship, proclamation of the Gospel, and acts of charity, we take up this work.

LOVE: Christian love is more than feelings of affection we might have for another person; it is an imitation of Jesus' sacrificial love for us, a love that seeks the good of the other above our own. Also called Christian "charity," it is "the theological virtue by which we love God above all things for his own sake, and our neighbor as ourselves for the love of God" (CCC 1822). (See John 13:34, 15:9, 12.)

MAGISTERIUM refers to the living authority of the Catholic Church, carried out by the pope in union with the bishops, to teach on all questions of faith and morals, as well as to interpret with fidelity all practices of prayer and worship. (See CCC 85–87.) *For a whole library full of letters, articles, and other Church writings—plus an online* Catechism—*go online to "Vatican.va."*

MARKS OF THE CHURCH: The four characteristics (or "marks") that define the Church are that it is *one* (see CCC 813–814), *holy* (see CCC 823), *catholic* (see CCC 830–831), and *apostolic* (see CCC 857). *See also* CATHOLIC *and* CHURCH.

Glossary continued ...

MARRIAGE is a lifelong covenant of love between a man and a woman, elevated by Christ to the dignity of a sacrament (Matrimony), the purpose of which is to provide for the spiritual and physical well-being of both spouses, as well as the procreation and education of children. (See Genesis 2:18-24; CCC 1601.) *See also* MATRIMONY.

MARY, BLESSED VIRGIN: As a teenager living in ancient Israel, Mary was chosen to become the mother of the Messiah, Jesus Christ. She was conceived without sin and lived in a continual state of grace. At the crucifixion, Jesus entrusted his mother to his beloved disciple (likely John), making her mother of the whole Church, a role she continues to fulfill to this day. (See Luke 1:26-38; CCC 487–494.) *See also* MOTHER IN THE ORDER OF GRACE.

MASS: The Mass has always been the center of the life of the Church. The two main parts are the Liturgy of the Word (Scripture) and the Liturgy of the Eucharist (Holy Communion). The word "Mass" comes from the Latin word *missa*, meaning "to send," and is also the root of the word *mission*. *For a brief history of the Mass, see CCC 1345–1358.*

MATRIMONY: The marriage of baptized Christians is called the "Sacrament of Matrimony" and is ordered toward the good of the spouses and the procreation and education of children. Matrimony is a vocation and a lifelong covenant established between one man and one woman. (See CCC 1601.)

MEDITATION is a type of prayer, a quest to understand and respond to all God is asking of us in order to grow in our relationship with him. (See CCC 2705.)

MORTAL SIN occurs when a gravely sinful act is committed with full understanding and consent of the will. If not repented, it deprives the soul of sanctifying grace, which is needed to enter heaven. (See CCC 1855–1861.) *See also* HELL *and* JUDGMENT.

MOTHER IN THE ORDER OF GRACE: Mary is the Blessed Mother of Jesus, mother of the Church, and our mother. (See John 19:26-27.) The Church's model of faith, love, and obedience, she cooperated at every stage of Jesus' redemptive work. (See CCC 967–970.)

MYSTERY refers to a truth revealed by God that we can describe in theological terms but cannot understand fully. Some prime examples include dogmas such as the Trinity, the Incarnation, and the Eucharist. God is infinite, so anything concerning him is a mystery to our finite human minds. *See also* PASCHAL MYSTERY *and* ROSARY.

NATURAL LAW: The law that is written on our hearts and in the very nature of things. (See CCC 1954–1960.)

NATURAL REASON refers to the human power to figure something out, as opposed to "revelation," which is what we know because God has told us. (See CCC 50.) For example, using our reason, we can judge right from wrong and observe order and beauty in the world, which tells us that it was created by God.

ORIGINAL SIN: Adam and Eve chose to disobey God, and the consequences of their personal sin affects the entire human race "by the transmission of a human nature deprived of original holiness and justice" (CCC 404). It is important to remember, though, that human nature is *not* totally corrupted. As the *Catechism* states, "Baptism, by imparting the life of Christ's grace, erases original sin and turns a man back toward God but the consequences for nature, weakened and inclined to evil, persist in man and summon him to spiritual battle" (CCC 405). Due to a special, unique ("singular") grace conferred upon her by God, Mary was conceived without Original Sin, a dogma known as the Immaculate Conception. As a result, Jesus was born without Original Sin (See CCC 602).

PARACLETE: This word means "counselor" or "helper." This is how the Lord referred to the Holy Spirit when he promised to send the "Spirit of truth" to the apostles after he returned to heaven. (See John 14:17; CCC 692.)

PASCHAL MYSTERY: The mystery of salvation through the life, Death, Resurrection, and Ascension of Jesus Christ is described as "paschal" because of the deep connection between our celebration of the Eucharistic sacrifice and the Jewish celebration of Passover. (See CCC 512, 542.) *For more, search online "Pope Paul VI" and "Live the Paschal Mystery."*

PEACE is one of the fruits of the Holy Spirit. It is experienced as a calm and often joyful sense of trust in God. Peace in society can only be achieved and maintained through respect for the dignity of the human person at every stage of life and does not refer merely to an absence of war. (See CCC 2304.)

PENANCE: In order to grow in faith and love, Jesus invites us to accept the ordinary sufferings (crosses) of life and to discipline ourselves with sacrifices called "penance" (i.e. prayer, fasting, and almsgiving). Accepting penance does not mean that we have not been forgiven, but rather that we recognize that sin has damaged us and that we want to overcome sin's effects in our lives. (See CCC 1473.) *See also* ALMSGIVING.

PENTECOST celebrates the descent of the Holy Spirit upon the apostles that occurred nine days after Jesus' Ascension. (See Acts 2.) Sometimes Pentecost is described as "the birthday of the Church" because the Holy Spirit made it possible for the Church to take up Jesus' work of communicating the message of salvation to the world. (See CCC 1076.)

PERPETUAL VIRGINITY OF MARY: Conceived solely through the power of the Holy Spirit, Jesus was "born of the virgin." Yet Mary also remained a virgin throughout her life, as a model of a life completely dedicated to God. (See Matthew 1:20; CCC 506.)

PERSONAL SIN: See "sin."

PRAYER is "the raising of one's mind and heart to God or the requesting of good things from God" (St. John Damascene). God made us to be in loving relationship with him, and prayer is the communication with God that sustains and deepens our relationship with him. (See John 8:8-11.) Prayer can be vocal, mental, or contemplative. (See CCC 2558–2561.)

Glossary continued ...

PURGATORY is a state of purification and preparation for those who die in a state of grace, but whose souls are not yet perfected. Like the guests in the parable of the wedding feast (see Matthew 22:1-14), we must first be cleansed and healed of the effects of our sin before entering heaven. (See CCC 1030–1032.)

RECONCILIATION means to set things right after we have caused harm to our relationship with God or others. The Sacrament of Reconciliation (Confession) provides forgiveness of sins, restores us to the state of grace, and heals and strengthens our souls. (See CCC 1450.)

REDEMPTION is the primary purpose of God the Father's saving plan for the human race (see CCC 763), accomplished through the sacrifice of his only Son, Jesus Christ (see John 3:16). Jesus, the pure, innocent Lamb of God, through his passion and death, atoned for our sins. (See CCC 571.)

REDEMPTIVE SUFFERING: When we experience pain in our lives, Jesus invites us to face that suffering with courage, offering it back to God by faith. In this way, our sufferings can be spiritually united with his cross for our spiritual benefit and that of others. Jesus showed us by his example that our sufferings have value and that we can participate in his saving work. (See CCC 1505, 1521; Colossians 1:24; 2 Corinthians 1:5-7.)

REVELATION is derived from an ancient Hebrew word that means "to unveil or uncover" and refers to the ways God makes himself and the mysteries of the faith known to us through Scripture and Tradition. (See CCC 50.) *See also* MYSTERY.

RITUAL: A ritual is a ceremony that is performed according to a plan, in a particular order, and that usually expresses a profound or solemn meaning. Liturgical rituals allow us to express our love of God and our deep reverence for his presence in the Word of God, the Eucharist, the priest, and the community.

ROSARY: The Rosary is an important and spiritually powerful Marian prayer that involves meditating on the mysteries of our faith. The joyful, luminous, sorrowful, and glorious mysteries of the Rosary depict events in the lives of Jesus and Mary. (See CCC 971.)

SACRAMENTAL GRACE: When administered and received in a valid and appropriate manner, each of the seven sacraments conveys a particular sacramental grace that nourishes the supernatural life of the soul. (See CCC 1129, 2003.) *See also* SANCTIFYING GRACE.

SACRAMENTALS are objects or signs that "sanctify" (make holy) moments of daily life, and which help us to pray and to receive with even greater devotion the graces of the sacraments. Holy water (Numbers 5:17), relics (Mark 6:56; Acts 19:11-12), and the Sign of the Cross are all examples of sacramentals. (See CCC 1677–1679.)

SACRAMENTS: Sacraments are efficacious signs that give us God's grace and allow us to partake in his divine life. They were given to us by Christ, who entrusted them to the Church, which dispenses them by his authority and by the power of the Holy Spirit. (See CCC 1084.)

SACRAMENTS OF HEALING: Penance and the Anointing of the Sick are the two sacraments of healing. They continue the work of Jesus Christ, the Divine Physician, who forgave sins and healed the blind and the lame. (See CCC 1421.)

SACRAMENTS OF INITIATION: The *Catechism* refers to the sacraments of Baptism, Confirmation, and the Eucharist, which "lay the foundation of every Christian life" (see CCC 1131, 1212), as "Sacraments of Christian Initiation" (or simply "Sacraments of Initiation"). It is through these sacraments that Christians are given a share in God's life and are strengthened and nourished as they strive to become holy. Adults preparing to enter the Catholic Church follow the Rite of Christian Initiation of Adults (RCIA). "The Christian initiation of adults ... reaches its culmination in a single celebration of the three sacraments of initiation" (CCC 1233).

SACRAMENTS OF SERVICE: The *Catechism* refers to the sacraments of Holy Orders and Matrimony as the "sacraments at the service of communion" (or simply "Sacraments of Service"). The graces of these sacraments strengthen the recipient to fulfill his or her vocational calling, living and acting as a sign of God's faithful and sacrificial love in the world. (See CCC 1534.)

SACRED: Whatever is connected spiritually with God and dedicated to a profound religious purpose, like the Scriptures or the chrism used in our sacraments, is called "sacred." *See also* SACRAMENTALS.

SACRED SCRIPTURE: The seventy-three books of the Holy Bible are called "Sacred Scripture." Sacred Scripture is one of the two channels (along with Sacred Tradition) through which we receive what God has revealed to us for our salvation. (See CCC 81, 105.)

SACRED TRADITION: See TRADITION (SACRED).

SACRIFICE means to give up our own wants for the good of others or to make up for a wrong done; request a favor; or express gratitude or love. In the Holy Sacrifice of the Mass, we participate in the perfect sacrifice Christ offered on our behalf to save us from our sins. (See CCC 2100.)

SALVATION: Through the life and Death of Jesus Christ, we are saved from our sins and offered the hope of heaven. The sacraments of the Church are the primary means by which we receive salvation. (See CCC 1129; Mark 16:16.)

SAME-SEX ATTRACTION: Sexual attraction toward the same gender. The Church distinguishes between same-sex attraction (SSA), which is not sinful in and of itself, and acting on that attraction, which is always sinful (as is any sexual activity between unmarried persons). Every person is unique, unrepeatable, and worthy of love. However, the particular love expressed by sexual union is to be shared only between a husband and a wife (man and woman) for the purpose of union and procreation. Same-sex attraction is a reality for many, and we are always called to love those struggling with SSA as brothers and sisters in Christ. Yet all non-married persons (including those struggling with SSA) are called to live chastely and to refrain from all sexual activity. (See CCC 2357–2359.)

SANCTIFYING GRACE is a free gift of God's own life, received at Baptism for the healing and sanctification of our souls. Those who commit mortal sin can lose this grace, but it can be restored through the Sacrament of Reconciliation. (See CCC 1856, 1999–2000.)

Glossary continued ...

SEAL: A seal is a permanent spiritual "mark" on our souls. Because the sacraments of Baptism, Confirmation, and Holy Orders have a sacramental character that imparts a "seal," these sacraments can be received only once. (See CCC 698, 1121.)

SEAL OF CONFESSION: Because of the importance and private nature of the Sacrament of Reconciliation, priests are strictly bound, under threat of severe penalties, to maintain absolute secrecy about anything revealed in the confessional. These secrets are "sealed" by the sacrament; this is sometimes called a "sacramental seal." (See CCC 1467.)

SEXUALITY: The ability to express the complementary differences of our gender, rooted in our very human nature as male or female, according to God's plan.

SIN is a deliberate thought, word, deed, or omission contrary to God's plan that offends God and harms ourselves and others. (See CCC 1849–1854.) *See also* MORTAL SIN *and* VENIAL SIN.

SOCIAL JUSTICE: We help to bring about social justice when we live by the "Golden Rule" and work with others to make society a more just place, tending to both the physical and spiritual needs of all. (See CCC 1929–1933.)

SPIRIT (SOUL): A soul is the life principle in a body. All living things have a "life principle," or a "soul," but the human soul is also a spirit, which means that it has the power to know and to choose, and that it will live on after it separates from the body at death. At the end of time, our souls will be reunited with our bodies in the general resurrection. (See CCC 362–368.)

SPIRITUAL MATURITY refers to the degree to which one is conformed to Christ. This type of maturity does not always correspond to a person's age; children can attain spiritual maturity beyond their years. (See CCC 1308.) Growing in maturity is a lifelong process involving humble surrender to the will of God and an acceptance of suffering.

SPIRITUAL MOTHER: In imitation of Mary as our spiritual mother (our mother "in the order of grace"), all women can pray for, encourage, comfort, and guide those who are not their biological children. (See CCC 501.) Similarly, all men can be true "spiritual fathers." *See also* MOTHER IN THE ORDER OF GRACE.

SUPERNATURAL refers to anything that operates through power that is beyond the known laws of science and nature.

SUPPLICATION is a form of prayer and means to request something of God humbly and earnestly. (See CCC 2702.)

THANKSGIVING is a form of prayer in which we express our gratitude for gifts received from God, especially the gift of his Son, Jesus, who died to save us from our sins. The Greek word *Eucharist* means "thanksgiving." (See CCC 2637–2638; 1 Thessalonians 5:18; Colossians 4:2.)

THEOLOGICAL VIRTUES: Faith, hope, and love are the theological virtues described by St. Paul. (See 1 Corinthians 13:13.) They are infused into our souls at Baptism to make it possible for us to relate to God now and to live with him forever in heaven. (See CCC 1812–1829.)

TRADITION (SACRED) refers to the living transmission of the Word of God. The teachings of the apostles and all that was entrusted to them by the Lord are transmitted to us through the Church's doctrine, life, and worship. (See CCC 75–78, 81.)

TRANSUBSTANTIATION describes the complete change that occurs in the bread and wine during the consecration at Mass. When the priest speaks the words of Christ at the Last Supper (see Matthew 26:26-28), the bread really and substantially becomes the Body of Christ, and the wine becomes his Precious Blood. (See CCC 1374–1376.)

TRIBUNAL: A tribunal is an ecclesiastical (Church) court made up of one or more competent judges who consider all testimony, applying canon law (i.e., the law of Church) and rendering a declaration or verdict. Most of the work of local (or diocesan) tribunals concerns annulment cases. *See also* ANNULMENT.

TRINITY: The Blessed Trinity is the central mystery of the Christian faith (see CCC 234), the belief that the Father, the Son, and the Holy Spirit, three distinct Persons, are one God and share in a single divine nature.

UNITY: One of the "four marks" of the Church, its unity, or oneness, is a reflection of the unity of the Blessed Trinity. Christ established the "one" Church, and all are called to be part of it. (See CCC 763, 813–822, 836.)

VENIAL SIN: Sin that wounds but does not destroy the divine life in the soul. Unlike mortal sin, which can normally be forgiven only in the Sacrament of Reconciliation, venial sin may be forgiven by a worthy reception of the Eucharist. (See CCC 1394, 1862–1863.) *See also* SIN *and* MORTAL SIN.

VIATICUM (literally "with you on the way") is what the Church calls a person's last reception of the Eucharist. Because Jesus is the "resurrection and the life" (John 11:25), he has promised us that if we eat his Body and drink his Blood, we will have eternal life. (See John 6:51, 54; CCC 1524–1525.)

VIRTUE: A virtue is a habit of acting in a way that is pleasing to God. (See CCC 1803.)

VOCAL PRAYER can be used privately or in groups and involves speaking directly to God. We can memorize and use traditional prayers, such as the Our Father or the Hail Mary, or we may address God in our own words. (See CCC 2700–2704.)

VOCATIONAL DISCERNMENT is the process of seeking our true purpose in life and involves preparing ourselves to hear the call of God, preferably under the guidance of a spiritually mature person. Our greatest happiness will be found in our faithfulness to God's plan. (See Jeremiah 29:11.)

Catholic Prayers

How to Pray the Rosary

The Rosary is a devotion directed to Jesus, through and with his Mother, Mary. It focuses on four sets of "mysteries" based on the life of Christ and the Blessed Mother. As we pray the scriptural prayers on the beads (the Our Father, Hail Mary, and Glory Be) we should keep in mind Jesus' warning to not let our prayers become repetitious babbling or empty phrases (Matthew. 6:7). As you meditate on each mystery, it sometimes helps to recite the prayers more slowly, to ensure you are *praying* and not just *saying* the prayers.

1. **Make the Sign of the Cross**

2. **Pray the Apostles' Creed** – Crucifix

   I believe in God, the Father almighty, Creator of heaven and earth, and in Jesus Christ, his only Son, our Lord, who was conceived by the Holy Spirit, born of the Virgin Mary, suffered under Pontius Pilate, was crucified, died and was buried; he descended into hell; on the third day he rose again from the dead; he ascended into heaven, and is seated at the right hand of God the Father almighty; from there he will come to judge the living and the dead. I believe in the Holy Spirit, the holy catholic Church, the communion of saints, the forgiveness of sins, the resurrection of the body, and life everlasting. Amen.

3. **Pray an Our Father** – 1st bead

   Our Father, who art in heaven, hallowed be thy name; thy kingdom come, thy will be done, on earth as it is in heaven. Give us this day our daily bread, and forgive us our trespasses as we forgive those who trespass against us; and lead us not into temptation, but deliver us from evil. Amen.

4. **Pray three Hail Marys** – 2nd through 4th beads

   Hail Mary, full of grace, the Lord is with thee. Blessed art thou among women, and blessed is the fruit of thy womb, Jesus. Holy Mary, Mother of God, pray for us sinners, now and at the hour of our death. Amen.

5. **Pray a Glory Be and the (optional) Fatima Prayer** – 5th bead

   Glory be to the Father, and to the Son, and to the Holy Spirit. As it was in the beginning, is now, and ever shall be, world without end. Amen.

   O my Jesus, forgive us our sins, save us from the fires of hell, lead all souls to heaven, especially those in most need of thy mercy.

6. **Announce the first mystery, then pray the Our Father.**

7. **Pray ten Hail Marys while meditating on the mystery on the next ten beads (a "decade").**

8. **When you get to the next single bead, pray the Glory Be and the (optional) Fatima Prayer. Announce the second mystery while on the same bead.**

9. **Repeat steps 6-8 for each of the three remaining mysteries.**

10. **After you've finished the fifth mystery and are back to the centerpiece, finish the Rosary by praying the Hail, Holy Queen ...**

Hail, Holy Queen, Mother of mercy, our life, our sweetness, and our hope. To thee do we cry, poor banished children of Eve; to thee do we send up our sighs, mourning and weeping in this valley of tears.

Turn, then, most gracious advocate, thine eyes of mercy toward us, and after this, our exile, show unto us the blessed fruit of thy womb, Jesus. O clement, O loving, O sweet Virgin Mary.

Leader: Pray for us, O Holy Mother of God …

All: That we may be made worthy of the promises of Christ.

Leader: Let us pray.

All: O God, whose only-begotten Son, by his life, death, and resurrection, has purchased for us the rewards of eternal life, grant, we beseech thee, that meditating upon these mysteries of the Most Holy Rosary of the Blessed Virgin Mary, we may imitate what they contain and obtain what they promise, through the same Christ our Lord. Amen.

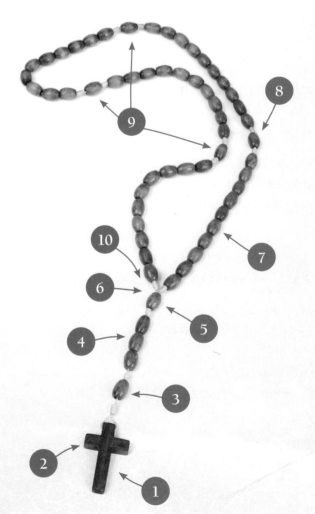

Joyful Mysteries (*Monday, Saturday*)

The Annunciation: Luke 1:26-38
The Visitation: Luke 1:39-45
The Nativity of Jesus: Luke 2:6-12
The Presentation of Jesus: Luke 2:25-32
The Finding of Jesus in the Temple: Luke 2:41-50

Sorrowful Mysteries (*Tuesday, Friday*)

The Agony in the Garden: Luke 22:39-46
The Scourging at the Pillar: Mark 15:6-15
The Crowning with Thorns: John 19:1-8
The Carrying of the Cross: John 19:16-22
The Crucifixion: John 19:25-30

Glorious Mysteries (*Wednesday, Sunday*)

The Resurrection: Mark 16:1-7
The Ascension: Luke 24:45-53
The Descent of the Holy Spirit: Acts 2:1-11
The Assumption of Mary: Luke 1:46-55
The Coronation of Mary: Revelation 12:1-7

Luminous Mysteries (*Thursday*)

The Baptism of Jesus: Matthew 3:13-17
The Wedding at Cana: John 2:1-11
The Proclamation of the Kingdom: Mark 1:14-15
The Transfiguration: Matthew 17:1-8
The Institution of the Eucharist: Matthew 26:26-28

Additional Catholic Prayers ...

Memorare

Remember, O most gracious Virgin Mary, that never was it known that anyone who fled to thy protection, implored thy help, or sought thy intercession was left unaided. Inspired with this confidence, I fly to thee, O Virgin of virgins, my Mother; to thee do I come, before thee I stand, sinful and sorrowful. O Mother of the Word Incarnate, despise not my petitions, but in thy mercy, hear and answer me. Amen.

Prayer to St. Michael

Saint Michael the Archangel, defend us in battle.
Be our protection against the wickedness and snares of the devil.
May God rebuke him, we humbly pray,
and do thou, O Prince of the heavenly host,
by the power of God, cast into hell
Satan and all the evil spirits,
who prowl throughout the world,
seeking the ruin of souls. Amen.

Come, Holy Spirit

Come, Holy Spirit, fill the hearts of your faithful
and kindle in them the fire of your love.
Send forth your Spirit and they shall be created.
And you shall renew the face of the earth.

Let us Pray:
O God, who instructed the hearts of the faithful by the light of the Holy Spirit, grant us in the same Spirit to be truly wise and ever rejoice in his consolation, through Christ, our Lord. Amen.

St. Augustine's Prayer to the Holy Spirit

Breathe in me, O Holy Spirit, that my thoughts may all be holy.
Act in me, O Holy Spirit, that my work, too, may be holy.
Draw my heart, O Holy Spirit, that I love but what is holy.
Strengthen me, O Holy Spirit, to defend all that is holy.
Guard me, then, O Holy Spirit, that I always may be holy. Amen.

The Divine Mercy Chaplet

Using a rosary, begin with the Sign of the Cross, one Our Father, one Hail Mary, and the Apostles' Creed.

On each Our Father bead, pray:

Eternal Father, I offer you the Body and Blood, Soul, and Divinity of your dearly beloved Son, our Lord Jesus Christ, in atonement for our sins and those of the whole world.

On each Hail Mary bead, pray:

For the sake of his sorrowful passion, have mercy on us and on the whole world.

Repeat above prayers on each decade. End by praying three times:

Holy God, Holy Mighty One, Holy Immortal One, have mercy on us and on the whole world.

Stations of the Cross

The Stations of the Cross is a devotion based on fourteen events from the passion and Death of Christ. At each station, you reflect on the event and prayerfully contemplate Jesus' suffering, death, and Resurrection. Most Catholic churches have the stations along the walls of the nave (where the parishioners sit).

1. Jesus is condemned to death.
2. Jesus takes up his cross.
3. Jesus falls the first time.
4. Jesus meets his mother.
5. Simon of Cyrene helps Jesus carry the cross.
6. Veronica wipes Jesus' face.
7. Jesus falls the second time.
8. Jesus meets the women of Jerusalem.
9. Jesus falls the third time.
10. Jesus is stripped of his garments.
11. Jesus is nailed to the cross.
12. Jesus dies on the cross.
13. Jesus is taken down from the cross.
14. Jesus is laid in the tomb.

Notes

Lesson 1: "Why am I here?" (An Introduction to *Chosen*)

Lesson 2: "What makes me happy?" (Discovering God as the Source)

1. Jean M. Twenge, *Generation Me: Why Today's Young Americans Are More Confident, Entitled—And More Miserable Than Ever Before* (New York: Simon and Schuster, 2007), 87.

2. See *Catechism of the Catholic Church* (CCC) 358.

3. See John 3:16.

4. See Matthew 5:3-12.

5. See 1 John 4:19; John 13:34-35, 14:15, 15:12-17; CCC 1823.

6. See CCC 1716.

7. See Galatians 5:22-23; CCC 736.

8. See CCC 2304.

9. St. Augustine, *Confessions* 1,1,1: J.P. Migne, ed., *Patrologia Latina* 32, 659-661 (Paris, 1857-1866).

Lesson 3: "What's your story, God?" (A Look at Salvation History)

1. See Matthew 28:20.

2. See CCC 1849–1851.

3. See CCC 234.

Lesson 4: "How do I know God is real?" (Understanding Divine Revelation)

1. See Isaiah 62:5; John 3:29; Matthew 25:1; Mark 2:19.

2. *Reader's Digest*, January 1963, 92.

3. See *Dei Verbum* 8; CCC 75–83.

4. *Nostra Aetate* 2.

5. During the sixteenth-century Protestant Reformation, Luther and Calvin wrongly rejected some of those books, which is why the Protestant Bibles do not have all seventy-three books.

Lesson 5: "Who is Jesus?" (The Person and Mission of Christ)

1. *Jesus Freak.* Mark Heimermann and Toby McKeehan, dc Talk (Los Angeles: ForeFront Records/ Virgin Records, 1995).

2. Check out Dr. Peter Kreeft's book, *Yes or No,* to see this whole argument.

3. See CCC 464.

Lesson 6: "Why be Catholic?" (Discovering the Church Jesus Founded)

1. In the United States in 1870, no seminary would accept a black candidate to the priesthood; Bishop Healey of Boston, the only other Catholic clergyman of African descent, had studied abroad and was believed to be Irish Catholic by all but his closest friends.

2. See John 17.

3. See John 15:16, 20:21; Luke 22:29-30.

4. Bishops, priests, and deacons are all referenced in Scripture. The principle of apostolic succession is found in the first chapter of the Acts of the Apostles, with the story of Matthias, who replaced Judas among the apostles. (See also 1 Timothy 3:1 and Titus 1:5.)

5. See Matthew 16:19.

6. See Isaiah 22:22.

7. See CCC 857.

8. See CCC 775 and 830–831.

9. See *Lumen Gentium* 15-16; CCC 817–819.

10. See CCC 889.

11. See *Lumen Gentium* 12.

12. See *Dominus Iesus* 13-14.

13. See CCC 846.

14. See *Lumen Gentium* 8; *Dominus Iesus* 16.

15. See CCC 889.

16. See *Lumen Gentium* 15-16.

17. See *Ut Unum Sint* 3.

18. See *Gaudium et Spes* 22.

Lesson 7: "Where am I going?" (A Look at the Four Last Things)

1. See Matthew 5:29, 25:41-46; Luke 16:23.

2. See 2 Peter 3:9.

3. See Mark 16:16; John 3:3-5.

4. See 2 Timothy 2:12-13; Romans 11:22; 1 Peter 1:15-17.

5. See James 1:17.

6. See CCC 1033.

7. See CCC 1022.

8. See CCC 1030–1032.

9. See Revelation 21:27.

10. For Scripture references to purifying "fire," go to 1 Corinthians 3:13 and 1 Peter 1:7. From the start, the early Christians took up the Jewish tradition of praying for the dead. See also CCC 1030–1032.

11. See 1 Peter 3:21.

12. See John 6:51-55.

13. See Galatians 6:9; James 1:2-4.

Lesson 8: "How do I get there?" (The Power and Purpose of the Sacraments)

1. St. Thérèse of Lisieux, *The story of a Soul: The Autobiography of St. Thérèse of Lisieux, Third Edition*, trans. John Clarke, O.C.D. (Washington, DC: ICS Publications, 1996), 14.

2. See Genesis 3:8.

3. See CCC 1129 and 1131.

4. See CCC 1131.

5. See CCC 1129.

6. The Catholic Church makes a distinction between public revelation and private revelation. Public revelation pertains to what is contained in the deposit of faith and must be believed by Catholics. Private revelation, in contrast, are the revelations made in the course of history that do not add to or form the deposit of faith. Some private revelations have been recognized by the authority of the Church; however, strictly speaking, Catholics are not required to believe in private revelation. (See CCC 67.)

7. See Matthew 26:17-30; Mark 14:12-25; Luke 22:7-30.

Lesson 9: "When did my journey begin?" (Baptism, Your Initiation into God's Family)

1. See Matthew 3:13-17; Hebrews 8:6-7.

2. See Romans 6:4.

3. See Colossians 2:11-14; John 3:3-5; CCC 804 and 1267.

4. See Galatians 3:26-27; CCC 790.

5. As descendants of Adam and Eve, we are born into Original Sin. This is not through any fault of our own; we inherited our fallen human nature and come into the world desperately needing God's sanctifying grace restored in us. (See CCC 404, 1263.)

6. See CCC 1257.

7. See CCC 1213.

8. See CCC 1263.

9. See CCC 1423, 1427, and 1431.

10. See Genesis 3.

11. See CCC 1261.

12. See CCC 1258.

13. See CCC 1260; *Lumen Gentium* 16.

Lesson 10: "Why tell my sins to a priest?" (The Healing Power of Confession)

1. See CCC 1466 and 1589.

2. Carol Glatz, "Master of metaphor: Pope Francis can weave a vivid tale." *Catholic News Service,* April 4, 2013.

3. See CCC 1456–1458.

4. See CCC 1790–1793.

5. Pius XII, encyclical, *Mediator Dei:* AAS, 39 (1947) 548.

6. See CCC 1466.

Lesson 11: "How does God help when it hurts?" (Anointing of the Sick and Redemptive Suffering)

1. See CCC 405.

2. St. Thomas Aquinas, *Summa Theologica* III, 1,3, ad 3; cf. *Romans* 5:20.

3. See CCC 1514.

Lesson 12: "Who is the Holy Spirit?" (Meeting the Third Person of the Trinity)

1. See John 4:10.

2. See John 7:38.

3. See John 14:16, NAB.

4. *Roman Missal,* Pentecost, Sequence.

5. See CCC 687 and 702.

6. See CCC 683–684 and 2818.

7. See CCC 363.

8. See Exodus 13:21.

9. See Exodus 31:18.

10. See Luke 1:35.

11. See Matthew 3:16.

12. See Acts 2:3.

13. See John 16:13; CCC 696–701.

14. See John 14:16, 15:26, 16:7.

15. See CCC 688.

Lesson 13: "What does the Holy Spirit do for me?" (Gifts for the Journey)

1. See Isaiah 11:2-3; CCC 1831.
2. See CCC 799 and 951.
3. See CCC 2003.
4. See Galatians 5:22-23.
5. See CCC 1829.
6. See Isaiah 11:1-3; CCC 1831.

Lesson 14: "Why I have been *Chosen?*" (Sealed and Sent in Confirmation)

1. See CCC 1299; *Ordo Confirmationis* ("Rite of Confirmation"), 25.
2. See John 10:10, NIV.
3. This word is frequently translated "foremost" (1 Timothy 1:15).
4. See Acts 7.
5. See Acts 8:14-19, 19:1-6; CCC 1285 and 1316.
6. See CCC 1313 and 1314.
7. See CCC 1297–1301.
8. See 2 Corinthians 1:21-22; CCC 1303.

Lesson 15: "Why do I have to go to Mass?" (Encountering Jesus in the Eucharist)

1. *Spirit of the Liturgy*, 137.
2. See John 14:3.
3. See CCC 1342.
4. See CCC 1366.
5. See CCC 2177–2178.
6. See CCC 1357.
7. See CCC 1069.
8. See John 13:1-15.
9. See CCC 1346.
10. See CCC 1382–1383.

Lesson 16: "What does it mean to say, 'I do'?" (Marriage, a Sign of God's Love)

1. Wendy Shalit, *Girls Gone Mild* (New York: Random House, 2007), 278.
2. John Paul II, address, 22 November 1986, Auckland, New Zealand. As quoted by López, ed., *The Meaning of Vocation* (Princeton, NJ: Scepter Publishers, 1997), 19.

3. John Paul II, address, 1 October 1979, Boston, Massachusetts. As quoted by López, ed., *The Meaning of Vocation*, 19-20.

4. See CCC 1643.

5. See CCC 2358.

Lesson 17: "Who's calling?" (Holy Orders and Vocational Discernment)

1. Thanks to Rory O'Brien for writing the story of Michael Monsoor for us.

2. See 1 John 4:8.

3. See Mark 12:30-31.

4. See CCC 1141, 1268, and 1547.

5. See CCC 1548, 1566, and 1570.

6. See CCC 1120 and 1552.

7. See CCC 1545.

8. See CCC 1536–1538.

9. See CCC 968.

Lesson 18: "Are you talking to me?" (Getting to Know God Through Prayer)

1. See CCC 2567.

2. See CCC 2721.

3. See Matthew 6:9-13.

Lesson 19: "Who is Mary?" (Meeting the Mother of God – and Your Heavenly Family)

1. *Mother Teresa.* Prods. Ann & Jeanette Petrie. Narr. Richard Attenborough. Petrie Productions, Inc., 1986. DVD.

2. See CCC 490–493.

3. See Acts 1:14.

4. See John 7:3-5.

5. See Luke 1:42.

6. See CCC 962.

7. See CCC 532.

8. See 1 Timothy 2:5.

9. See CCC 2116–2117, citing Deuteronomy 18:10 and Jeremiah 29:8.

10. See Matthew 17:1-6.

11. See Deuteronomy 34:7.

12. See CCC 828; 1 Corinthians 4:16.

Lesson 20: "What would Jesus do?" (The Beatitudes as a Path to True Happiness)

1. See CCC 1718.

Lesson 21: "Do I have what it takes?" (Building Virtue – Your Spiritual Workout)

1. See CCC 1805–1809 and 1813–1829.

2. See Genesis 4:7.

3. See CCC 1804.

4. See CCC 1806–1809; Wisdom 8:7.

5. See 1 Corinthians 13:13.

Lesson 22: "Why wait?" (God's Plan for Love and Sex)

1. Karol Wojtyla, *Love & Responsibility* (Ignatius Press: San Francisco, 1993), 172.

2. See CCC 2332.

3. John Paul II, address, 29 April 1989, Antananarivo, Madagascar. As quoted by Pedro Beteta López, ed., *The Meaning of Vocation* (Princeton, NJ: Scepter Publishers, 1997), 28.

Lesson 23: "How do I build the kingdom?" (Saying "Yes" to the Mission of Christ and His Church)

1. See 1 Thessalonians 5:17.

2. See 2 Timothy 2:24-25.

3. See Luke 10:25-37.

4. See Matthew 7:12.

Lesson 24: "Where do I go from here?" (The Journey Continues)

1. For three years, Savio was a student of St. John Bosco. When Savio died in 1845 at the age of fifteen, Bosco was so impressed with Dominic's holiness that he wrote a biography, *The Life of Dominic Savio*.

2. *Spe Salvi* ("On Christian Hope") 49.

Leader's Notes

1. John Paul II, October 8, 1995.

2. John Paul II, Toronto, July 28, 2002.

3. John Paul II, "The definitive aim of catechesis is to put people not only in touch, but also in communion and intimacy, with Jesus Christ," *Catechesi Tradendae*, 5. (Quoted in the General Directory for Catechesis, 80.)

4. *Familiaris Consortio* 39.

5. Barna Group. "Americans are most likely to base truth on feelings." (February 12, 2002). (barna.org/barna-update/article/5-barna-update/67-americans-are-most-likely-to-base-truth-on-feelings).

6. http://www.vatican.va/holy_father/francesco/speeches/2013/march/documents/papa-francesco_20130322_corpo-diplomatico_en.html.

7. Cf., CIC, can. 989; Council of Trent (1551): DS 1683; DS 1708.

8. This is the first of five precepts (or "positive laws") of the Church. Confessing sins and receiving the Eucharist at least once a year, at Easter, are the second and third precepts (see CCC 2042).

9. See CCC 1346; *Sacrosanctum concilium* 56.

10. St. Thérèse of Lisieux, *Manuscrits autobiographiques*, C 25r.

11. John Paul II, World Youth Day 2002, Downsview Address, 5.

12. http://www.usatoday.com/story/news/world/2013/03/14/pope-francis-profile/1985945/.

Acknowledgments

With gratitude to the long chain of disciples from the Ascension of our Lord to the present day, who were responsible for handing on the faith to me, most of all, to my parents.

To my children—I pray they will grow strong in the Truth, the Life, and the Way, and share Jesus with the world.

To my wife, Natalie, my greatest ally in working for the kingdom, at home and in the world.

To Archbishop Chaput and to all the good shepherds who lay down their lives for the sheep and administer the grace of Confirmation to them.

To Ron Bolster for putting his unparalleled expertise in catechetics at the service of this project.

To Chris Cope, Patrick McCabe, and Steve Motyl, whose talent and devotion chiseled *Chosen* into a world-class program.

To Nick DeRose and Philip Braun, who made the videos a work of art.

To the writers, editors, and designers, for putting their gifts at the service of the New Evangelization: Heidi Saxton, Colin and Aimee MacIver, Lisa Mladinich, Maria Johnson, Lora Brecker, Michael Flickinger, Stella Ziegler, and Mike Fontecchio.

To Jim Beckman, Scott Anthony, Annamarie D'Innocenzo, Fr. John Rapisarda, and Eddie Cotter, who helped us craft the *Chosen* curriculum.

To all of our presenters, for sharing the gift that they are with young people.

And finally, to Matthew Pinto who has touched countless lives from behind the scenes at Ascension Press and who believed in me and in this project enough to make it a reality.

I'm so very grateful.

Christopher J. Stefanick